Biblical Captivity

Biblical Captivity

Aggression and Oppression in the Ancient World

ROBERT KIMBALL SHINKOSKEY

RESOURCE *Publications* • Eugene, Oregon

BIBLICAL CAPTIVITY
Aggression and Oppression in the Ancient World

Copyright © 2012 Robert Kimball Shinkoskey. All rights reserved. Except for brief quotations in critical publications or reviews, no part of this book may be reproduced in any manner without prior written permission from the publisher. Write: Permissions, Wipf and Stock Publishers, 199 W. 8th Ave., Suite 3, Eugene, OR 97401.

Resource Publications
An Imprint of Wipf and Stock Publishers
199 W. 8th Ave., Suite 3
Eugene, OR 97401
www.wipfandstock.com

ISBN 13: 978-1-62032-006-8

Manufactured in the U.S.A.

All scripture quotations, unless otherwise indicated, are taken from the Holy Bible, King James Version®, KJV®. Copyright © 1611.

Contents

Abbreviations vii
Introduction ix

1. War and Oppression—Daily Bread of the Ancient Israelites 1
2. Religious and Political Violence in the Ancient Near East 24
3. Falling into Captivity and Rising Out of It:
   The Foundational Stories 48
4. The Constitutional Tradition of Ancient Israel 87
5. Captivity Through the Old Testament Eras 115
6. Captivity in New Testament Times 148

Bibliography 199
Index 203

Abbreviations

ABD   Anchor Bible Dictionary. Edited by D.N. Freedman. 6 vols., New York. 1992.

ANET Ancient Near Eastern Texts Relating to the Old Testament, Edited by J.B,. Pritchard. 3d. ed. Princeton:Princeton University Press, 1969

BCE   Before the Common Era (i.e. BC)

CE   Common Era (i.e. AD)

GNB   Good News Bible

JPS   Jewish Publication Society

KJV   King James Version

NRSV New Revised Standard Version

OCB   Oxford Companion to the Bible. Edited by Bruce M. Metzger and Michael D. Coogan. New York: Oxford University Press, 1993

REB   Revised English Bible

Introduction

THIS ESSAY WILL DEMONSTRATE that the Bible is a sophisticated record of an ancient national political history, featuring a constitutional law system, the Decalogue,[1] aimed at diminishing political and religious violence. Many claim that the Bible encourages violence intentionally, or at least theologically. We will make clear that much of the violence that is chronicled in early Israelite society is not partisan, religion-inspired violence or God-inspired violence. It is usually natural violence (what modern insurance policies call "acts of god"), utterly typical political and military adventurism (local, tribal, regional, and national), internal political oppression of the sort well understood in the ancient Near East (including political wrangling and warring among sons of the king over the problem of succession), or secular wrangling over economic resources, like water wells, flocks, fields, and roadways. These kinds of violence draw religious people and parties into it from time to time, certainly. But such violence is quite evidently not required or inspired by the God of the Exodus and the ancient constitution of the land, shot through as it is with various means to forge domestic peaceableness and tolerance, and quiet, independent living among the "nations."

What violence is required by the God of the Exodus and by the laws promulgated at Sinai, aside from the initial conquest/ displacement of political parties inimical to constitutional government, is military defense of the land and its people against outside aggression, and revolution in defense of the constitutional laws themselves, once those laws have been overrun from within by the leaders of the political and religious parties. Murder of political or religious innocents (ethical

---

1. See *Do My Prophets No Harm*, 85–86, for a summary of the political content of the Ten Commandments.

Introduction

people), and offensive-imperial war against neighboring idolatrous nations, is proscribed by the Sixth Commandment against killing.

Bible critics point to the slash-and-burn vocabulary of the Bible to undergird their attribution of a militant and destructive mentality to the God of Sinai and the prophetic writers. However, the frequent mention of the curse of "death" by the God of the prophets, psalmists and historians of Israel, is typically metaphorical, or extremely premature, as in the frequent statements of "surely ye shall die," if you do or don't do one or another thing. For example, God told Adam and Eve that they would surely die if they ate the fruit, but Adam seems to have lived an extremely long life instead. (Gen 2:17, 5:3–5)

The promises of "death" to the citizenry if they neglect the provisions of the Decalogue (Deut 27) are simply predictions of unhappiness, dissolution (and perhaps even early death) as a consequence of self-defeating actions in contradiction to the political lifestyle prescribed by the Decalogue. While God predicts that false prophets must die (Deut 18:20), we do not hear of the actual untimely physical demise of any such prophets outside the circumstance of war or revolution in the Old Testament. In fact, Jeremiah and others re-iterate there are many of these prophets flourishing quite handily and happily throughout the nation. We might best interpret the law as legitimating the rough handling of false prophets only during the time of revolution—something like the period of time of the Elijah/Jehu revolt against oppressive Baalists and the Baal-invested Ahab monarchy. The death of the "firstborn" of Egypt is very likely metaphorical as well, as the firstborn nation in ancient Near East terminology refers to the most mature and cosmopolitan nation, which reputation Egypt (the Rome of its day) was rapidly divesting itself of at the time of the mad Pharoah of Moses' day. Israel, in fact, was becoming God's new firstborn nation. (Exod 4:22)

Among religionists, there are as many views on the subject of Bible religion as a motivator for violence as there are researchers on the topic. Bible commentators are particularly interested to explain or criticize the violence surrounding Joshua's activities in Canaan, often described as "genocide" prescribed by God. I will list just three views here: the Canaanites had become spiritually corrupt and the land needed to be purged to make place for a more moral society that might easily be corrupted if the worst of the Canaanites remained;[2] Old Testament

---

2. Cowles, *No Mercy*, 63–94.

Introduction

warfare involved preparation for God's work that was to play out among a chosen group, and this preparation required that the spoils of Canaan (property) taken during the conflicts sustained during settlement had to be turned over to God (the priests), and the lives of any recalcitrant inhabitants sacrificed to him, as ancient Near East custom often prescribed;[3] Old Testament doctrines of violent treatment of enemies were real and unfortunate, but were fortunately superseded by the New Testament doctrine of love of enemies.[4]

To this list we add several notions from ancient Near Eastern secular ideology which may help explain some instances of Bible violence. Old Testament violence demonstrates the rules of international law by which a neighboring nation who badgers, oppresses, or kills unlawfully must be severely punished so as to prevent further rogue activities of the sort;[5] law and custom allow for killing not only of soldiers but women and children, since they are not really innocent bystanders, but are commonly used as aides-de-camp;[6] and insecure, despotic kings (outside and inside Israel) enjoyed cruelly killing as many of their traditional enemies as they could, and took pleasure in turning people's homes into ashes and fields into wastelands.[7]

It is our position that religion, God, and God's sacred places and peoples are all part of the overall political culture and identity of a given Near East nation or group of nations, and thus theology is commonly dragged into the political or military fray either to bless or curse the cause of other individuals, parties, and nations. But such theology is not always the centerpiece of military activity, as is presumed for the medieval Christian crusades against Islam, for example. This essay takes the position that theology can be either a primary, secondary, or negligible factor in inspiring the use of force. In ancient times, some reference to

---

3. Ibid, 161–187.

4. Ibid, 13–44.

5. This might well apply to Canaan. The propensity for raid and rapine by the petty kings of Canaan is evident in the Gen 14 story of Lot's capture by a coalition of such kings.

6. The apocryphal story of Judith and the Biblical story of Esther shed some light on this notion.

7. While the Assyrian kings enjoyed this kind of reputation as a rule, other ancient Near East despots did as well.

Introduction

a deity was customarily made not only in most war-making but also in most other acts of state, whether domestic or international.[8]

The position that we take in this essay is that Bible religion and politics are intended to operate in separate spheres, to be mutually supportive, but to form not a unitary but a binary political system, roughly akin to the two-kingdom theory of a number of sects of Protestantism.[9] The secular powers hold sway in their realm (the public, or crown realm), and the religious powers hold sway in their realm (the private, or cultic realm). For example, there is abundant evidence of a tradition of separation of church and state in ancient Israel, so that governing compacts and subsidiary laws can safely be classified as non-theocratic documents.[10] In most cases the secular realm takes chronological and constitutional precedence over the sacral realm, as it does throughout the Near East.

This is why the Bible is so opposed to the general system of Baalism. It is not because it is a religion, but because it is a civic constitutional (or unconstitutional) system based on idolatrous (unrestrained) monarchy, with a culture that is enamored with unrestrained sexual ethics (Num 25:1, 3), encourages relative ignorance as demonstrated by means of popular attachment to astrology and sorcery (Isa 47:13; Dan 2:2), practices intolerance and even enslavement of minority sects of religion (1 Kgs 18:4), and allows privilege and a level of centralization of government and concentration of aristocratic wealth and religious luxury[11] inimical to a people who suffered under such a system for 400 years.[12] The House of Seti in Egypt worshipped the Egyptian equivalent of Canaan's Baal, so the Hebrew exiles were well acquainted with this system before they left the Delta region and understood they would see it again along the way and in Canaan as well.

It is an unfortunate irony of fact and history that political mono-ethics (the system of representative government and its accompanying

---

8. This has been particularly well documented in Hittite treaty documents.

9. Eidsmoe, *God and Caesar*, 10–18.

10. The next essay in this series will deal with the evidence of political separation between the two spheres.

11. Amos 8:4–6; 2 Kgs 23:4.

12. The term "baal" is generically applied to any inhumane political or religious system, as evidenced by the fact the related term "Baal Zebub," or "Beelzebub," is the name given to Satan by Jesus. (Matt 12:26–27)

Introduction

concern for human rights), and religious mono-theism (the civic religious system associated with such political ethics), actually support pluralism and tolerance in politics and religion, because the terminology seems to dictate the opposite. But this is not the usual thinking among students of the Bible. For example, Regina Schwartz says what many suspect. She believes that monotheism is inherently violent, since it is based on an exclusive arrangement with a deity who supplies an identity, a law, a land, favored kinship relations, and a nation for followers and punishes any who are, or become, outliers from this specially protected relationship.[13]

Based on the flawed notion that the Bible is a book of religious history, Schwartz makes the aggressive claim that God consciously promotes violence among the sons of men by setting up conditions of rivalry between and among them. These sons (Cain and Abel, Jacob and Esau, and the brother nations who follow from them) are a Freudian-style threat to their earthly fathers, and to the Heavenly Father as well, all of which fathers wish them to destroy each other in order to protect their own sovereignty.[14] But such sibling rivalries evidently have legs of their own, quite aside from any attribution of their insecurities to God. In fact, much of Bible god-talk is bland attribution to a deity whom the ancients believed created the world and therefore took responsibility for whatever people happened to do to each other in that world, whether for good or for evil. God, of course, counseled the good, but believed he could not force people to be good, other than by providing punishments which fit the crime.

Schwartz sees treaty instruments and international marriages as peace instruments, while God's commandment for Israel not to enter into friendship treaties, matrimonial alliances, or commoner marriages with foreigners, potentially promotes violence. That is because monotheism's resources are scarce, and there are not enough to go around to share one society with another.[15] Israel spurns sharing of land, people, and other resources and instead violently holds on to its own. Unfortunately, the author misses the point that identity formation and national boundary formation and the wars that result from the violation of those

---

13. Schwartz, *Curse of Cain*; in fact such behavior is more clearly aligned with the secular imperialism of the rogue kings in Israel, as least in the post-Judges period.

14. Ibid, 110.

15. Ibid, 89, 91–97, 101.

Introduction

boundaries are most often civic, political, and military in nature, rather than religious. In addition, those boundaries can serve a good purpose in creating space for variant political systems to get out of each other's faces and live alongside each other in peace—the message of so many foundational stories in the Pentateuch.[16]

Indeed, Hector Avalos expands Schwartz's assertion and states that religion in general is "inherently prone to violence" because it creates scarce ecclesiastic resources that have to be protected and fought for: scripture, sacred space, group privileging, and salvation.[17] But much of Bible-based scripture/law, sacred space, group privileging, and salvation, while packaged in religious sounding language, is civic in nature, when one considers the Hebrew lexicon it draws from. The great commandments/laws are political in nature; the sacred space of the national temple is dual-purpose space, with the greater part of that space devoted to non-denominational activities and gatherings of citizens; group privileging results from ordinary sociological dynamics; and salvation is most often secular deliverance (matters of national security, civil rights, economic policy, etc.). These resources are certainly scarce among the nations, but if held abundantly in Israel, are certainly offered to all neighbors of the Israelites freely and warmly.[18]

While many religious denominations promote proprietary salvation, group superiority, special pilgrimage sites, and a monopoly on correct scriptural interpretation, the Bible does not support such machinations, and in fact lobbies against them and in favor of pluralism instead. The only mono-chromatic system worth fighting for is Israel's civic system, which also fits into a system of international law and is designed to bring domestic tranquility, international peace, and personal happiness. Avalos misreads the content of Decalogue law in ancient Israel, and misses the Biblical historical doctrine that ethical political activity, prophetic scriptural activity, hallowed land, and chosenness is a hope and an expectation for many diverse populations across history.[19] Scripture is closed and opened again many times in Israel when new prophets come along, and each time those prophets argue for toleration and peace within a restored constitutional frame.

16. See for example Gen 13.
17. Avalos, *Fighting Words*, 18.
18. Isa 49:6.
19. See Shinkoskey, *Do My Prophets No Harm*, 42–59; also Amos 9:7.

Introduction

Avalos, on the other hand, sees violence as necessary and natural since the whole system of theism is premised on an unverifiable system of belief which invites people to violently compete for resources in order to remain special. Religious belief may be unverifiable, but political leaders can be tracked and criticized or impeached or overthrown, and a historical records left of their abuses of power, as in the Book of Kings. Something like the Decalogue system of government had been tested in both Near-East, Far East, and Mediterranean systems of law at or before the time of the Hebrew system of consensual government.[20]

There is, on the other hand, the temptation for the state to transform genuine constitutional limits on aggression into religion-assisted violence in the service of oppressive or imperial minded leaders. This is commonly associated with systems of autocracy where the king usurps mainstream religious functions and marginalizes minority religious groups or all religious groups, and can even substitute a cult of his/her own personality for legitimate religion. This is the very definition of the idolatry mentioned in the second commandment.[21] This is the system that leads to violence against neighbors and against one's own citizens, and it has characterized much of religious-inspired violence in Israel (ancient and modern), Christianity, and Islam.

Despots use systems of alliance with aristocrats or autocrats in friendly or vassal nations, often cemented by cross-national marriages, to reinforce political or economic control. Treaty alliances are often forced upon nations as a result of threatened or actual conquest, and require the subjugated nation to go to war to protect that suzerain's often broad, and often illegitimate, interests throughout the community of nearby nations. It also invites the vassal nation to trust in the intentions and the protective capacity of the superior nation to deliver them from evil. On the other hand, the monotheism of the Bible discourages defaulting to protectionist strategies offered by power broker nations, and to rely instead on the humane constitutional law of one's own nation and a neutralist position with respect to the warring propensities of

20. See, for example, the Laws of Manu in ancient India, the Code of Hammurabi, the doctrines of Confucius, and the teachings of Buddha, and the Twelve Tablets of early Rome.

21. The eighteenth century English dissenter Richard Price, friend of Thomas Jefferson, warned that fawning before royalty produced "idolatry as gross and stupid as that of the ancient heathens." He thus inadvertently re-discovered exactly what the Bible writers had discovered at a much earlier time. See Cohen, "God Spare," 56.

neighboring great nations. If war comes to one's own shores and lands, then the people can surely fight, but it is much less likely to come if the nation minds its own business and treats other nations with equanimity.

When political leaders co-opt the political and religious traditions of the ancestors, they are happy to do it if they can get away with it. Such are Ahab and Jezebel, Rehoboam, Manasseh, and King Mesha in Moab (who tried to co-opt Baalam). This pattern can be found in the medieval world at the time of the Holy Roman Empire, and in the instances in the modern world of totalitarian secular dominance over religious communities throughout the globe.

The human rights culture in ancient Israel, as it is everywhere it pops up throughout history, is self-consciously resistant to violence and war. Israel's constitutional provision for tolerance of variety in political and religious views (the first commandment) is the most fundamental of anti-war, anti-violence thinking and living, but it is hard to maintain and even to remember in the swamp of daily life and economic greed. In order to stress the need for maintenance and periodic restoration of this kind of legal system, the Bible details the neglect of constitutional precepts by its kings and periodic efforts by democratic-oriented reformers and revolutionaries to re-enthrone them.

As against the Meshas and Ahabs of the Biblical world, the literary prophets are extraordinarily pacifist, pluralist and populist in their approach to domestic and international politics. They uniformly look toward the day when the masses are well educated enough in human rights and responsibilities to diminish the need for regulatory behavior by the state over each citizen with respect to politics and religion, and when the community of nations can beat the swords into plowshares and get into the flow of peaceable living again. They teach Hebrew constitutionalism and detail the backsliding going on and the necessary contribution that each of the ten precepts makes to maintaining and promoting peaceable living. They start civic movements remembered in Hebrew history as "remnants" or "sons of the prophets." They restore what they believe is the original legislative intent of the constitutional law.

Introduction

THE DUAL MENACES OF THE ANCIENT WORLD

In this book we pay paramount attention to the First and Fourth commandments, the dual solutions to ancient Near East dual menaces of ancient autocracy. We also elaborate to a degree the Second, Sixth, and Tenth commandments as they relate to the prevention of political and religious violence and oppression.

Early literary man learned that free speech and free labor were frequently suppressed or obliterated by powerful governments in the Near East world. This is the source of the Bible's passionate interest in providing for liberation from politico-religious and economic repression.

Moses and his people in Egypt experienced the rapid disintegration of their right to religious worship and self-directed labor. They attempted to rectify that in the civic constitution enacted at Sinai and in Canaan. However, even within the relatively benign confines of a representative government, oppression was hard to overcome. For example, Saul exterminated the priests of Nob, David attempted to use a national draft registration (a "census") to conscript citizens of the nation into a standing army, and Manasseh oppressed many in Israel. Critics or domestic movements arose to challenge or correct these abuses.

So, too, the people of Gilgamesh took corporate action to force political changes, as did the Egyptian people under Akhtoy I, and the people of early Rome at the time of Tarquin. From time to time, laws were enacted by reformers in large states like Mesopotamia to broaden labor and worship rights. The policy of "corvee," or state-directed civilian or military labor conscription, was a hotly debated and frequently reformed policy in the Near East.[22] The point of this book is to show that Bible writers were well aware of political, economic, and religious oppression in their regional milieu, and wrote in opposition to it.

This is the second in a series of texts which sees the Decalogue as ancient Israel's constitutional law solution to political injustice of the type experienced in Egypt and later within its own national boundaries. The first essay was published earlier in March, 2011, by Wipf and Stock Publishers, and is titled *Do My Prophets No Harm: Revelation and Religious Liberty in the Bible*.

In that essay we argued that the Bible sees theo-political prophecy as an ancient expectation for ongoing Israelite culture. God lives and

---

22. Weinfeld, *Social Justice*, 9–10, 16.

Introduction

desires to right floundering nations by inspiration provided through prophets, whose activities ironically take place mainly in the secular rather than the ecclesial sphere. Not incidentally, the wisdom tradition and literature in the Bible suggests there is much for mankind to learn about the earth and its natural environs and sciences, and such learning is facilitated both by ordinary scribes and prophets (learned men and women making no claim to theophany), and high Prophets (those making a sustainable claim to theophany). We introduced the idea that oracular revelation, academic/scribal inquiry, and liberality in political expression were thus to be protected by law in ancient Israelite society by means of the First Commandment. Humankind might then benefit both from God and from its own innate capacities, and communities might dwell in quiet independence rather than be decimated by war.

We will take particular care to emphasize that prophetic movement and constitutional kingship (i.e., popular, but ultimately secular civic activity) are not only the biggest aid to freedom, but once corrupted, as they inevitably are (when lesser scribes and pundits, or despotic successors, replace the great rulers and prophets and neglect or misconstrue their historical records and doctrines), those instrumentalities become a grave threat to freedom in the ancient world. As an example, David's faith and politics are initially helpful in relieving the oppression of Israel's tribes by neighbors and by their own king, but his own early ethical strength is corrupted and he begins to use tyrannical methods and privileges instead, as seen in the stories of his purging of political (and sexual) rivals, his aborted effort to organize a powerful standing army, and his encouragement of state temple building.[23] Lesser prophets rule, and teach the citizenry to "prophesy no more." (Amos 2:11–12) That is, there is to be no more criticism of the system, as it is operating currently for the best good of the people.

HAVE MODERN NATIONS LEARNED THE POLITICAL LESSONS OF THE BIBLE?

The fundamental political problem and solution elucidated by the Bible has not been any better understood or propagated in the modern world of Renaissance, Reformation, Enlightenment, and nationalist

---

23. 2 Sam 7:1–17.

Introduction

self-determination than in the ancient world of great king empires or the medieval world of the Crusades. We can see this currently in the pattern of religious and political violence across the decades and nations of the twentieth and twenty-first century world.

The airplane attacks on the U.S. World Trade Center in New York City on September 11, 2001 were arguably motivated by radical Muslim opposition to U.S. military bases erected on a long-term basis in the Middle East, and a persistent Christian insinuation of in-your-face superiority over Islamic culture. The attacks on the twin towers were preceded by episodes of religious violence by Christian anti-abortion activists in America, Islamic subway bombs in France, Hindu-Buddhist subway nerve-gas incidents in Japan, Irish Catholic bombings in Britain, Sikh car bombings in Delhi, India, Tamil and Sinhalese militant bombings in Colombo, Sri Lanka, al-Qaeda-related bombings of Bali nightclubs in Indonesia, and regular violence in Palestine by militants in both Jewish and Muslim communities and governments.[24] Before these, notable incidents of religious-based strife have taken place between Sunni and Shiite sectarians during the long tenure of Saddam Hussein in Iraq, and have continued well after the American war of conquest and occupation there beginning in 2003. Similar conflicts simmer in Iran, Syria, and other Arab countries.

Concern rages in Europe and in the United States regarding persecution of Christian groups in Muslim countries. Pope Benedict XVI believes Christians are now suffering greatly in Asia, Africa, and the Middle East.[25] Secretary of State Clinton adds that not only Christian groups, but Middle East minority Muslim groups are under attack.[26] After Mubarak's abdication in Egypt, Christian-Muslim clashes have broken out in the vacuum of power there.[27] Violence between Christians and Muslims in Sudan form much of the background for the ongoing humanitarian crisis there, and many similar factors apply to the ongoing crisis in Somalia. The United States Congress conducts hearings on Muslim organization activities in America and takes testimony from law enforcement and Homeland Security representatives on the topic.[28]

24. Juergensmeyer, *Terror*, 3.
25. D'emilio, Frances, "Pope calls Christians the Most Persecuted."
26. Associated Press, March 5, 2011.
27. Hendawi, Hamza, "Christian-Muslim Clashes in Egypt Kill 13."
28. Shane, Scott, "Hearing Puts Muslim Group in Hot Seat."

Introduction

There is a renewal of religious enmity and terror in Ireland between Protestants and Catholics.[29] As I write this, clergymen representing Greek and Armenian clergy clash inside a holy shrine at Bethlehem, the traditional birthplace of Jesus.

In the latter part of the twentieth century, religious rivalry was evident in the Hutu political massacre of Tutsis in Rwanda, and the war between Orthodox Christian Serbs and Bosnian Muslims in the former Yugoslavia. Before that, and going back in time, it was evident in the sacralized political and military pogroms directed against Jews in Hitler's Germany, America's Protestant-backed war against Catholics in Puerto Rico during the Spanish-American War of 1846–48,[30] the violence directed against "pagan" native populations in the New World by Christian colonial empires, the holy wars following the Reformation, The Christian "Reconquista' of Spanish lands in the hands of an Islamic empire,[31] and the 500 years of the Inquisition.

Political violence after the Bible is as easily motivated by secular (cultural, ethnic, economic, imperials) notions as by religious, and is particularly characteristic, as always, of jealous and egotistic kings and emperors in their fits of expansive empire-building. Secular factors were in play in the Persian-Roman wars, the Roman expansion in Britain, the Germanic wars against both the western and eastern Roman empires, the many early Slavic wars, the Islamic wars of expansion (such as the Ummayid Caliphate's dealings in Iberian Spain), the Byzantine empire and its wars, the Bulgarian and Russian empires and wars, the Magyar invasions and occupations, the Viking conquests, the adventures of the Holy Roman Empire, the Danish and Norman kingdoms and wars, the Mongol conquests in Eastern Europe, the empire of Poland-Lithuania, and the African autocratic wars in Mali, Axum, Ghana, Songhai, and Great Zimbabwe.

Early modern and modern iterations of these medieval venues and themes can be seen in the 100 Years War between Britain and France, the wars and oppressions of the Hapsburg empire and the Ottoman and Safavid empires, the Spanish empire in the New World, the Romanov dynasty and its depredations, British colonies in India and in Kenya, Napoleonic Italy, and France under the Nazis.

29. *Yahoo! News*, April 4, 2011.
30. Herring, *Colony to Superpower*, 318–19.
31. Ellis and Esler, *World History*, 218.

Introduction

The dual menaces of state-mandated labor and state-suppressed political and religious conscience is still well represented in the world of twentieth and twenty-first century autocrats. The military conscriptions of young, politically immature conscripts into national imperial wars they little understand, at the behest of political powers they stand little chance of resisting, applied not only to the conscripts of and religious purges by adventurist dictators in the middle twentieth century Europe, such as Lenin, Stalin, Mao, Kim Il-Sung, Castro, and Pol Pot, but also to America's supposedly benign wars of "intervention" or conquest in twentieth century and early twenty-first century in the Philippines, Viet Nam, Bosnia, Kosovo, Afghanistan and Iraq.

Furthermore, the seething reserve of indignation about the increasingly capricious and capacious economic and political suppression of the middle and poorer class by aristocratic, one- or two-party political systems in the capitalist world precipitated not only the American Tea Party movement, but also the Arab Spring and Occupy Wall Street movements and similar movements across Europe and Asia. Much of this political violence is animated by such secular values as military technology, economic gain, and political will, but the cultic sector of society is as culpable in many ways as the civic sector in inciting it. This book, together with *Do My Prophets No Harm*, hopes to provide an antidote to the way of thinking that either overemphasizes the role of religion, or de-emphasizes it too much. The problem is not authentic religion per se, but political use of religion as a club and disengagement of religious people from constitutional literacy and ancient history.

The point of this book is to demonstrate that the Bible is well aware of the decimating effects of political- and religion-based conflict in general and is deeply devoted to doing something about it. But while the Bible encourages civic activism directed at limiting central political power, and thus curbing its ability to inflict pain on its citizens and its neighbors, the mainstream churches in powerful nations of Europe and the Americas settle for securing the peace on the Lord's Day, while defaulting to opportunist politicians to rule the larger community like rogues the other six days of the week. De-politicization of the Bible message—turning its characters away from their political, legal, and international interests and turning them into Sunday soldiers-only encourages some minority communities of believers to disengage from the civic sphere. Other communities of believers use their superior

xxi

Introduction

access to public processes to dominate, discriminate against, or persecute minority political and religious groups. Both groups miss the essential Bible message. The sacralizing of Biblical concepts and narratives that are clearly civic, even secular in nature, serves to turn the thematic focus of political pluralism into one of political and religious uniformity, the very xenophobic and monolithic worldview the Bible's characters continually struggled to free themselves from.[32] The framing of the Biblical history in ecclesiastic rather than broad constitutional governmental terms has enabled institutional Christianity not only to marginalize and discriminate against minority religious groups but to justify European and American interference with other nations.

In this essay we will review the Exodus story and outline the characters and constitutional events that gave birth to Israel's earliest laws and policies. We note that the historical reports of Bronze and Iron Age civilization, in both the Near East and the northern Mediterranean, provide other examples of arduous migrations, either voluntary or forced[33], and violence done to human rights, and that Israelite resettlement was just one of many responses to that violence and violation. But if this particular ancient history is to be understood as an effective prologue to modern history and western lore, its enduring political message must be better understood.

In chapter 1 we review the Bible's emphasis on captivity in the patriarchal stories, during the sojourn in Egypt, in the wilderness and in settlement in Canaan. We review a variety of cultural and legal solutions for preventing captivity and ameliorating oppression. In particular, we outline a new interpretation of the Decalogue and its First Commandment, which we view as directing attention to the rule of humane law—a body of law closely association with the God who presided over the liberation of early Israel from oppression in Egypt.

In chapter 2 we study the story of life under great king captivity in the superpower nations outside of Israel, which demonstrates the validity of the events and personalities chronicled in the Bible. In chapter 3 we look more in depth at foundational (primeval, patriarchal, and Exodus) stories of the problem of political and religious violence, and some late Bronze Age solutions. In chapter 4 we also look at political and constitutional law solutions springing from the Exodus and Sinai experiences.

32. Horsley, *Jesus and Empire*, 5–14.
33. For biblical reports of these, see Shinkoskey, *Do My Prophets No Harm*, 50.

Introduction

In chapter 5 we look at external aggression and internal oppression throughout the time of the confederacy and the monarchies in Israel, down through the time when Judea was a colonial dependency of great nations, taking note of prophets, priests, reformist kings, and ordinary people who stood up to confront and roll-back these forms of captivity. Finally, in chapter 6 we look at Jesus and the apostles and find they are aware of the basic problem of religion-inspired violence and oppression, and that essentially they uphold the same solutions that authors, editors and compilers of the Hebrew Bible did.

This particular interpretation of Biblical thought and story-telling sends a powerful message of encouragement to modern societies oppressed under similar circumstances, whether by military dictatorship, utopian communist dictatorship, or dictatorship by exploitative aristocracies and priestly political parties.

I was amused to find this statement by James Barr in his article on "Politics and the Bible" in the Oxford Companion to the Bible: "The Bible is not a purely religious book."[34] I agree wholeheartedly with this sentiment. In fact, I had thought to introduce this book with a similar, yet more radical statement: "The Bible is not a book about religion." Thinking better of this second statement, I hit upon "The Bible is not a book primarily about religion." I suspect this compromise position will still raise the hackles of many.

The Bible is indeed a book about the regular oppression of political and religious conscience and of economic opportunity. In particular it is about the roughshod handling of Hebrew religion and Hebrew democratic political society and its various forms by the internal and external political powers of the Mediterranean and Near Eastern world over a lengthy period of time. The story of Hebrew culture is the story of all religious culture. The story of Hebrew nation-building is the story of all nation-building. The story of Hebrew philosophical and political thought is the story of all sentient thought. The Bible story is the story of a highly politicized people who, in the beginning, happened to support both a mainstream church and a number of minority cults along side each other. It is a story of how these religious groups and the tribal partisans who sponsored them got along in polite society, much more than it is about the content of the religious beliefs and liturgies of the specific denominations.

34. Barr, "Politics and the Bible," 599.

1

War and Oppression: Daily Bread of the Ancient Israelites

The Bible presents a coherent political science that can be teased out of the wild variety of religious interpretations of its pages. The chronological flow of political events is something like the following: the earliest well-storied ancestors of Israel, Abraham and his group, migrate to high ground in Canaan to get clear of the tidal flows of oppression and violence which typify the riverside monarchies of their Mesopotamian homeland. These monarchies marginalize or dominate new or minority religious culture. We are lead to understand that the norm of culture since earliest times in the kingdoms dotting the Tigres and Euphrates rivers is aggressive control and insensate retribution for actual or perceived injury or offense. (Gen 4:14–15, 24; 6:4–6, 11–12; 11:6–8) The earliest race of men within memory were "giants" who were men of war—"Mighty men . . . men of renown." (Gen. 6.4) In fact, the tendency of polytheistic, political cultures to war one against another was so marked that "The earth was filled with violence."[1] (Gen. 6.11) In the very ancient Song of Lamech, the householder tells his wives he favors

---

1. John J. Collins maintains than Mosaic monotheism and pre-Mosaic polytheism can be viewed as having equally brutal records in this regard. To this assertion we answer "yes and no, but mostly no." See Collins, *Justify Violence?*, 2, and Shinkoskey, *Do My Prophet No Harm*, 85.

aggressive vengeance at a kill rate of "seven and seventy fold"—490 times—for the loss of one falsely claimed life.[2] (Gen 4:23–24)

God, on the other hand, is opposed to barbarous violence.[3] He encourages his prophet messengers to situate themselves and their peoples in a location where they can institute a more tranquil culture. So it was that God gave Abraham stark and memorable advice under the instant circumstance of Mesopotamian history: "Get . . . out of your country." (Gen 12:1) There was an ever-present threat, as we know from extra-biblical sources, of the overrunning of Chaldea by neighboring city-states, and also of internal usurpation and overthrow of the monarchies there.[4] Abraham and his family were to substitute this barbaric lifestyle with a pragmatic one that stressed co-existence with peaceable peoples, and violence only in order to defend themselves: "I will bless them that bless thee, and curse him that curseth thee . . ." (Gen 12:3) This is a formula for intra-clan, cross-clan, national, and inter-national religious peace in an extremely pluralistic world, and a call to consequence (curse) for misuse of that policy. In the Bible we see examples of correct use as well as abuse of the policy in all four kinds of settings, as we see below.

Four generations of the clan live independently, and relatively peaceably,[5] in Canaan, before, due to environmental hardship, they relapse into socio-political life in a great king setting in Egypt. There the tribes descendant from Abraham are treated to the political and economic oppressions, and the diseases, of urban river culture. (Amos 4:10; Exod 5:3, Exod 7-10; Hos 9:3, 13:9–11; Rev 11:8) The oppressiveness of that society is ultimately amplified even further under the ministrations of a particularly xenophobic and cruel Pharoah, who denies them freedom of religion and freedom of economic determination. (Exod 1:22, 2:15, 3:7, 5:6–14; Exod 11-14; Acts 7:34)

---

2. Brueggemann, *Genesis*, 66.

3. In Israel, as in other politically ethical cultures in the ancient Near East, the job of the ruler or the ruling party is to enact justice, together with religious and economic freedom. Violence against free labor and the gods of the people is considered to be bad form. Shinkoskey, *Do My Prophets No Harm*, 113.

4. Shinkoskey, *Do My Prophets No Harm*, 112.

5. One exception is the captivity of Lot; another, the story of Dinah, Shechem, and the sons of Jacob.

War and Oppression: Daily Bread of the Ancient Israelites

Moses then re-enacts Abraham's migration by removing a group of followers from Egypt and leading them back to the relatively inaccessible and thus protected frontier of the Canaanite highlands where the people of Abraham might have freedom again. The ancestral legal constitution for ensuring political independence and domestic tranquility is re-discovered at Sinai, (Exod 19-20, 34) relied upon in travels in the wilderness before settlement, (Lev 24; Num 11–16, 21, 25, 30–31, 36) and formally re-enacted once the group organize for political life in the land of the ancestors. (Deut 27, Josh 8) That legal solution involves coexistence with reasonable ethical cultures and seemingly offensive, but ultimately defensive engagement against those who wish to dominate others politically. More particularly, that solution suggests a division of the land so all the tribes may have an economic base and control over their own lives, flocks, and government, outside the pale of central government domination.[6]

This path of allocation of land, and thus political power, among all capable citizens of the land, after all, is the path that allowed Cain and his descendants to prosper even after the debacle with Abel (Gen 4:12, 16–17); that rescued the descendants of Noah after the great flood (Gen 11:8); and that Abraham took with Lot when their two groups fell to infighting. (Gen 13) So it was, then, that Joshua divided the land among the frequently squabbling tribes who entered Canaan for the second time in the family's long history.[7] (Josh 14–21) The legal structure, for good measure, specified that there be rules for reversion of the land to descendents of the original holders according to special rules, if it was expropriated under hardship or violence. (Lev 25; Deut 15)

Under the decentralized governance of this national federation of tribes, one tribe/region might come to the aid of another if they should so desire, but not if they should not desire. (Judg 5:17) The national confederation's status of isolationist independence among the nations (Num 23:9) and the pattern of informal interaction with other nations rather than formal diplomatic treaty and alliance, was the norm during the time of Judges, and was not subverted until early in the time of Kings. (1 Kgs 11) After settlement in Canaan, the tribes could safely

---

6. See Habel, *The Land Is Mine*, and Brueggemann, *The Land*.

7. One's mind runs to the time of the American "judges." Roger Williams and his followers ran from an intolerant Massachusetts to find land and breathing room in Rhode Island.

3

enact local statutes for clan and family government and apply the accumulated wisdom of humankind to the problems at hand. (Exod 20:12; Deut 5:16; Micah 4:4)

Israelite chronicles in oral and written form narrate accounts of broad constitutional problems and solutions, as well as local legislation and judicial decisions enacted by the new nation. These accounts summarize a worldview which contemplates two great political pathways, two ways to do government: one leading to blessing (peace, happiness, success, pluralism, profitability, freedom), and the other to cursing (war, sadness, failure, loss, force, oppression). The original Mosaic covenant of government enacted ten humane constitutional statutes, which, if enforced, would lead to blessing. Any equivocation with those laws sets the society on a course toward fulfillment of the curses of bad government. (Deut 27–28)

But even in well protected Canaan, at first smaller powers, during Judges, and greater powers, during Kings, encroach on Israel's land and liberty, often inspired by the gods of their cultures. The Amorite Sihon, for example, wars against the gods of the high places of Moab and against their tutelary god Chemosh. (Num 21:26–29) Moab, in turn, uses Balaam to curse Israel in behalf of Chemosh. (Num 22:5–6) Later, Assyria's gods lead the way against Israel. (2 Kgs 18:33–35; 19:17, 37) Moreover, Israel's own leaders eventually begin to act like autocrats and impose imperial hardship on the people as well.

Early transgressions of the Decalogue's "covenant" or constitutional law of progressive political localism revolve around acceding to the political ideals of the indigenous Canaanites, whose constitutional culture is known as Baalism, or "idolatry"—basically, abdication of religious and political pluralism in favor of the autocratic preferences of glorified, despotic, and sometimes hereditary leaders. This confusion of values leads to a loss of control over land, livestock, and liberty. The early settlers have plenty of occasion to taste the cursings enumerated in Deuteronomy (Deut 27) at the hands of aggressive polities like the Midianites, Amalekites and Philistines, and at the hands of their own wayward rulers, like Abimelech, son of Jerubbaal (Gideon). Abimelech is truly the first example of ruinous political idolatry after Israel crosses Jordan. (Judg 9)

But once elective kingship is organized in Israel, and particularly once traditional forms of Near East kingship begin to dominate Israel's

War and Oppression: Daily Bread of the Ancient Israelites

culture after the unified kingdom is divided into north and south, Israel sees in stark relief how great king flirtation can change a nation, bringing with it standing armies, unstable government, and alliances with "friendly" governments that quickly and easily turn unfriendly. Reaping the harvest of their constitutional mistakes is nowhere better memorialized than at the moment Rabshakeh delivers the Assyrian great king's message to them at the walls of Jerusalem during siege. (2 Kgs 18:28–35) Political boasting, seduction, caprice, threat, all that their early culture sought to banish from their communities, was now knocking at the door in spades. Meanwhile, the literary prophets had given interminable advice to Israel and Judah to avoid foreign entanglements and curb the strength of her own kings, but to little avail. Israel had turned hell-bent toward perpetual war and total captivity, and was soon to experience all that she had lusted after.

Our concern in this chapter, and in those following, is the political psychology of early Israel and the extraordinary fear of over-weaning government, whether that of neighbors in the ancient Near East, or of their own. We will see that the historical narratives, the polemical writings of prophets, and the laws of the society reflect this meta-political concern. It is thus a desire to construct and maintain a socio-politico-economic culture resistant to political domination that pervades the pages of the Bible. Religion, in a general way, is both a solution and a problem to Israel in the constitutional challenge which they face in the ancient world.

We have outlined in the first essay of this series the idea that the Ten Commandments constitute secular constitutional law. Those statements of government formation and operation are intended to deal with political violence in general, but more particularly with religious and cultural violence, which seems to be at the root of most political and military violence. The Decalogue does not "establish" a favored denominational religion, but rather only establishes a set of politico-cultural ethics—proper verses improper civic religion. It acknowledges that both worldview and behavior are political in nature, something that the modern concept of "civil religion" acknowledges as well.[8] Included in Decalogue civil religion or social life, much as in modern constitutional society, are monogamy, marital fidelity and sexual continence, nurturing, instructing and mentoring of children whether or not

---

8. See Bellah, "Civil Religion," 1–22.

gifted with wealth or physical wholeness, and excluded are polygamy (largely), adultery, temple prostitution, human sacrifice of unblemished children or marginalization/exposure of disabled children.

The Bible and its Decalogue acknowledge that religious practice, which is properly a matter of individual or small group belief and expression, can easily be pirated from localized or regionalized conclaves of faith and made into the sole legal possession of a political high priest, often a monarch, who then governs both imperial cult and imperial state, and may ultimately substitute personality, personal polices and whim for the constitutional precepts of the ancestors.

This process is translated as "captivity" in the King James Bible. It can happen at the hand of a political ruler or at the hand of a religious ruler, and can happen at the hand of a conqueror who brings his own religious orthodoxy along with him and imposes it on his new conquest. I understand such words as "take (into captivity)" (Hebrew laqah, meaning "take, capture"), and exile (Hebrew galut, meaning "deportation"[9]) to refer to externally-imposed conditions of captivity. I understand such words as bondage (Hebrew aur, moser, ebed), as well as practices such as labor conscription, taxation and other economic manipulation such as indentured servitude, and neglect of traditional ancestral political ethics and rights, to refer to internally-imposed conditions of captivity.[10]

The story we have outlined to this point suggests our overall thesis. The Bible is not a book about religion in particular, but rather is a book about political science, constitutional law, and the religio-scientific worldview in general. There are certainly religious people who take center stage in the book, but their cult activities and beliefs are not usually at issue unless they are abusive toward constitutional/ethical values. Their civic activities are the real focus of the stories about them,

---

9. Smith-Christopher, *Theology of Exile*, 9.

10. The theme of religion-rooted conflict and captivity, unfortunately, is not well represented in academic and confessional writing and teaching. For example, the KJV terms "captive," and "captivity," and the English translations—"deport"/"deportation"—used by other Bible translations such as NAB, GNB, NEB, and JPS cannot be found as entries in the Anchor Bible Dictionary. The term "exile" used in the NRSV does have an entry in the ABD, but only refers the reader to "Israel, History." It appears, then, that international imperialism is not understood to be a significant historical reality in the ancient Near East or in the Bible, or, alternately, that it was not an important topic in the study of religion at the time of publication of the ABD.

War and Oppression: Daily Bread of the Ancient Israelites

including their propensity either to tolerate or denigrate other religions or peoples. The Bible's numerous references to God represent ancient Near East literary phrasing rather than statements of orthodox faith. The Bible is, in fact, about the long Israelite hill country experiment with secular constitutional government, a system of political organization and citizen responsibility framed by the Ten Commandments and aimed at limiting the reach of popular rulers into the lives of ordinary people. Even the Psalms, so full of worshipful prayer and devotion, are most often situated in a context of civic concern for the well-being of the community. Many, indeed, are lamentations over various internal and external forces which distress the nation.[11]

Love of freedom, and *fear* of orthodox or politicized religion, in fact, is the pre-eminent concern of "the law and the prophets," as well as the historical narratives and the New Teatement. The canon writers express antipathy toward priestly government imposed either by external control (conquest, tribute) or by internal oppression (slavery, repression of rights, reduction of property).

Another way of saying this is that the Bible is concerned about civic solutions to the violence and oppression so rampant in the ancient world, so that precious land, clan and local government structures, and intellectual freedoms can be maintained.

Religion is a powerful force for organization of the political systems. The Bible does not dispute this. The Bible sees, however, that religion, as a corporate, civic institution, exercises power relationships and can be as corrupt as any other institution in society.

Israel's ancestors experienced harm at the hands of institutional religion in its sojourns in Mesopotamia, Canaan, and Egypt. Israel's own citizens also experienced harm and oppression at the hands of its own occasionally domineering political and religious institutions.

In this chapter we will look at Israel's own experience as it was remembered and written by the prophets and historians of its culture in the corpus of the Bible. In chapter 2 we will explore the notion that Israel's memory of the harshness of the ancient political world and its ecclesiastic bedfellows is well evidenced in extra-Biblical sources as well.

---

11. Anderson, *Old Testament*, 512–17.

CAPTIVITY IN THE BIBLE AND ITS PREVENTION IN ANCIENT ISRAEL

The pervasiveness of religion-swathed conflict and war in the ancient world, and the perniciousness of its consequences in all periods of time chronicled, is a major theme of both the Hebrew and Christian testaments. Such violence is most often tied to a single socio-political source—either despotic kingship or autocratic tyranny (the oppression meted out by reformist usurpers). It begins with Cain and Abel, a story of murder tied to a quarrel over religious sacrifice. Because Abel's sacrifice was preferred by God over Cain's, Cain killed Abel and usurped his place in the world. (Gen. 4.3–4, 8) Israel again quarrels over religion when Joseph's brothers sell him into slavery and take his place of pre-eminence in the family after he announces a close connection to God and his superiority over the older brothers. (Gen 37:1–1; 49:22–26) In Egypt, Pharaoh is not only political ruler, but also high priest in the temple of the dominant god, and is thus the only one accorded access to its holiest precincts. Aggregating both public and private power into his own hands assures that his power is unchecked, and he abuses it against the minority religious culture of Joseph's descendants in Egypt.

Just before Israel enters Canaan, the King of Moab hires a prophet to discredit the culture of political and religious freedom found in migrating Israel by pronouncing God's curse against it. His plan is to marginalize that culture and provide a basis for aggression against Israel. (Num 22–24) Early on in the life of the northern kingdom, Ahab and Jezebel persecute great numbers of the priests of Israel's God Yahweh, in order to establish a predominant place for the imported Phoenician god Baal. (1 Kgs 18:4) When Assyria besieges Jerusalem, Rabshakeh boasts that the God of Israel is not able to stand up against the King of Assyria and his god Nisroch any more than the gods of Hamath, Arpa, and other lands are able to. (2 Kgs 18:30, 19:37) Given this unfolding biblical rendition of history, both early and later Israel are determined not to use religion and politics as a club against their own people or other nations. Moses' God is a God of religious and political freedom and this God does not engage in unilateral aggression or marginalization of individuals or groups.[12]

---

12. For four different views on the subject of God and Canaanite "genocide" see Cowles, *No Mercy*. For the author's own views, see *Do My Prophets No Harm*, 115–17.

War and Oppression: Daily Bread of the Ancient Israelites

The Exodus story itself is about both external and internal captivity—a minority culture not indigenous to the kingdom is held captive and subjected to the depredations of the House of Seti (also Seth, or Sethos). This kind of oppression, though not as severe, is known among the patriarchal ancestors who first lived in Canaan. There they labored against the threat of local kings, as seen in the story of the aggressive kings who captured Lot (Gen 14), the coastal monarchies who quarreled with Isaac over properties and water wells (Gen 26), and the inhabitants of Shechem who menaced the daughters of Jacob. (Gen 34)

The long history of her culture is one bloodied by intolerance and aggression. Pharaoh refuses to recognize Israel's right to worship and to regulate economic policies for her own people, and after relenting somewhat, then races after the itinerant worshipers into the desert in an effort to exterminate them. (Exod 14) Assyria obliterates the independent existence of the northern kingdom after denigrating the God of the southern kingdom during the siege of Jerusalem, as we mentioned above. (2 Kgs 19:6) Nebuchadrezzar carries off to Babylon the civic-religious emblems of the Jerusalem temple after denying Judah a reasonable measure of independent political activity. First Ptolemaic Greece, then Seleucid Greece acquire Judea and environs as a client state, and apply varying degrees of rigor in their political, economic, and religious demands of the area, the worst of which produces the revolt of the Maccabees and a brief period of independence. Rome then appoints and maintains puppet Jewish priest-leaders who studiously ignore and subvert the political tradition of popular ancestral prophet-leaders by killing their modern counterparts, such as John the Baptist and Jesus of Nazareth.

Cross-religion political aggression and intolerance, whether stemming from forces external or internal to the nation, is seen in terms of loss of life, land, cherished possessions, freedom of action, and also in terms of the debilitation of the intellectual capacity of both the oppressor and the oppressed. In the name of religious orthodoxy, or in order to maintain politico-religious hegemony, great disasters within her memory befall Israel's nation.

After crossing Jordan and re-inheriting their relatively isolated ancestral homeland once again, the Israelites were nevertheless still menaced by the strong-man city-states of Philistia, Mesopotamia, and Syria, and later by the empires of Assyria, Babylon, Greece, and Rome.

Biblical Captivity

Israel held fast to the political ethic of local government until the time of David's son, when the internationalism and bureaucratic centralism of Solomon got her into trouble with Egypt. In fact, Israel was nearly destroyed by Shishak in 950 BCE. (2 Chron 12) Her political behavior then went downhill over the next 200 years until the north was conquered by Assyria, and the south by Babylon a century later. Much of the history to this point was given shape at or near the time of the final demise of the independent nations of Moses in Canaan around 700 and 600 BCE, and thus could be edited to reflect the lapses of a people consumed by neglect of constitutional political principles.

The Bible takes care to enumerate lives lost, details of dispossession of lands, homes, and animals, the suffering and captivity of men, women and children. The Bible's frequent body counts are rarely published in the manner of the triumphalist victory odes of Near Eastern monarchs, but rather in order to underscore the illegitimacy of the political practices of those who do the killing, or the failings of its own people who lust for blood and treasure, or the irresponsibility of those who subjected themselves foolishly to danger, or the consequences to foreign forces threatening local lands and freedoms, or to underscore the political price of defending those lands and freedoms. (Num 16:35; Josh 10:11; Judg 20:21, 25, 35; Judg 21:10; 1 Sam 4:10, 21:11; 2 Kgs 10:7, 21:16) It also provides numerous examples of psalmic lamentation tied to these losses. The writings of the prophets, in particular, link the backsliding ignorance of the people and their leaders regarding the foundational laws relating to political and religious pluralism to their increasing vulnerability to external aggression and internal injustice. What goes around comes around. Bible writers find that aggression is often meted out against minority religious groups, the disenfranchised, outcasts, slaves, and those critical of institutional political and religious power, and this leads to grave consequence.[13]

The text of the scripture is generous in its suggestion of solutions to the problem of religion-based political tension and violence. Those solutions are cast both in personal piety and corporate, socio-political terms. Policies for prevention and amelioration of religious violence spring from the earliest patriarchal traditions of the tribes of Israel, and in part, from the socio-economic milieu of their "country" way of life. Abraham, for example, demonstrates socio-political deference

---
13. Albertz, *Israelite Religion*, 77.

War and Oppression: Daily Bread of the Ancient Israelites

to the preference of Lot, in the case of conflict between their respective extended-family retinues. On the civic level, the new confederate nation of Israel institutes provisions to protect the varied interests of its citizens. Poor and foreign residents are to be treated civilly and not deprived of economic or intellectual rights. Cultic leaders in Israel are to mimic the lives of the landless and the lifestyle of the itinerant workers and thus demonstrate God's affinity with these people. In fact, in conflicts involving dominant parties who try to suffocate the lives of marginal citizens, God one-sidedly takes up the cause of the underdog, the socially oppressed, and offers a way to liberation, assuming they are willing to uphold his laws.[14]

Aside from the direct prohibition of killing in Israel's national Decalogue constitution (the sixth commandment), which is the mainstay of its anti-violence constitution, a political theory of a government system able to accomplish both the prevention and cure of religious violence is evident in the pages of the Bible. The three basic elements are land, political/national independence, and a central government limited by means of strong local government and justice-oriented constitutional law. The best overall method to maintain independence and prevent aggression and domination is that brand of law chosen by the founders of the nation—democracy in government and in religion. Those policies must protect prophets, place the same behavioral limits on government leaders as on citizens (Deut 17–18), and limit intrusion into religious affairs. (Lev 8; Num 6)

Limited government is accomplished by means of broad distribution of power throughout society and a balance of power at each level of government. This was achieved initially by a balance of power between the tribal affiliates of the confederacy during judges, and the weak, or occasional, central government. Once kingship took hold, the power of the King was balanced by the power of the national assembly and judiciary, and by the traditional tribal and town assemblies and judiciaries.[15] (Deut 16:18–20) It was also achieved by means of a "two kingdom" political science which balanced the private, cultic world against the public, governmental world.

In this book we suggest that the reading of the Decalogue as a religious document which encourages a close association of shrine and

14. Ibid, 52.
15. Albertz, *Israelite Religion*, 72–76.

state, is a clear misreading of the text and a misunderstanding of the political contexts enumerated by its historians. Ancient Israelite clans, sages, and historians, understood all too well what real fusion of sacred and secular was all about, and shunned it implicitly and explicitly. Israel was not a theocracy at any time during its long history. Moses separated cult and state in the beginning when he took over secular judgment and invested Aaron with ecclesiastic duties. The Bible sees such separation, maintained down through the period of judges and kings, as the surest and best way to promote religious diversity.

Archeology demonstrates that the cult of Yahweh was manifest in a wide variety of denominations throughout all periods of Israelite history, from the founding days of the patriarchs, through the wandering in the wilderness, and during the period of judges and kings down through the Palestine of Jesus' day. The literary prophets, while seeming to promote a sort of purist Yahweh religion, were, in fact, promoting a return to the freedom politics and local government of the God who liberated Israel from theocracy in Egypt. They objected to a civic manifestation of "nature" religion in their culture, which often invited priestly usurpation of the civic sphere or civic usurpation of the priestly sphere. What appears on the surface to be a centralization of cult in the days of Hezekiah and Josiah is better described as a re-definition both of the civic ethical parameters of religion (as exemplified by reformed practices at the renovated national cathedral) and a political re-configuration of the government of the nation toward greater localism.

Although there is a temptation to rely upon state religion even during the period of Judges (Gideon, near the end of his life), only with the advent of tyrannical or hereditary monarchy, and not always then, do we find considerable temptation to fusion of cult and crown, and the railings of the prophets against the oppressions which that system places on the people. Limited intrusion into religious affairs is accomplished by legal enactment of a human right to free expression, and separation of cult and state, both of which policies can be traced to the First Commandment.[16]

Israel's first commandment enacts a broad right to political and religious liberty, rather than a harsh limit upon such liberty, as is suggested by its seemingly partisan religious language. When the north secedes from the south and sets up its own independent civic and

16. Shinkoskey, *Do My Prophets No Harm*, 94.

religious shrines there, there is no civil war, in good measure because both sides understand that the regions of the country are historically and constitutionally empowered to act independently in political and religious matters according to local laws and circumstances—to govern their own "tents" and "see to (their) own house(s)." (1 Kgs 12:16) In fact, God prohibits religious civil war by means of a message from a prophet. (1 Kgs 12:21–24) Policies curbing religious expression are permissible only when foreign or domestic political parties promote or impose a return to the primitive and politically slavish nature religion originally banished from cultural life by the constitutional law of the nation.

The story of the Bible is the painstaking chronicle of Israel's occasional respect of the commandment promoting political and religious freedom and localism (the first and fifth commandments[17]) and her socio-economic success, and the more frequent neglect of the commandment and the precipitous reversals of her fortunes. Even when Israel respects free exercise, the problem of religious tension does not go away, it just eases. Political and religious factions and schisms replace conquest and civil war as the outcome of religious disagreement. But these are preferable to war.

The theme of religious tension and its proper resolution is of such importance that the Bible text frames much of the reporting of great moments in the past in these terms. With this new understanding of the Biblical problem and solution in tow, quite different parts of the narrative come to the fore than those traditionally cherished. For example, it is not the westward crossing of the Jordan by all of the tribes into Canaan that is the historic moment, but the eastward crossing of the same river by a two-and-a-half tribe sub-group, as we see below, that is the truly instructive event. It is no longer the exotic story and tempestuous personality of Sampson that occupies center stage, but the seemingly pedestrian information about Sampson's father and mother that emerges as truly significant.[18]

The narrative links these scenarios and others to what may be called the secular or civic salvation of the nation, the peace and happiness of its people. It also specifies a vehicle for discerning the problem

---

17. The first commandment to love the God of freedom promotes pluralism; the fifth commandment promotes local home rule by means of the depth and breadth of empowerment of family government.

18. Shinkoskey, *Do My Prophets No Harm*, 98, 138.

and promoting the solution. God acts in concert with highly intelligent individuals called prophets, who seem to fall along a continuum line as to their actual ethical strengths. Pedestrian prophets are marginally learned political citizens or scribes, pundits who may hold to any one of a number of religious beliefs, and who assert political views in and around the court because of the freedom given them to do so. The best lawyers, some capable Levites and priests, and, later, well respected rabbis, are middling sorts of prophets, who do their best to interpret sacred histories and records without benefit of oracular communication with God. Literary high prophets are a much rarer breed of commentator, as they enjoy a connection with the divine which a small group of followers, initially, and later a much larger group of followers, corroborate by their testimonies. Together with their followers, the high prophets analyze the existing deficiencies of the society in terms of respect of the commandments and initiate reforms which affect the consciousness of the people and modify the constitutive laws of government. Prophets are political animals who make their mark in the secular sphere, though they clearly exercise private devotional lives, usually independent of the mainstream religious denominations of which they are critical.

One early and major challenge to the constitutional way of life is seen in the story of the tribes who settle east of Jordan in Canaan. Once the twelve tribes agree to separate to their lands, the two and a half tribes quickly push the envelope of solidarity which unified the tribes. They erect a public altar east of Jordan. This causes a constitutional crisis. The act forces all twelve tribes to evaluate the level of liberality intended by the Decalogue regarding regional sovereignty and local religious independence. Joshua and the other tribes interpret the act as a declaration of independence, a giant step toward menacing the people and the values of those settling west of Jordan, and organize for war.

The two and a half tribes, ultimately, however, satisfy their compatriots that their intent is not to secede from the tribal confederacy, nor to establish a frame of regional government based on nature worship or any other cultural pattern inimical to the constitutional values of the Decalogue. (Josh 22) The separatist tribes do, however, exercise their tribal prerogative to organize religious worship according to a local pattern particular to their needs, and will use the altar to signify their legitimate regional interests in the confederacy. In effect, the eastern tribes ask the western tribes to bless their particularistic local efforts in interpreting Yahweh politics and religion, while at the same time they bless the overall effort of the confederacy with their support, rather than curse it. (Gen 12:3)

This story serves to underscore the notion, as we mentioned above, that the Bible is not primarily a book about ecclesiastic doctrine or ritual. It is, however, concerned with reasonable limits on ecclesiastic diversity and on political uses of religion. The two and a half tribes demonstrate that political and religious localism introduces tension into constitutional government, but it is a tension and diversity that can and must be tolerated as long as it does not subvert the fundamental political ethics of the covenant itself. The story mirrors the larger narrative of the Bible about the political and social lives of a democratic-oriented group of ancient people, their struggle to originate and maintain a civic constitutional law, and the type of leadership they look to for the governance of their communities and nation. Government under the judges is decidedly clan—and family-based, and even during the time of kings there is still heavy emphasis on a decentralized judiciary, local decision-making in "the gates," and separation of the functions of priests and officers of state.

In the pages below, we will outline broader concerns about religious violence and political aggression in the ancient Near East (chapter 2), return to the story of Israel and explore her deep-seated fear of captivity (chapter 3), and then explore specifics about the constitutional solution she developed to prevent it in her own society (chapter 4). But first we review in a general way the breadth of the scripture's commitment to limiting political and religious violence and control.

CAPTIVITY A CONCERN OF EVERY BOOK IN THE BIBLE

We have said that the pervasiveness and perniciousness of religious conflict and captivity and its solution is a defining theme in the Bible. Like the attention given to oracular revelation, this theme is found in each major grouping of books of the Hebrew Bible (e.g., Torah/Pentateuch, Prophets, and Writings) and New Testament (Gospels, Letters, and Revelation), and each individual book of the major groupings as well.

In the Introduction we suggested that captivity for Israel falls into two major types—external and internal. External captivity refers to conquest and deportation, a situation often accompanied by the besieging and toppling of the capital and the ransacking and destruction of its temple. A second form of external captivity occurs when a nearby nation puts pressure on local socio-religious norms. This can result from the formation of friendship or parity alliances and certainly from vassalage or suzerainty alliances with other nations. Isaiah, for example, rues Ahaz's alliance with Assyria and Jeremiah rails against Judah's alliance with Egypt. Both point out the effect which those alliances have on the laws and worship practices of the nation.

Internal captivity comes in two forms as well. First, the people turn responsibility for governing families and communities, church and economic ventures over to an ever boastful and incompetent central government. In doing so, they neglect or abandon the foundational commandments and place their hopes in rich and elegant princes who promise security and prosperity. This leads to the second form of internal captivity, competition between mainstream and minor denominations of religion, often involving religious repression and violence—persecution by the currently favored belief system of those not currently in favor.

The Pentateuch was compiled in stages, having as its goal the preserving of the story and the tradition of the people against the forces of religious and political jealousy and aggression. Awareness both of the threat and severity of captivity in the ancient world and the variety of methods traditionally used to prevent or overturn it fills the pages of those five books.

Genesis tells the foundational story of religious jealousy between Cain and Abel, and how socio-political rivalries play out in the violence in the world at the time of Noah. Abraham's wanderings are inspired by pursuit of both a place and a principle for peaceful coexistence with clan members and with neighboring tribes. The stories about the way in which Abraham and Isaac disguise their wives as sisters are not examples of the arrogant self-interest of the patriarchs, as some would have it. They are, rather, pointed reminders of the inflammatory nature of inter-tribal relations in a nomadic society. They demonstrate the political negotiation and social manipulation necessary to deal with the insecurity occasioned in the heart of the local ruler by a nomadic and charismatic prophet-prince and his beautiful and sophisticated female partner. It is yet another creative method used to prevent the outbreak of violence.

The Book of Exodus is focused entirely on a story of internal political captivity of a people by a particularly insecure and oppressive king. The book of Numbers deals with the religious conflicts and schisms which occur within the Exodus party itself, and also the politico-religious threat posed by the Amalekites. Leviticus presents a socio-political code of laws and ethics related to "holiness," a way of life based on individual self-government and protection of the rights of others so that peaceful economy and social life may prevail. Deuteronomy presents a formula for charismatic government designed to promote individual and clan responsibility for welfare of the neighbor and to sustain the high level of engagement in that process envisioned in the ancestral laws.

Joshua details the early tendency toward religious jealousy among the tribes during in-migration to Canaan, one major example of which is the schism between tribes settling east and west of Jordan. Judges relates a 200-year history of politico-religious jealousy among and between Canaanite kings and Israelite settlers, and Israel's efforts to repulse the imperial forces of the nations outside of Canaan.

The two books of Samuel are concerned with the Philistine threat of conquest of Canaan, the internal captivity of the mainstream religion by the decrepit priestly dynasty of Eli, and King Saul's usurpation of other cults which rose to challenge Elide corruption. It also presents the story of the rise of the charismatic political dynasty of David and his refreshing of the original civic laws and national church of Moses.

The books of Kings and Chronicles detail the 400 year history of the monarchies of Israel—the waxing and waning of the enforcement of the covenant laws. These cycles of "evil" and "good" parallel Israel's drift in and out of self-imposed captivity. The result of internal ethical decline is external conquest and suffocation of Israel's social culture first by Assyria and then by Babylon. The Psalms celebrate free exercise of political and religious rights during good times, and lament restriction or repression of those rights during oppressive times. It reflects highly individualized persecutions of the prophetic voices who penned many of the psalms.

The book of Ruth is a story about a particularly delicate form of socio-economic predicament that is a by-product of a largely patriarchal society, and whose solution is found in the laws of clan solidarity. It is also about the beauty and strength of religious understanding and cooperation that serves as an antidote to religious jealousy and violence. Esther is the story of life in foreign captivity under Persian leaders, wherein religious rivalry explodes in great fury even under the relatively benign worldview of the Persians. Ezra and Nehemiah are books about the restoration of the privilege of temple worship and recovery of properties in the ancestral homeland.

The books of the sixteen literary prophets are aflame each one of them with encouragement of the people to prevent captivity by honoring the ethical beliefs and practices of neighbors, and challenging the political powers when they overrun Decalogue legal prescriptions relating to limits on central government. Their literatures are declarations of independence and freedom from internal and foreign powers which corrupt the capacities of the people. The wisdom books—Job, Proverbs, Ecclesiastes, and Song of Solomon—are about the political and civic science of prosperity, self-government and thoughtful engagement by individuals with the natural and political worlds round about them. They stress man's own capacity for responsible self-government, irrespective of personal belief about divinity.

The four New Testament gospels, Acts, the general and special letters, and the underground visionary political essay of Revelation, all bear proper witness to the statement of civic mission given by Jesus at Nazareth: the purpose of Father and Son together is to heal the poor and the broken-hearted who are reeling from the blinding and bruising consequences of socio-economic and political captivity. (Luke 4:18–19) The gospels detail the untimely demise of John the Baptist in the heady environment of political jealousy and curbs on political speech occasioned by Rome and the Herodians. John's death leads Jesus to teach a civic gospel, challenge the political and religious authorities of colonial Syro-Palestine, and prepare his disciples for his own inevitable and brutal death. The acts and letters detail the struggles of apostles against intolerant mainstream Judaism, pagan culture, and other Christian charismatics who challenge their authority. Revelation is a thinly disguised broadside directed against imperial Rome, similar to the final chapters of the book of Daniel, which are directed against imperial Greece.

THE VOCABULARY OF FEAR

The curse of ancient captivity is not only chronicled and featured in every book of the Bible, but is deeply embedded in the vocabulary of the text as well. In fact, there is an extensive lexicography relating to captivity that dominates the parts of speech—the subject matter nouns, the active word verbs, and the descriptive adjectives of the Israelite language.

There are a great number of words related to distress, harm, oppression, abandonment, exploitation, aggression, bondage, and exile, and an equally large number of words expressing relief, wellness, redemption, restoration, enfranchisement, peace, release, and return.

The words used to communicate these critical events can be grouped into a chronology reflecting the all-too-painful cycle of events detailing political, economic, and social captivity repeated over and over again in the history summarized by Deuteronomistic and Chronicalistic historians.

The editors and compilers of the canon, and the authors of its principle discernable sources, describe the ever-present pressure on their free way of life by using a variety of distress-type words which denote the psychological fear of losing remaining liberties and possessions. Those writers understand present concerns to result from some recent event of corruption, bondage, aggression, or persecution remembered from the historian's own experience, or from the experience of parents or grandparents, handed down in the oral or written lore of the culture. This process resembles in many ways how the modern Jewish "holocaust" or "Shoah" memory is kept alive today in Jewish communities, several generations after its actual occurence. In Biblical times, national festivals like the Festival of Booths recalled the experience of slavery in Egypt, and the festival of Purim recalled the captivity in Babylon.

In effect, then, the writers of the canon express a kind of post-traumatic stress on behalf of the nation, a recurring nightmare about large events in the past, re-enacted when similar events trigger that memory and those fears in the present.

In the Bible there is a large vocabulary used to express the recurring pain of adverse events in the recent past, such as misery, suffering, plight, cry, sigh, cry out, lament, afraid, anguish, vexation, affliction. There are many words that relate to abandonment as well: forsake, cast

Biblical Captivity

off, cast out, turn the back. We will examine the Hebrew word yr' (fear) as representative of the post-traumatic pain that is the lot of a people oppressed from within or held in external captivity.

The word yr' can be found in verb, adjective, and noun form.[19] It occurs a total of 436 times in the Old Testament.[20] Its original meaning seems to have been "to shiver, shake." The kinds of fear expressed relate to fear of sinister socio-economic threats (Jer 42:16, famine; Isa 24:17, pit, snare), of defeat by enemies in combat (Exod 14:10; Deut 2:4; Josh 10:2; 1 Sam 7:7; 2 Kgs 10:4), of death by political means (Gen 26:7; Gen 32:11; Deut 13:11; 1 Kgs 1:49; Jer 26:21; Jonah 1:5; Dan 1:10; Neh 6:13), and of the martial power and deeds of kings. (Ps 45:5) Many synonyms exist, including Hebrew words which express anxiety, shaking, terror, and dread. The people, on the other hand, are encouraged to "fear" God, so that political oppression and external aggression in the community will not result in hot "fear" of defeat and debasement (Ps 25:12–13, Prov 3:25–26), but rather punishment of the evildoers. (Ps 52:6–7; Ps 64:7–9)

The next chronological stage, after fear of encroaching impoverishment, is the actual expropriation of rights, lands, and family members at the hands of internal power-mongers and external imperialists, who nibble away at what does not belong to them by raiding villages or cities. This stage is memorialized in the litany of words surrounding the concept lqh (take, capture[21]). Semantically-related Hebrew/English cognate words include grasp, seize (lkd[22]), trap, snare, plunder, take away, carry off (Isa 57:13; Jer 15:15); to be taken away, capture, rob, steal, consume (Zeph 1:2; Isa 7:20), and destroy (Gen 18:2; Ps 40:14). Other related concepts are tribute, affliction, pressure, vex, tribulation, trouble, spoil, humble, impose, claim, pay, prey, burden. This, in effect, is the economic imperialism phase of captivity, perpetrated by encroaching external powers nipping around the edges of one's national territory, or by one's own monarchs, oligarchs, or aristocrats taking things that do not belong to them because they can get away with it.

The word lqh means, fundamentally, to take or seize manually. It implies a rude and instantaneous assault on personal property or

---

19. Jenni and Westermann, *Theological Lexicon*, 568–569.
20. Ibid., 570.
21. Also "rush upon," Hoffmeier, *Israel in Egypt*, 34.
22. Jenni and Westermann, *Theological Lexicon*, 649; Ellis, *Biblical Hebrew*, 272.

War and Oppression: Daily Bread of the Ancient Israelites

territory, often the objects being food (1 Kgs 14:3), money/purse (Prov 7:20), cities (Num 21:25; Josh 11:16; Amos 6:13), land (Deut 3:8; Judg 11:13), and religious property. (Judg 18:24; 1 Sam 4:11) It also means to take life. (Ezek 33:6; Jonah 4:3; Ps 31:13, 104:29) The word also finds use in "take vengeance" (Isa 47:3; Jer 20:10), in the sense of God overthrowing those who perpetrate oppression, and taking an individual out of detention. (Jer 38:10)

The next step in the cycle of captivity is large-scale military hot war, a time of great physical activity and harm. This often happens concurrently with the previous step. In this regard we find English Bible words such as smite (Hebrew nkh), pluck up, tear, blast, cut down, waste, stroke, dashed to pieces, rip open, hew down, heap, waste, cut out, sweep, tread down, thresh, winnow, besiege (Hebrew hnh[23]). Closely associated with the physical activity of the falling down of human beings is the running from the scene of battle or the impending scene of battle. The Hebrew word we examine here reflects the all-too-frequent outcome of hot war, the act of fleeing. The Hebrew word "nus" (to flee) refers to flight from immediate danger. The Hebrew word "brh" (flee) refers to pre-emptive flight from coming danger.[24] Cognate words like refuge, flight, banish, drive away, and to become homeless derive from the same stem. The word in its most fundamental sense means "to remove oneself quickly from a region of danger," as avoiding destructive battle. (Job 20:24) One is often fleeing enemies (Exod 14:25), pain and suffering (Isa 35:10), or immoral behavior. (Gen 19:20, 39:12) Often one flees in the sense of emigration (brh) to avoid danger. (Judg 9:21)

Use of the word flee is suggestive of the range of implications a word can have for political fleeing in Israel. The ancients in Canaan lived in perpetual readiness to run from enemies. Often they ran from the countryside to one or another walled town or city for security. Often they fled into the untracked hills and mountains to hang out until danger passed. At times they left the nation altogether until things stabilized. Job describes the lot of early man. His life is short and full of fear: "Man that is born of a woman . . . cometh forth like a flower, and is cut down: he fleeth also as a shadow . . . ." (Job 14:2)

Civic flight at the approach of an enemy is an extraordinary panic: "Ye shall flee like as ye fled from before the earth quake in the days of

---

23. Hoffmeier, *Israel in Egypt*, 34.
24. Jenni and Westermann, *Theological Lexicon*, 725.

Uzziah . . ." (Zech 14:5) Jeremiah warns, "Gather yourselves to flee out of the midst of Jerusalem . . . for evil appeareth out of the north, and great destruction." (Jer 6:1) Indeed it is the job of a prophet to serve as a political watchman, as if on the walls of the city, to warn the people when political alliances are about to become political disasters. But if a prophet is reluctant, he may run from the task. Of Jonah it was said, as it was often said of the whole nation, "He fled from the presence of the Lord." (Jonah 1:11)

The condition of internal captivity to heathen lifestyle is as bad as external flight from an armed enemy: "The wicked fleeth when no man pursueth." (Prov 28:1) Hosea reminds that flight from the commandments, from the judgments against backsliding, brings the consequence of destruction, or "woe," as much as the "woe" of war: "Woe unto them! For they have fled from me." (Hos 7:13) Furthermore, "He that fleeth . . . shall not be delivered." (Amos 9:1)

Life lived in exile captivity is even worse yet that living in fear on one's own land. It is one of extreme vulnerability and insecurity: "I will send faintness into their hearts in the lands of their enemies; the sound of a shaken leaf shall chase them; and they shall flee as fleeing from a sword; and they shall fall when none pursueth." (Lev 26:36) Many will die untimely in captivity: "And ye shall perish among the heathen, and the land of your enemies shall eat you up." (Lev 26:38)

Matthew's account of the early family life of Mary and Joseph indicates the couple were no strangers to the volubility of political life and the depredations of tyrants in Palestine. An angel told Joseph in a dream, "Take thy young child and his mother, and flee into Egypt." (Matt 2:13)

The final outcome after all the fearing, taking, and fleeing from military or political blasting are the great apocalyptic curses mentioned so often in the canon, which we examine in chapter 4: exile, bondage, famine, pestilence, torture, death. Here we examine the Hebrew words "golut" (exile) and "moser" (bonds, shackles). The words "bonds" and "bondage" are used in the Bible to suggest captivity and oppression, not merely shackles and imprisonment. We are introduced to the larger scope of the word in Exodus: "The Egyptians . . . made their lives bitter with hard bondage." (Exod 1:13–14) In fact, Egypt is then referred to as "the house of bondage." (Exod 13:14) The Psalmist sees bondage in terms of personal suffering at the hands of those who persecute, and longs for release. (Ps 116:16) He has been "greatly afflicted' (10), and subject to, or nearly subject to "trouble and sorrow" (3), and "death." (8) Stephen judges that Egypt brought Israel "into bondage, and entreat(ed) them evil four hundred years." (Acts 6:7) Paul tells the Ephesian elders that "the Holy ghost witnesseth in every city, saying that bonds and afflictions abide me." (Acts 20:23) Here Paul suggests he comes under constant limitation of his freedom due to arrest and prosecution. Such persecution is religio-political in nature; he speaks of "my bonds in Christ." (Phil 1:13) Christ has taught men to esteem freedom (Gal 4:9; 5:1), but much of the world still remains "in bondage under the elements of the world." (Gal 4:3) Paul suffers "trouble, as an evildoer, even unto bonds" because he teaches Jesus was "raised from the dead." (2 Tim 2:8–9)

There are a number of synonyms related to exile that are liberally dispersed throughout the Bible text. The word "captivity" is used widely, particularly in the King James Version. (Judg 5:12; Deut 30:3; 2 Kgs 24:15; Isa 5:13) The words carried off/carried away (2 Kgs 17:6), expelled (Josh 23:5), banished (2 Sam 14:14), removed into (Deut 28:25), thrust out (Deut 33:28), scattered (Hab 3:14), dispersed (Esth 3:8), displaced/removed (Isa 10:31), moved/removed (Deut 28:25), and gone into captivity (Isa 5:13), are used as well.

These final destinations of desolation and destruction, in turn, give rise to new worries and fears of recurrence of such trauma and loss in a future date. But in the meantime, there are those who counteract fear with courage: words such as stretch out (one's hand), boldness, adamant, wall of bronze, strengthen, not bend, confidence, encourage, honor, judge, loose, overcome, withstand, and zeal. Many counteract taking with restoring, redemption, possessing, preserving, delivering, binding up, healing, awaking, dedication. Fleeing is countered with standing up, establishing, being steadfast, continuing, vigilance, setting aright, answering, diligence, refuge, fulfilling, keeping, planting, remaining, running (ironically). Exile is overcome with passing over, moving, turning, return, remnant.

2

Religious and Political Violence in the Ancient Near East

According to Israel's prophets and historians, the special political election of Israel was real and visible (Isa 42:1, 45:4; Ps 89:3; 1 Chr 16:13), but was quickly and easily neglected. Most of the time the lives of her citizens, the laws of her communities, and the thinking of her leaders were very much like the lives and times of other ancient Near East peoples. (Deut 30:15, 31:29; Num 14:27) There were only very brief periods of Decalogue-oriented kingdom building which took place among the followers of prophets and in the administrations of reformist monarchs. Israel as a community in Canaan approached the glory of the Sinai dream culture, with its heady socio-political awakening and activism, perhaps only a few times in Judges and Samuel, and arguably twice in Kings and Chronicles (during the reigns of Hezekiah and Josiah)—a mere handful of generations out of thirty or more before the Babylonian exile. Much of the rest of the time, Israel ignored her own grand constitutional system and wandered about in the political wilderness of partisan or autocratic hegemony. She mistreated her own citizens economically, politically, socially, and religiously and made alliances with heathen nations that committed the "elect" nation to wander far outside the constitutional interests of her people. This happened, to be sure, when the northern kingdom allied herself with Egypt against

Assyria, and later when the southern kingdom allied herself with Egypt against Babylon, thus triggering almost total destruction of her tenuous ethical civilization. (see chapter 5)

The broader ancient world waffled, like Israel, between progressive concepts of government and primitive, autocratic situations. Autocratic conditions resulted both from imperial dynastic kingship and from reform-talking governments lead by usurpers or oligarchic cliques which were ostensibly "democratic," but operated as a practical matter in a tyrannical fashion outside the scope of humane written law. Both these kinds of government were well-known in the world around the ancient nation of Israel. Their systems (in Biblical terms) of "judgment" (government) were, unfortunately, often characterized by the use of power against their own people or against neighboring nations in a variety of heavy-handed ways: restriction of freedom, political interference, compulsory service, tribute, confiscation of land, forced emigration, and other forms of economic exploitation, subordination, or terror.[1]

Classical political theorists and operatives like Heraclitus, Thucydides and Polybius in Greece, and Virgil, Pompey and Julius Caesar in Rome, expressed the idea that it is natural and right for the stronger power to dominate the weaker.[2] In this they are not different from modern political theorists such as Machiavelli and Lenin, modern capitalist colonial monarchs like Britain and France, and the United States in the twentieth and twenty-first centuries. Neither are they different from strong-arm kings who prated about the world scene well before the classical period—the likes of the early Mesopotamian imperialists Lugal-zaggasi, Sargon of Agade, Ur-Nammu, Shulgi, and Hammurabi; the Egyptians Menes, Tuthmose III (the Napoleon of ancient Egypt[3]) and Ramses II, the Hittite expansionists Hattusilis I and Mursilis[4], and the later Assyrian and Babylonian imperialists.

The ancient Greek political philosopher Heraclitus glorified the notion of natural superiority of one faction over another and the benefit of war to both the victor and the vanquished. He wrote, "Justice is strife." By this he suggests that justice among the community of nations

---

1. Garnsey and Whittaker, *Imperialism in the Ancient World*, 4.
2. For Thucydides and Polybius, see Ibid, 5.
3. Bauer, *History*, 212.
4. Gottwald, *Politics*, 20.

can best be apprehended by means of intolerance of the inferior by the superior. Furthermore, war is good for the citizenry: "War is the father of all things and is the king of all."[5] His theory ably represents the international philosophy of primitive polytheistic imperialism, as opposed to the polytheism of ethical pluralism which ancient Israel endorsed. Interestingly, this primitive theory was not without its advocates at the time the United States set out to place its martial stamp upon the world either. Theodore Roosevelt, for example, wrote, "I should welcome almost any war, for I think this country needs one."[6] Randolph Bourne, a contributing editor to the "progressive" magazine *The New Republic* and a critic of World War I, summarized the view of many at the time: "War is the health of the state."[7] By time of the post-World War II period, it became apparent that "war is the health (more particularly) of the President," as each new American President rescued a failing domestic policy or a personal conduct disaster by means of a roaring military romp or two on foreign soil.

In the first chapter, we asserted our contention that imperial violence and domestic oppression rooted in religion affected the nations of the ancient world in the same way it affected Israel. The gods of the nations had a war-like character whether for offensive or defensive purposes. Even Yahweh was known as a warrior who fought for the freedoms he wanted his people to enjoy. Fighting to obtain the resources of others, or to defend one's own resources, was a chapter of ancient history without an ending. The traditions of Old Kingdom Egypt suggest that human beings followed a pattern of inter-necine violence much like that expressed in the stories about their gods. Horus, worshipped in southern Egypt, and Set, worshipped in Northern Egypt, made rival claims as to rulership of all of Egypt and engaged in violence against one another. The kings of the Second Dynasty raised one or the other of those heavenly names in battle as they made similar claims to rulership of the land nearly 2,000 years before Moses.[8]

Because the gods constantly bickered in heaven, it was permissible, even wholesome, for nations to bicker on earth. War was waged in support of a group of one or more gods opposing another group of one

---

5. Quoted in Klassen, "War in the New Testament," 868.
6. Quoted in Healy, *Cult of the Presidency*, 48.
7. Ibid, 64.
8. Bauer, *History*, 67.

or more gods. For example, the Homeric epics note that when Achilles went into battle his shield boasted the emblems of both Ares and Pallas Athena, opposed as the two major gods of Mycenaea were to the gods of Troy. The Roman governor Pontius Pilate caused an uproar among the Jewish population when he ordered Roman troops into the sacred city of Jerusalem bearing depictions of Roman gods on their military standards.[9] Gods jealous of one another acted in heaven like petty kings and queens did on earth. They acted out their anger against other societies.

There are a number of standard ways that religion is invoked in political conflicts in Israel and in the ancient Near East. Often the deity is consulted as to whether war-making is propitious or not.[10] The war-making party, as we mentioned above, usually displays some emblem of the deity during battle, which is believed to inspire fright in the enemy and concern about the righteousness of the enemy cause. (I Sam 4–5) Before going to battle, political interests in Egypt and Urgarit participated in religious rites in order to convince themselves and their sometimes reluctant people of the righteousness of the cause. Before undertaking travel, nomadic or emigrating populations typically undertook similar rites as well.[11] The Israelites' rite of the Passover was a quasi-religious, quasi-political rite serving a similar function.

On the other hand, when societies such as Israel proposed the existence of only one God, it was a theological and political advance from primitivism because one God was not quite as capable of warring against himself as a mob of gods were against each other. The European wars between Protestants and Catholics, and present conflicts between Sunnis and Shiites, demonstrate that wars between monotheist parties are still a very real possibility. However, the declaration in Deuteronomy 6.4 that there is only one heavenly ruler—"The Lord our God is one Lord"—echoes the First Commandment idea that the citizenry and the people of the earth ought to live at peace with one another. When they look to no other God than the one who brought them out of Egypt, they look to the peace that is possible in a world of political and religious rights and pluralism. This God supports peace through law, and, if necessary, uprising against oppression. There is no heavenly or earthly justification for the warring of one people against another

9. Horsley, *Jesus and Empire*, 47.
10. Hiebert, "Divine Warrior," 877.
11. Kitchen, "The Exodus," 705.

Biblical Captivity

unless to recover freedom of political and religious thought and action, in imitation of that which was accomplished by the people of Moses during the Exodus. The unethical political violence that undermines the freedom of people from time to time in all civilizations of the earth cannot be laid at the feet of this God.

Aside from Moses during ancient times, there came along political theorists and reformers of a similarly ethical and anti-domination political nature during the classical period, such as Hesiod, Demosthenes and Aristotle in Greece, and Livy, Tacitus and Cicero in Rome, who argued for a balance of power and pluralism within the nation, and restraint in relations with other nations. We might also reference modern theorists like Locke, Blackstone, and Jefferson, and very early reformers like Urukagina in Sumer, Pepi II in Egypt, the Chinese sage kings, and the prophets of the other monotheist-type traditions of the Near East, including Islam.

The job of political rulers, in the ancient view of the ethical kings of Sumer, Akkad, Egypt, the northern Mediterranean, and the Far East, is to redeem the oppressed, not to exploit them. In Mesopotamia, for example, the king was to institute "misarum," meaning justice, or equity.[12] In Israel, proper governing is often translated "judgment." It refers to the duty of both positive attendance upon righteous government (enforcing rights), and a meting out of negative consequences against those who suppress rights. (Deut 1:17; 1 Sam 8:3; Neh 9:13; Isa 5:7; Jer 22:3; Matt 10:15) The very distress one designs to impose upon another will eventually come back to bite the designer himself: "When thou shalt cease [for a moment] to spoil, thou shalt be spoiled." (Isa 33:1) Especially heinous is aggression without cause: "Woe unto thee that spoilest, and thou wast not spoiled." (Isa 33:1) In Israel, political karma is also reflected in the law of talion—an eye for an eye, and a tooth for a tooth. In 2,500 BCE Sumer, the penalty for breaking a contract was the breaking of teeth, so the later metaphor had an earlier basis in physical reality.[13]

When democratic polities like ancient Israel grace the human stage, they seem to mimic the very ancient traditions of tiny villages huddled about the great river beds of the Near East and Far East (before those villages grew to powerful city-states), dedicated to economic

12. Weinfeld, *Social Justice*, 26.
13. Westbrook and Wells, *Everyday Law*, 34.

and political progress by means of irrigation, cultivation and consent of the governed.[14] In the early civilization of the Indus valley in India, the earliest kings, like the generous Manu, were men of the people who protected the weak.[15] Early Hindu writings, somewhat like the book of Deuteronomy, warn that powerful kings steal wealth and decision-making away from families.[16] China, too, lived in early times in peaceful localism along the Yellow and Yangtze rivers, and remembered sage-kings dedicated to just rule, at least until the time of her "unifiers."

The basic idea is peace through rule of ethical law. But the efforts of reformers are usually relatively short lived as against the efforts of usurpers and conquerors, who advance a variety of seductive ideas for dominance, one of which we saw above in the idea that war breeds discipline and helps a people accomplish great things.

In Israel's day, city-kingdoms now claimed the great river resources of Egypt and Mesopotamia and all-too-frequently proclaimed a right to imperial extensions of their rule. Israel mimicked the serenity of small-scale civilization and family rule by wandering through the wilderness, avoiding aggressive kings, and eventually by settling in the hill country of Canaan, where they shunned the depredations of hereditary kingship in favor of limited, popular magistrates called "judges."

The classical Greek tradition, at about the time of the advent of the Golden Age of representative government in the sixth and fifth centuries before Christ, seems to have carved out a similar niche as well. In pre-Homeric times, the war god Ares was accorded great favor. But by the time of the writing of Euripides and Aristophanes, the malice and evil of war as usual was demonstrably protested. In the early stages of the civilization of man, Hesiod writes, there was little war. Only later did Ares gain ascendency. But over time Athena then struggled to marginalize Ares. On temples of religious groups devoted to peaceful living, and in the writings of the democracy-oriented writers, Ares is given the denigrating nick-name Eualios, the "war-like one."[17]

---

14. Bauer, *History*, 30.
15. Ibid., 32.
16. Ibid.
17. Klassen, "War in the New Testament," 868.

JUSTIFICATIONS FOR AGGRESSIVE IMPERIAL ACTIVITY IN THE ANCIENT WORLD

Justifications of ancient imperial conquest or internal oppression can be grouped to a small handful of arguments, which have since withstood the test of time: the natural hegemony of the powerful; defensive or buffer-zone imperialism[18]; and economic imperialism. At the root of each of these three rationales is the idea that the deity supports and authorizes the hegemony. If the nation is strong, it is because its god(s) is strong. The nation is powerful and aggressive because the deity is powerful and aggressive. If the deity is mostly peaceable minded, but still wishes to protect his territory, he may annex territories round about him. If the deity is in need of water, or grain or workers, he may send armies much further afield to find and secure those resources. Also, at the core of these three rationales is the idea of the vitality of one particular nation within a family of related nations. In each region of the earth there is one nation which is "firstborn," that is, having a long tradition of superior development and culture that tends to dwarf other, lesser developed nations. In the ancient world the firstborn nation was the greatest nation, not only economically but ethically. It was the nation favored of God to raise up other nations round about because of its evident experience and superiority, in the way an older sibling might help to raise a younger one, to bring moral order into a world characterized by immaturity and chaos. (Jer 31:9)

The humane version of the "firstborn" theory posits the worth of a sort of humanitarian, benevolent colonialism and justifies efforts to be of use or of service to other nations. An enlightened society may well play the role of the firsborn by means of example, negotiation, and trade, thus interacting with other nations without using military persuasion. In the ancient world, Babylon was such a firstborn culture, exercising brotherly encouragement to cities about it. But in the eighteenth century BCE, for example, Hammurabi claimed that the high god En-Lil, ensconsed at Nippur, affirmed the right of his city, Babylon, to extend its rulership over all of Mesopotamia. Hammurabi did so by military conquest, however, not by voluntary confederation. The less

---

18. Garnsey and Whittaker, *Imperialism in the Ancient World*, 2. For example, King David extended the borders of the unified monarchy in order to put neighboring monarchies who often attacked Israel back on their heels; see 2 Sam 8.

humane version of the firstborn nation concept, of course, suggests that the firstborn nation deserves not just respect from lesser nations, but also adoration, gifts, and political subservience to its rulers and its god. This stage often comes on the heels of the more benevolent stage, after an imperial nation has suffered resistance and insults at the hands of the nations it merely desired to reform and protect.

Egypt, like Hammurabi's Mesopotamia and like the United States today, saw herself as in a position of manifest destiny to lead the entire world. Egypt's leader wrote that Amun "appointed me (Amenhotep III) to be "Ra of the Nine Bows' (leader of the nations of the earth)." New Kingdom Egypt ventured out into the nations "to bring moral chaos to order" in foreign nations.[19] She sought, for example, to subject Mitanni to the "good god" of Egypt.[20] Many ancient rulers, in fact, entered the capital cities of other nations in order to relieve those peoples of the oppressions of their own rulers. Merodach-baladan, from Ur of the Chaldeas, is one early exponent. He entered Babylon from the south to liberate the city from the Assyrian leadership supplied from the north. Soon after, Sargon II of Assyria returned the favor by liberating Babylon from its new Chaldean master.[21] The Persian Cyrus, too, liberated Babylon from the neglect of her people by Nabonidus. Imperial Rome, as well, found a way to "liberate" Greeks from Macedonian oppression. The Roman consul Flaminus writes of his act of political mercy, "The entire human race will revere the Roman name after the gods only."[22]

All this is reminiscent of statements about America as "leader of the free world" today. The American president has effectively become "President of the West," in addition to being President of the United States. President Kennedy positioned the American post-World War II presidency in the company of ancient regimes like Hammurabi's and Amenhotep III's, which aimed at being the good policeman of the entire globe: "We shall pay any price, bear any burden, meet any hardship, support any friend, oppose any foe, in order to assure the survival and the success of liberty."[23]

---

19. Garnsey and Whittaker, *Imperialism in the Ancient World*, 8.
20. Ibid, 14.
21. Bauer, *History*, 378–80.
22. Quoted in Bauer, *History*, 640.
23. Quoted in Healy, *Cult of the Presidency*, 86.

Biblical Captivity

Later on in the time of the New Kingdom of Egypt, however, the god's tone about Egypt's relationship to the "Nine Bows" changed. It moved from assertive to aggressive and menacing. Of Ramses III it was written, "Thy father [the god] sends thee forth to destroy the Nine Bows."[24] When the child-like nation does not take direction from the parent nation, it must be punished. A Neo-Babylonian building inscription asserts, "I [Nebuchadrezzar] called into me the far dwelling peoples over whom Marduk my lord had appointed me . . . that they should bear his yoke . . . ."[25] The same kind of deterioration of interfaith and inter-political relations internationally can take place with respect to minority groups inside a given polity. The disaffection of Ramses II with Israelites in Goshen may well have reflected the difficulty he was having with their counterparts still living in Canaan. This scenario still plays out in the imperial stories of modern nations as well. A recent Congressional hearing during the Obama administration aimed to place Muslim groups in America in a more defensive position than what they occupied during the G.W. Bush administration.[26] This certainly reflects the difficulty America is having with groups abroad unwilling to acquiesce to America's hope for national obedience to the protector of freedoms of the Western world, and her hope for economic support of the firstborn.

A variation of the parent vs. child nation theory of imperialism (or older brother vs. younger brother theory) is effected under the circumstance of two religious traditions that see themselves as equals, essentially twin siblings of equal sophistication. We will examine the Bible's theory of sibling rivalry in chapter 3, and touch upon its extra-Biblical correlates here. In Egypt during the Amarna, age just prior to the time of Moses, there was demonstrable competition between such Gods as Amun and Aton. Mesopotamian history demonstrates similar competition and violence between Enlil and Sin. In Israel there was open competition between Yahweh and Baal as well. Israel dealt with the inevitable conflicts between the one God of heaven and the many gods of nature by defining an ethical or cultural boundary between them rather than a simple geo-political boundary. Baal, for example, seems to have been tolerated in Israel during those times when and

24. Garnsey and Whittaker, *Imperialism in the Ancient World*, 11.
25. Bauer, *History*, 67.
26. Shane, Scott, "Hearing puts Muslim group in hot seat."

places where he and his people acted reasonably. (Judg 2:13) Israel, on the other hand, rose up against Baal when the oppressions associated with Baalism became intolerable. (Judg 6; 2 Kings 9–11)

Throughout history we find much economic motivation in the imperial adventure. In ancient Sumer, some 1,500 years before Moses, Gilgamesh of Uruk mastered the great cities of Sumer and gained access to their resources—copper and water—and also the holy city of Nippur, where the priests blessed and legitimated the rule of kings.[27] Gilgamesh rallied his reluctant forces forward to the north with the cry: "There are many wells to be claimed."[28] This was a time-honored goal for making war. In much the same way Enmerker, a predecessor of Gilgamesh, had used the name of the god Inanna to declare war against Aratta, seeking the precious metals of that kingdom.[29] In Egypt, the deity Amun prodded and encouraged the Pharoahs to obtain cedars from Lebanon, turquoise from the mines of Sinai, and incense from Punt to present to the god in support of temple sacrifice.[30] The deity also wished for subjugated nations to provide food for the fatherland, as Nubia was asked to provide for Egypt.[31] The United States fights wars in the Near East and the Far East (Viet Nam) under the banner of Jesus, in order to stabilize the flow of inexpensive oil to the cities of the American hinterland.[32]

If the establishment of local military garrisons on the soils of many nations doesn't always free up local resources for consumption by the firstborn, the simple expedient of military conquest often does the trick. Usually, the conquered nation then provides skilled workers and stone or metal resources that will aid in maintaining military activities of the neighboring power. Thus Egypt smites Sinai for its copper, vital for making bronze weapons, just as Sumer forages militarily among the mining cities of the mountains to the northeast.

It is this economic aspect of imperialism—the concentration of great wealth in the hands of one or a few greater rulers—that Israel saw as perhaps the most virulent form of "idolatry." Great kings confiscated silver and gold mines and used the wealth to mint coins on which they

27. Bauer, *History*, 52–59.
28. Ibid, 54.
29. Ibid, 55.
30. Garnsey and Whittaker, *Imperialism in the Ancient World*, 10.
31. Ibid, 31.
32. See Kiernan, *America: The New Imperialism*, 301.

stamped likenesses of their own faces, or throne names and insignia. The conquered nation, at such times, effectively was invited to acknowledge the grand ruler as though he were a substitute for the local deity altogether.[33] Such monetization practices, could be used to purchase the military support of mercenaries to keep the king or tyrant propped up in power, and its citizens mired in destitution and slavery.

The kings of China understand centralized religion and politics the same way as other monarchic civilizations. King Mu, around 900 BCE, was reminded by his wise advisers that the kingdom is like an onion, with five rings. As the king's army forages outward from the capitol city, the vassal hinterlands should normally be required to provide fewer and fewer resources for the regency and its cult the further away from the center they are located. If the king presses his luck with far-flung territories, the loyalty of those lands might well falter in a politically unpleasant way.[34] Only in the case of particularly powerful kings, does an ancient regime attempt to accomplish what the Assyrian rulers undertook. For example, Tiglath Pileser wrote that he undertook to subject far-away kings "who had never known subjection."[35]

The ancient battle against the imperial element of political life assumed a sort of cosmic proportion for those on the defensive against it. Israel resorted to a protective God who battled against the primordial elements of chaos, darkness, and the dangerous depths of the sea and the monsters who lurk there. One can be sure those elements are but metaphors for the unpleasant kings and polities of the ancient world. Many of the psalms extol a God who "ensures the failure of any natural or historical threat to Israel's security and well-being"—in effect, the monsters both of the deep and of the land.[36]

THE CRUELTY OF THE IMPERIAL GODS

Religious imperial war is such an important function of kingship that one or more of the gods of the pantheon is often saddled with the job of specializing in it. Thus Inanna, Ningirsu, and Marduk take on the task in Mesopotamia, Hadad in Syria, Agni in ancient India, Baal in Canaan,

33. Lewis, *Ancient Tyranny*, 110.
34. Bauer, *History*, 304.
35. Ibid, 287.
36. Hiebert, "Divine Warrior," 878.

Dagon in Philistia, and Janus in Rome.[37] These and other territorial gods often tangle with one another to obtain slaves, land and natural resources. Serious civil strife or international war between gods, as we mentioned above, resulted from the combative directives of the oppositional gods Horus and Seth in Egypt, Enlil and Sin in Babylon, and Yahweh and Baal in Canaan.

Often, one god will proclaim that he favors a particular principality over another. For example, Inanna announces that she prefers Uruk to Aratta (Elam), a statement issued in diplomatic correspondence that essentially amounted to a declaration of war against Aratta and an alliance with Uruk.[38] If, on the other hand, a god can declare war, it can also declare peace. In fact, it is a commonplace in the ancient world that a national or international god mediated the boundary disputes of nations. Thus the Sumerian judge god Sataran decided an important boundary dispute between Lagash and Umma in Sumer.[39]

Often, a great god takes special care to nurture a particular nation, giving it confidence of victory. For example, a Sumerian war shout reminded the enemy, "The great gods created Uruk."[40] Often it is claimed that the superior or aggressive god despises the god and people who are the enemy. Kings of the First Dynasty of the Old Kingdom of Egypt left evidence of the violence of their administrations, as the decapitated warrior bodies demonstrate on the Narmer Palette.[41] Later, one of those First Dynasty kings sent militias outside the kingdom to "the east" to subdue peoples there.[42] This was a habit and passion of many of the Pharaohs of Egypt in later dynasties. Not long before the time of Moses, Egypt itself was conquered and subjected to foreign rule for a century by the Hyksos. The Hyksos were a Syro-Palestinian people regularly disturbed by Egyptian military activity in the Levant. This reversal of roles was an early example of the Israelite historical scientific notion of "taking captivity captive." An ethical God will eventually turn oppression against a firstborn people who exploit their own or others. What goes around, politically, comes around. This works, too, when a

37. Prichard, *Concise Atlas*, 68–69.
38. Bauer, *History*, 55.
39. Ibid, 90.
40. Bauer, *History*, 58.
41. Ibid, 26.
42. Ibid, 62.

nation such as Israel reneges on friendship treaties with brotherly nations like Babylon. For example, Jeremiah indicates that Babylon was used by God to despoil Israel after such a betrayal. (Jer 39:11–14; 2 Kgs 24:10—25.10; 2 Chr 36:6–19)

An inscription relating to the military campaigns of Thut-mose III of Egypt speaks of foreigners in a way which hints at the lengths of aggression to which despotic kings are wont to go: "These enemies whom Re abominates . . ."[43] We will see below, this concept of "abomination" (hate) was applied to the Israelites in Egypt, and lead to the great economic and intellectual cruelty meted out against the children of Jacob. Thut-mose III, a self-confident imperialist, led campaigns through Palestine and to the north and east almost every year for twenty years against the abomination of "eastern" Asians.[44] He proudly records the outfall of his conquests: "Now the children of the princes and their brothers were brought to be hostages in Egypt."[45] The king has in mind permanently enlarging his kingdom: "His majesty . . . set up his stela in Naharim, (thus) extending the frontiers of Egypt . . ."[46]

Thut-mose justifies his imperial activities as a trust given him by the god of Egypt: "the victories of my majesty, through the plans of my father [Amon-Re], who entrusted to me all foreign countries." He spoke of "victory . . . which this good god performed."[47] Thut-mose's propensity for land and slaves was facilitated by means of his control of the agencies both of cult and state. The priesthood could not easily check his ambition, since he controlled their livelihoods as well as that of his own soldiers, to wit: "His majesty commanded that [the victories which his father Amon had given to him] should be established upon a monument in the temple which his majesty had made for [his father Amon] . . ."[48]

Neo-Assyrian kings gloried in imperial violence, as demonstrated by reliefs depicting them luxuriating near the severed heads of foreign combatants, and writings mentioning the festooning of city walls with the bodies of rebels and the hanging of conquered politicians in cages

43. "The Annals In Karnak," *ANET*, 235.
44. "The Asiatic Campaigns of Thutmose III", *ANET,* 234.
45. "Sixth Campaign," *ANET*, 239.
46. "The Annals in Karnak," *ANET*, 240.
47. Ibid.
48. Ibid, 235.

suspended at the gates of cities.[49] Assyria frequently cut down trees and burned crops, in a scorched earth policy that makes Sampson's burning of wheat in Philistian fields seem paltry. (Judg 15:4) The Assyrians dug up graves of the honored dead and even carried away fertile top soil in carts in an effort to erase the memory and any traces of the existence of the local population.[50] Tribute money exacted from the provinces was used to support the King's temple his huge standing army, and to build lavish cities. Neo-Assyrian rulers appealed to that paragon of very ancient Assyrian imperialism, Sargon I, who had himself maintained a large standing army, fed daily from the larders of his quivering subjects.[51] The Bible attests the cruelty of Babylon's Nebuchadnezzar, who killed the children of Judah's king Zedekiah before his face, before putting out the eyes of the rebellious colonial leader himself. (2 Kgs 25:6–7)

Political monsters, as Israel's apocalyptic writing demonstrates, are often associated with the dictators who menace life in the Mediterranean world. The emperor of Rome, for example, was described in only a thinly veiled fashion by the writer of Revelation as a "dragon" of the deep.[52] (Rev 19:11–21) One historian suggests, "Israel's poets knew existence as a struggle to survive and recognized threats from both natural and political realms . . ."[53] God becomes king of the universe by virtue of his laws banishing violence and oppression. It is clear that while the periodic flooding of the earth threatened physical existence from time to time, political dictators just as regularly threatened civic existence and free worship.

While we have mentioned a number of rational justifications for imperial oppression and violence, we must now report here that most often ancient despots did the dirty deed of mayhem and murder simply because they could get away with it and because they enjoyed it so much. In fact, it was because aggression and captivity was so capricious and brutal that ancient societies feared it so much. Ancient fear of ancient economic, intellectual and physical captivity/slavery is visible even today in the modern world from one continent to another in the surviving forms of massive earthen mounds, stone and wooden walls,

49. Kuhrt, *Ancient Near East*, 2:517.
50. Smith-Christopher, *Theology of Exile*, 50.
51. Ibid, 51.
52. Hiebert, "Divine Warrior," 879.
53. Ibid, 877.

and moats. Across the globe, ancient peoples "streamed in" to walled cities to protect their cultures from political marauders. The stone age culture tutored bronze and iron age militants in the ways of domination, apparently. The ancient graveyard uncovered at Jebel Shahaba near the modern Sudan-Egypt border reveals that more than 40% of the skeletons of men, women and children there either had stone weapons embedded in their bones, significant cut marks in those bones or bone fractures due to stone weapons.[54]

Autocratic imperial dynasties have been found from the 4th millennium BCE onward in Mesopotamia and Egypt. In the third millennium, Uruk undertook conquests of other city-states in Sumer. Reciprocal captivities are recorded between cities in Sumer and in Elam, and savage competitiveness characterized Lagash and Umma. In Old Assyria, Sargon imposed a military dictatorship on a great many communities in Mesopotamia. Old Kingdom conquests are evident between the northern and southern kingdoms in Egypt, and between Egypt and Nubia to the south, and were particularly evident in the time of Senusret III in the early second millennium. Many traces have been uncovered of the imperial activities of Hatti and Mittani. The early sea-going imperialism of King Minos of Crete in the Mediterranean was followed later by the truculent conquests of the Sea People along the eastern Mediterranean in the late second millenium. The reciprocal war making and conquests of the Persians and Greeks are well known, as are the Peloponnesian Wars between Athens and Sparta, the Punic Wars between Rome and Carthage, and Rome's subsequent turn to aggressive expansionism in the late first millenium.

Many of these conquerors left triumphant boastings of their depradations. The Sumerian Lugulannemundu gloried in the "steady tribute" he imposed on Elam around 2,500 BCE. Eannatum of Lagash is buoyed up by the begging for mercy and great emotional distress that he imposed on the city of Umma: "They prostrated themselves, they wept for their lives."[55] The Assyrian Ishme-Dagan, taking the name of the war god Dagan, gloats that "I flattened the town [of Hatka] in one day", and then asks his subjects back home to "Rejoice!"[56]

---

54. Wendorf and Close, "History of Egypt (Prehistory)," 333.

55. Bauer, *History*, 90.

56. Ibid, 171.

The conquest art of the first "unifier" of early Egypt, Narmer, shows the king parading past the bodies of decapitated warriers.[57] In Sumer, the Stele of Vultures depicts vultures flying off with the heads of those conquered by the king of Lagash.[58] The king of Assur, the Assyrian Adad-nirari, gives vent to a stereotypical kind of chest-beating after upon imposing misery on nations and peoples: "Adad-nirari, illustrious prince, honored of the gods, lord, viceroy of the land of the gods, city-founder, destroyer of the mighty hosts of Kassites . . . who destroys all foes north and south, who tramples down their lands . . . who captures all people, enlarges boundary and frontier; the king to whose feet Assur . . . has brought in submission all kings and princes . . ."[59]

The development of mathematics in Mesopotamia was stimulated as much as anything by the need to record body counts, booty inventories, and numbers of formerly freemen and women taken captive as slaves.[60] Leaders were concerned that due diligence be taken by their administrations to record numbers of living captives, although rounding seems to have been permissible. Shalmaneser I boasts of taking 14,400 captives in 1,200 BCE. Tukulti-Ninurta boasts of enslaving 28,800 Hittite prisoners of war, and builds his capitol city with them. K'ang in China of the first millennium records, "I captured 13,081 men." In both the Near and Far East the number of dead is determined either by the number of heads carted back to the capital city,[61] the number of hands cut off, or, in the case of Saul's particular temperament, the number of foreskins removed from his uncircumcised Philistine adversaries. (1 Sam 18:25)

Ashurnasirpal reminds us that he threw a celebration with 70,000 invited guests and during the feast claimed to be: "Great king, king of the world, the valiant hero who goes forth with the help of Assur; he who has no rival in all four quarters of the world, . . . the powerful torrent that none can withstand . . . he who has overcome all of mankind . . . whose hand has conquered all lands and taken all mountain ranges."[62] Shalmaneser IV records the terms of economic tribute which

57. Ibid, 26.
58. Ibid, 91.
59. Ibid, 250.
60. Ibid, 45.
61. Bauer, *History*, 566.
62. Ibid, 337.

Biblical Captivity

he imposed on his enemy: "Heavy tribute for all time I imposed on them."[63] Sennacherib decorated Nineveh's new palaces with his subjugation art. Ashurbanipal, after him, burned and looted Susa in Elam, but then did his best to desecrate the entire ancestral civilization of the city by raiding the royal tombs and carrying off the bones of the kings into captivity in his native land.

The Medes and Scythians carried out atrocities against one another's cultures. When Sparta conquered Messene in 630 BCE, they took the people of the territory into slavery. They also took unilateral action against the Achaioi Phthiotai in 413 BCE, extracting money and hostages/captives.[64] The sixth century Greek warlord Alexander of Pherae dispensed with the notion of an anthropomorphic god altogether and worshipped the spear whose depredations got him the kingship in the first place. He tortured innocents, buried men alive, and exterminated entire cities by inviting them into a peaceful assembly, then cutting them down. He dressed political opponents in bear or boar skin and set dogs upon them.[65] Plutarch wrote that Alexander's actions, and presumably the object of his worship, "earned him the hatred of the gods."[66] Nebuchadnezzar deported populations of Israelites several times during his reign. Once Persia ousted Babylon, Cyrus's son Cambyses tried to outdo his father in imperial one-upsmanship, and conquered Egypt. After him, Darius carved his conquest art into a cliff overlooking the highway into Susa.[67] The emperor Asoka in India, before he changed his ways, boasted of taking 150,000 captives in the territory of Kalinga. Once a republican nation, imperial Rome took captives from all her conquests and used them as gladiators, killing them for sport and entertainment.

One can understand the cosmic proportions ascribed to conquest and captivity by subjugated peoples when one considers the immensity of the suffering which was often imposed upon the vanquished. Thutmose III, for example, relates: "I desolated his towns and his tribes and set fire to them . . . their (re-)settlement will never take place. I captured all their people, carried off as living prisoners, . . . I took away the very

---

63. Ibid, 363.
64. Garnsey and Whittaker, *Imperialism in the Ancient World*, 97.
65. Lewis, *Ancient Tyranny*, 135–136.
66. Ibid, 136.
67. Bauer, *History*, 508.

sources of life . . . their grain . . . and their groves . . ."[68] A thousand years before, Sargon I of Agade made clear to his foes that any thought of rebellion against his rule would not be tolerated. On the pedestal of a statue of himself, he asserted his ascendency in both civic and priestly realms and threatened punishment for rebels who would try to revert to self-government and pluralism. The thought of the personal pain and family horror outlined thereon must have made men shiver: "May Shamash destroy the potency and make perish every offspring of whoever damages this inscription."[69]

THE FEAR OF INTERNAL CAPTIVITY IN THE ANCIENT WORLD

In view of this Near East legacy, it is not surprising that Bible narrators demonstrated such a stark fear of captivity and a strident desire to overcome or prevent it by means of a strident emphasis on the humane constitutional law. They intended to provide a safe haven for their own citizens at home by refraining from "friendship" treaties with dynasts abroad. Friendship with despots was no picnic and Israel desired to avoid it. While some scholars have questioned the harshness of exile in Babylon, others see indications in the prophetic literature of Ezekiel and the book of Lamentations of a level of deranged sadness suggestive of post-traumatic stress syndrome.[70] The horrific curses/punishments promised vassal nations that rebelled against suzerains like those found in Esarhaddon's treaties are much like those promised unrepentant Israel by her prophets. The prophets' warnings were apparently not idle threats or unlikely scenarios, but rather simple reminiscences about the pattern of imperial business in the ancient world. The level of historical information about imperial activity and its effects was considerable. Nebuchadnezzar, for example, was known to campaign abroad almost yearly.

The Persians seemed somewhat more humane, but their bureaucratic methods of control were just as effective. They gave conquered lands to court patrons as proprietary estates, in the manner suggestive

---

68. "The Barkal Stela," *ANET*, 240.
69. "Historical Documents," *ANET*, 267.
70. Smith-Christopher, *Theology of Exile*, 89–94.

Biblical Captivity

of the governorship of Nehemiah.[71] When the Greeks swept into Palestine, some of their princes enacted reforms, while others were extremely harsh overlords, setting about to exterminate any memory of the ancestral laws relating to self-government, as did Antiochus Epiphanes in 167 BCE. Antiochus accepted a bribe to install a pro-Greek Judaic high priest in Judea, but not long after, the Jews were prohibited from practicing even this perverted form of their religion.[72] Finally, the harsh ruler installed a statue of a foreign deity in the Jerusalem temple, an abomination to the Hebrews and the cause of the Maccabean uprising. (Dan 11:31, 12:11; Macc 1-2) The House of Herod served the Roman occupiers of Palestine quite well, lapping up priestly and political offices for themselves, at the expense of the diversity customary in Israelite history, and oppressing minority religious and political leaders such as John the Baptist and Jesus of Nazareth. More radical political movements which sought self-determination were suppressed with equal or greater dispatch.

The earliest recorded whole units of Biblical literature—the civil defense victory "songs" found in Exodus 15, Deuteronomy 33, Judges 5, and Habakkuk 3—extol a God of freedom who releases Israel from early and localized versions of such vicious imperial aggression and captivity. The goal of life in Canaan is summarized thusly: "Israel shall dwell in safety alone." (Deut 33:28) In the time when Deborah arose to inspire Israel, oppression in Canaan was so severe that "In the days of Shamgar . . . the highways were unoccupied and the travelers walked through byways." (Judg 5:6) God's victory of local right against imperial might was surprising. The Canaanite cities expected their heroes to return having "divided the prey; to every man a damsel or two." (Judg 5:30) But God was successful in confronting impetuous power: "Thou has trodden down strength." (Judg 5:21) A theme for the remainder of Israel's days as a nation, and even beyond, was struck by the prophetess: "Awake, awake, Deborah . . . utter a song: arise, Barak, and lead thy captivity captive . . ." (Judg 5:12) One who is called by God must inspire resistance, work with others to turn the tables on the oppressors, and rectify freedom in the land.

The Bible narrative is highly suggestive of a common pattern of religious and political oppression and captivity in the ancient Near East,

---

71. Ibid, 53.
72. Coogan, *Old Testament*, 501.

which we will examine more thoroughly in the remaining chapters. When the people of one god are conquered and taken captive by the people of another god, they are typically deprived of two major natural freedoms or rights—the right to their own labor power and the right to the expression of intellectual belief or conscience. Subjugated people were often placed at forced labor at or near the shrine of a competing god, where they not only were forced to work for the new god, but at times obliged to convert to the religion of the god as well. The deprivation of the right to labor and the right to religious conscience was the general situation of the children of Israel under the reign of Ramses II, as elaborated in Exodus 1—13 (see chapter 3), and much later under the Seleucid prince Antiochus Epiphanes (see chapter 6). Some degree of deprivation of these dual rights were imposed on citizens by a few of Israel's own kings such as Ahab and Ahaz. Shalmaneser V of Assyria, and Nebuchadnezzar of Babylon, of course, deprived both those they exiled, and those remaining in the land, the full exercise of rights they had previously known. For example, there is evidence that the political and religious activities of both Ezekiel and Second Isaiah were suppressed during the Babylonian exile. Ezekiel, for example, clandestinely crafted a constitution for a future Judean state, and Second Isaiah used a pseudonym for his literary efforts. He also exhibited a frank monotheism that was likely to offend the polytheistic Babylonian culture.[73]

While Israel hated this kind of captivity and legislated against it for its own citizenry, there is at least one example of its application in their own national history. They enslaved the Gibeonites in the early days of the settlement to provide wood for a shrine of Yahweh. (Josh 9:22-27) The Bible story suggests that this particular event of religious enslavement was a moderately benevolent policy. Full enfranchisement was not possible since the Gibeonites had dealt deceitfully with Joshua. Long-standing policy under Israelite law allowed honest and peaceable aliens full citizenship rights of conscience. To deny constitutional rights and obligations to ethical people invites the very punishment sought for another.

Upon his accession to the throne of Babylon, Cyrus freed groups that the Babylonians had deported and held captive, such as the Israelites. (Isa 45) Ancient kings were at liberty, as well, to proclaim freedom for denominations not necessarily subjugated by captivity, but rather

---

73. Albertz, *Israelite Religion*, 413–436.

Biblical Captivity

subjugated by means of falling out of favor with the previous monarch. Pharaoh, on the other hand, was remembered as only grudgingly and momentarily providing religious liberty for the children of Israel, even when they were long-time residents of the nation. (Exod 1–12) However, some 700 years prior to Pharaoh's negotiations with Moses, Ishme-Dagan in Babylon released devotees of Enlil, Ninlil and Ninurta from forced labor at the hand of the previous king, so they might devote their service to the denominations of their choice.[74]

We mentioned above that the Bible views internal political oppression as a particularly important variety of captivity, a consequence of inattention to the Decalogue. It seems to form an intermediate stop on the way to full fledged external conquest, exile and slavery. In Israel, David, Solomon, and Rehoboam each escalate the amount of state-mandated labor (corvee) over that level characteristic of their predecessor. Israel's historians remember her early, power-hamstrung judges and priests as providing inexpensive, exemplary service to the nation, and her later power-infatuated kings and priests as a source of continuous and consequential evil in relation to the people. Notable are the stories of the captivity of the nation by the Benjamin tribe's House of Eli, the usurper priest Abiathar, the oppressor Rehoboam, the hapless despot Ahab attached to the puppet strings pulled by his foreign princess Jezebel, the cruel autocrat Manasseh, the later, tyrannical Hasmonean and Herodian dynasts, and the Sadducees with their high priestly families in tow. Certain classical historians of the extra-biblical world, like Polybius and Herodotus, see the internal politics of nations in a similar way. A nation makes the mistake of glorying in a single individual, as if that leader alone were responsible for all good things. The glory then goes to the head of the ruler, who acts increasingly erratically, violently, and misanthropically.

The broad brush of early Egyptian history is instructive. First Dynasty Pharaohs in Egypt compeled human sacrifice of servants to accompany them in service into the afterlife.[75] The First Dynasty internal political purge that took place at the time Semerkhet ascended to the throne not only removed people from the landscape, but all references to the prior Pharaoh Adjib from the monuments they were inscribed

---

74. Weinfeld, *Social Justice*, 82–83.
75. Bauer, *History*, 63–64.

upon.[76] This political carnage is responsible for the outbreak of civil war and the start of the Second Dynasty. The third and fourth dynasties are noted for enslaving large portions of their own populations.[77]

Herodotus, a Greek historian writing around 300 BCE, makes pointed reference to domineering Pharaohs of the Old Kingdom such as Khufu and Kahfre (Cheops). Khufu closed down temples and sanctuaries all over Egypt, in the fashion of twentieth century communists 4,500 years later.[78] Kahfre kept these policies in place, so he could be glorified alone, as his uncle was.[79] The two implemented a life-time of forced labor on virtually the entire population in order to build their immense pyramid tombs.[80]

The Middle Kingdom in Egypt was launched by one of the most savage Pharaohs known in Egyptian history, notes Herodotus. His name is Akhtoy I (Achthoes). The early historian Manetho mentions, "He hurt people all over Egypt."[81]

In Sumer, the First Dynasty of Kish evidences heavy control over the aspirations of its people. One inscription recalled that her king "made firm all the lands."[82] Rebellion by "elders of the land" is noted in Kish.[83] The revolutionaries eventually seek asylum in the Temple of Inanna, demonstrating that god's concern for political rights and rest from labor. A black hole in the Sumerian King List[84] points either toward an obliteration of a culture by one of its contumacious kings, or its opposite, a period of what historians are wont to call "anarchy," by which is suggested an absence of strong kingship, like the "intermediary periods" between autocratic dynastic kingship in Egypt.

Historian Sima Qian, Prefect of the Grand Scribes in second century BCE China, notices a cycle of political irresponsibility and dissoluteness in China as well. He sees that hereditary rule inevitably replaces popular rule, as Israel's historians noted as well. In China the

---

76. Ibid, 66.
77. Ibid, 79, 81.
78. Ibid, 85
79. Strassler, *Landmark Herodotus*, 175.
80. Ibid, 174; Bauer, *History,* 85.
81. Bauer, 147.
82. Ibid, 17, 21.
83. Ibid, 102.
84. Ibid, 4.

Biblical Captivity

pattern of dissoluteness characterized the Dynasty of Xia in the late third and early second millennium.[85] It also was the way of the Shang dynasty, which ruled throughout most of the second millennium. Even well into the Zhou period of the first millennium, the people were attentive to the importance of political pluralism. One song of wisdom from the period intoned, "To block people's mouths is worse than blocking a river."[86]

About the same time in Greece, Hesiod expressed a popular yearning not only for intellectual freedom, but also freedom from heavy labor conscription and taxation. He looked forward to the day when the people will "amid feasts enjoy the fruits of their labors."[87] The same sentiment issued forth from the pen of Micah about the same time in Israel: "They shall sit every man under his vine and under his fig tree; and none shall make them afraid." (Micah 4:4) Athens enacted a unique strategy for lengthening out periods of domestic tranquility. In a sort of turning-the-tables action, they exiled for 10 years any politician who obtained too much power, in order to cool his oppressive jets. They prevented him from taking his people into captivity by taking him into captivity first![88]

The efforts of populist reformers not withstanding, kings in the first millennium Near East continued to plunder their neighbors and their own people. Shalmaneser V imposed such heavy work requirements on his people that his successor Sargon II was forced to provide relief. This he did in part by harvesting the wealth of the northern kingdom of Israel, which he carried off to Assyria.[89]

The oppressive early kings of Rome such as Servius Tullius and Tarquin the Proud, were confronted by reformers like Romulus and Remus, who jump-started constitutional government in Rome. Roman government then alternated between constitutional monarchy and republicanism, before turning finally to offensive-minded international violence.[90] Before Rome could become an oppressive imperialist state ruled by Emperors, China beat them to the punch. The totalitarian Shi

85. Bauer, *History*, 36.
86. Bauer, *History*, 330.
87. Ibid, 361.
88. Ibid, 525.
89. Ibid, 374.
90. Bauer, *History*, 474.

Huang-ti, the first Chinese communist, in 231 BCE modeled his polity on the despotic socialist state of Shang Yang in Ch'in China some 130 years before.[91]

In order to derail the inevitable tendency of Egyptian-style or Chinese-style dictators to arise and control thought and labor in African or Oriental great king style, Israel enacted the Decalogue's first and fourth commandments, aimed, respectively, at free political and religious thought and free labor—liberation of minds and bodies. We will review the legal material in chapter 4 below, but first we review the ancestral tradition of peace and tolerance that inspired Israelite lawmaking in the first place.

---

91. Ibid, 566.

3

Falling Into Captivity and Rising Out of It: The Foundational Stories

THE BIBLE PRESENTS ITS readers with a psychological theory of aggressive rulership and political conflict. The theory can first be seen in dynamics of families like that of Adam and Eve, and Jacob and his wives. The children of those foundational figures engaged in religious and political jealousy and rivalry, like that of the larger-scale political families of Egypt, Mesopotamia and Israel. One sibling, or one ruler, less favored than another, desires to be adored like the favored sibling, and can think to accomplish it only by marginalizing, overthrowing, or killing the other and replacing him. While unbridled zeal is given to this lust in imperial societies, citizens of locally governed, ethical societies are bidden to be kind to one another and are fitted with a bridle of humane law to reduce their capacity to enact the primitive fantasy of superiority and retribution common to the thoughts and emotions of all. In such egalitarian societies, violence is sanctioned by law only to punish offenders, or, if necessary, to uphold or restore constitutional values as against those who would subvert them. Violence is discouraged and education, tolerance, and patience is encouraged—the gradual kingdom-building of the heart, mind and family, which makes use of the non-violent political tools available in every community.

Falling Into Captivity and Rising Out of It: The Foundational Stories

The Bible gives a good deal of insight into the causal factors relating to religious and political violence. The book leaves the reader with the strong impression that God and his prophets are realist pacifists and that typical politicians, with their religious supporters in tow, are often aggressive and violent fundamentally, that is, not for defensive purposes alone. The stories we explore below suggest that the God of the Hebrews does not cause or promote the violence that occurs regularly in its pages, but labors instead by means of law and leadership to enfranchise the kind of gentle, fruitful, mature power-sharing that Jacob and Esau, for example, ultimately achieve after a long period of friction and enmity. (Gen 33) God associates himself with efforts to defend and free victims of aggression and oppression.

While the patriarchal stories like that of Jacob and Esau give Bible readers the impression that the rivalries between brothers and neighbors are personal affairs involving just a couple of persons in rural/pastoral settings, these stories, in fact, are meant to apply to larger, more institutional kinds of settings that occur later in large cities and in relationships between political parties, economic classes, and nations. In fact, patriarchal figures such as Abraham, Isaac and Jacob are not merely heads of small households. Each one of them is a kind of prince, a politico-military leader who gathers around him a large extended family, a number or workers and servants, and a variety of neighbors who uphold the charismatic leadership of what amounts to a tribal political governor. Thus, when Lot is taken captive by a coalition of city-state kings in Canaan, Abraham is able to rally 318 of his own servants/workers to effect a rescue. (Gen 14:13-16)

When rivalry breaks out between brothers (Jacob/Esau, Isaac/Ishmael, Joseph and his brothers), between wives in a single family (Sarah and Hagar), or between relatives (Abraham and Lot), the causal factors and the preventative and restorative strategies suggested in those instances are then shown to be applicable in larger scale events later in the Bible story. Sibling rivalry is a well studied phenomenon in modern psychological analysis. It was also carefully studied by Bible writers attuned to the psychology of desire for material wealth, fame, position, and power observable in human events from the misty, pre-historic past down through the days of written history. The oral traditions circulating among the people and the written annals of kings assured that both the cold wars and the violent activities occurring in the families of the ancient royals and the ancient priestly families were well known among the common people. In this chapter we will examine one such extra-Biblical account, of an Egyptian named Sinuhe. His early life, playing out in the belly of an ancient superpower wracked by palace political intrigue, led to exile into Canaan in somewhat the same way that Abraham's resort there, Moses' migration there, and David's internal exiles, took place. The accounts about the lives of Abraham, Moses and David were likely preserved in both oral and written fashion just as those about Sinuhe were.

According to the Bible pattern, then, it is no accident that the great international rivalry which was bred out of a Biblical family squabble among two wives of Abraham (Sarah/Isaac/Israel vs. Hagar/Ishmael/Edom), played out in similar geo-political conflicts elsewhere in the Mediterranean world. For example, the brothers Romulus and Remus fought for power at the founding of Rome, and their progeny divided into city-states which subsequently fought over similar goals provoked by causes similar to the original quarrel.[1] It should also not be a surprise that sibling gods inspire their followers to bicker on earth, as the followers of Osiris and Set demonstrated in Egypt.[2] There is, in the pattern of rivalry behavior, a root of the very ancient practice of both religious magic and sacrifice by which practitioners try to outwit death, win advantage in battle, or put an end to famine or pestilence or some other suffering, by such means as transferring untoward outcomes to some animal, some other individual or some minority religious or political culture.

The modern American phenomenon of an aggressor bullying one who is different, or perceived to be less whole, is well represented in the Bible and its ancient milieu as well. Such an individual is often chosen as a scapegoat to carry the transferred individual or corporate insecurity, self-loathing, sin, or crime of another party. For his part, the scapegoat is perhaps more visibly scarred than the average, but otherwise is just one of the flock or the community. It is possible that this official transfer of guilt was thought to be a valid, even scientific, way to heal an ailing individual or society by making both the instigating and sacrificial parties "at one" with God and man. The scapegoat makes things "right." It is "right" that the inferior party suffers, in this way of proto-scientific

1. Bauer, *History*, 358.
2. Williams, *Violence and the Sacred*, 30.

thinking, perhaps because some internal moral defect led to his physical condition in the first place.

It is also possible that the scapegoat ritual and other manifestations of this behavior merely reflected an institutional mentality requiring that subordinates suffer for the dastardly deeds of irresponsible leaders. The mainstream individual or group further defiles the already wounded individual, or in some modes of sacrifice, an unblemished specimen, to enlarge its own superiority, satisfaction, or success, or to appease a higher power. In the most severe of such traditions, female or developmentally disabled infants are left to die, exposed to the elements, and the handsome sons or daughters of kings are sacrificed to the god. Those marginal infants who survive and mature are subject to the kind of discrimination that follows the maturation of "challenged" individuals on the margins of society in modern times.

A more responsible theory, enacted in the ancient ritual of the responsible ruler, requires that the captain suffer for the inadequacies of his shipmates. He goes down with the ship while his workers are rewarded with the life boat. This is enacted in the Bible in the suffering servant narratives of both the Old and New Testaments, and can be found also in the beliefs and actions of non-Israelite ancients like Abimelech and the good Pharaoh in the time of Abraham, both of whom believe they themselves must be held accountable for adulterous behavior as much as any commoner.

The ethical approach to the disabled is modeled well in David's kind treatment and political elevation of the lame Mephibosheth. (2 Sam 9) While the ancient institutional political norm is to sacrifice the happiness of the disabled and politically marginalized on the altar of insecure pride, the Biblical socio-political norm is to rescue the halt and poor by sacrificing personal advantage in favor of an ethic of equal access to respect and power.

The Bible encouragement to voluntarily sacrifice land, limb, and even life in a process of sharing power and wealth and standing up against illegitimate power—in effect exposing oneself rather than others to political, physical, and economic loss—has been shown to be effective in modern times as well. Tremendous political progress can be brokered by means of self-denial, as Ghandi demonstrated in twentieth-century India by the simple expedient of fasting and non-violent political action. Ghandi followed the model of Moses, who eschewed his early bent toward political violence in favor of humble and persistent petition and negotiation, and in the process won the political "life" or blessing/freedom of his people and the "death," or political embarrassment, of the firstborn of Egypt. Moses' story is an early example of the political outcome which the literary prophets and New Testament founders and apostles later try to convince their audiences is possible in the day of Roman occupation and priestly puppet government as well—with steady effort and organization the exalted can be abased, and the abased exalted. This transfer is done one person at a time, and one event or incident at a time.

For example, God does not want Abraham to sacrifice Isaac's life as a magical or royalist means to any end whatsoever, as many primitive societies were wont to do. He suggests it is enough to use an animal as a shadowy surrogate and simply approach God by means of the power of ethical behavior and personal entreaty. Jesus sides with and heals the heavily ostracized Gerasene mad-man, while the swine (representing the legions of oppressing Romans) have a come-uppance instead, as the bedeviling spirits of the mad-man now inhabit the bodies of the pigs, and cause them to run off the edge of a cliff.[3] (Mark 5:1-20) Here the spirit of insecurity and violence is extirpated from the primitive and oppressed, and is unmasked in spades in the ruler and oppressor. The spirit of real healing proceeds to infect the one who is the butt of jokes or in need of well-being, and the spirit of self-hate or self-superiority leads the violent to a violent death.

RELIGIOUS RIVALRY AND ITS SOLUTION IN THE PRIMEVAL AND PATRIARCHAL NARRATIVES

The purpose of this book is to give greater attention to a little discussed theme of the Bible—the perniciousness of religious conflict in the communities of the ancient Near East—and thereby give greater visibility to the variety of religious liberty laws enacted in those ancient societies. A clear concern of the Biblical narrative is God's persistent effort—calling of messengers, establishment of legal norms, encouragement of political action—to prevent or end this kind of violence. An important political idea runs throughout the two testaments: God's concern and

---

3. Williams, *Violence and the Sacred,* 13.

mandate for peaceful deference to the religious conscience of others. The first statement of this is found in the creation narrative. Mankind is created in the image of the peaceful, high God so as to be sovereign and humane in thought and action, unlike Mesopotamian mankind, who are said to be the physical offspring of subordinate gods who war constantly.

Key to discerning the heart of evil among human beings is to understand both the jealousy and the perceived superiority of people of sectarian faith. Such jealousy finds its earliest expression in the Garden of Eden, in the serpent's envy of God's ways and the claimed superiority of his own. After apparently establishing himself in a camp separate from God, the serpent introduces religious tension into the relationship between Adam and Eve. The earliest solution to the problem of religious confrontation among humankind is the accommodation of Adam's initial faith to that modified faith suggested by his partner Eve, or perhaps in the mutual accommodation of each to the faith of the other.

Once humankind is settled into life outside the Garden of Eden, we learn that it is God's intent to protect those who are different and who are perhaps just as insecure as those in the mainstream of social affection—one such as Cain. Cain is different because he tills the land rather than tends the flock like Abel. Israel, much later settled in Canaan with its twelve tribes and now parsing through its ancestral history for one or another political purpose, is still largely pastoral and is often at odds with the settled, agricultural city-states in Canaan and the Levant during Judges and Kings. Thus, this story makes sense to the instant audience and, incidentally, seems to mitigate in favor of a degree of tolerance of the religions of the Canaanites.

The story of the earth's first political murder is set in the context of jealousy over religious worship. Cain's sacrificial offering is rejected by God and Abel's is accepted. Cain then slays his brother in order, most likely, to take his place of leadership in the small, but rapidly growing society of agricultural workers in the primeval world. While Cain is socially marginal because of his occupation, he becomes even more marginal due to the (perhaps negligent) homicide of his brother Abel. Rather than bullying him for his difference or encouraging hasty blood revenge violence against him, God provides a reasonable identification for him as a as yet unconvicted felon, a "mark." God also exiles him from his homeland. This action, while a punishment, also seems to provide a refuge and home for him on the margins of society. In addition, any who would exact vengeance on him are to be subject to a heavy penalty. (Gen 4:15) Apparently, the exact nature of the homicide is not clear to the parties, and thus it may not have been fully intentional. God metes out both justice and mercy at the same time. This is an early foreshadowing of the later Israelite practice of designating sanctuary places, "cities of refuge," for criminal offenders so that cool and impartial justice can be provided rather than hot vigilante justice. (Exod 21:12–14; Josh 20)

In due time a third son of Adam is born. Seth is a kind of substitute for or restoration of the departed righteous Abel. The offspring of both Cain and Seth are presumably protected by the arrangement of Cain's exile. Cain is given a second chance in his new home, and sires a respectable nation of citizens, much as the felons emptied from England's prisons are given a second chance in the wilds of the eastern shore of the New World and manage to create a respectable polity there in the seventeenth century. God sides with whatever innocence and potential remains in Cain, and the reader learns that the bet was well placed in this case.

The enmity introduced into the world by Cain is in due time expressed in a somewhat different form by Lamech, who admits to his wives he has killed a man who struck him. He has done the deed and is clear and open about it. It is not clear whether he boasts of his retaliation against the young man, or if he personally suffers for what he has done. For example, the King James Version translates his confession as "I have slain a man to my wounding, and a young man to my hurt. If Cain shall be avenged seven fold, truly Lamech seventy and seven fold."[4] It seems that this refrain gives voice to the guilty feelings of the offending party as much as to a defense of the legitimacy of the act.[5] Lamech is an ethical man who has defended himself against violence. His punishment is his great mortification over the loss of a life, and, if anyone thinks he needs more, or kills him for it, the law ought to fall with vengeance on that man.

---

4. The GNB translation has it: "I have killed a young man because he struck me. If seven lives are taken for killing Cain, seventy-seven will be taken if anyone kills me."

5. Brueggemann, *Genesis*, 66.

Falling Into Captivity and Rising Out of It: The Foundational Stories

This brief portrait may be seen as a reflection of a level of social retribution and control necessary to curb the conspicuous level of violence in the ancient world.[6] Legal violence must be used to counteract gratuitous violence. Clearly, however, Lamech feels more innocent than Cain, since he suggests any knee-jerk repercussion for his act ought to be sentenced even more sternly than that specified for vengeance against Cain. (Gen 4:23–24) His is much more clearly an act of accidental or negligent homicide than in Cain's case.

Here we see in the very ancient world a differentiation something like that between premeditated homicide (the numerous examples of regicide in the Bible) and negligent homicide (Cain/Abel), and between negligent homicide and accidental or justifiable homicide (Lamech). There are higher and lower degrees of culpability and penalty for different levels of intent. This may be read as sensitivity to the perennial problem of sorting out levels and types of violence, whether religious, political, or criminal. There are justifiable forms of such violence and unjustifiable forms, whether inter-national or intra-national. The Bible aims to sort these out for the reader at any early stage in the book, so the reader can follow the flow of the political and ethical arguments that ensue. The Song of Lamech suggests there is a considerable tendency among early mankind toward unstudied blood retribution—the sort of provoked or unprovoked action of one rival against another for political or military or family gain. Several thousand years later, in fact, Jesus is still suggesting victims should refute the practice of unbridled vengeance by turning the cheek and thus handle violence privately with the same high level of diligence that Lamech suggests is appropriate for public officers to deter it in an earlier day: seven times seventy. (Matt 18:21–22; Luke 17:3–4)

In time, the nations and their peoples subject themselves to so much violence that God sends a flood to destroy them. (Gen 6–9) The pinning of responsibility for the great flood on God reflects early humankind's sense that things happen for a reason. The flood happened as a consequence of humankind's ill-treatment of one another. Even nature responds negatively to the violence committed on its soil. The Bible gives the sense that God accepts responsibility for the horrific event, even though he merely created the world and left it to operate according to laws of nature and constitutional law. Men who hate God,

---

6. Westbrook and Wells, *Everyday Law*, 73.

or who hate people and their humane laws, will pin it on him in order to aggrandize themselves or their views anyway.

The descendants of Noah make a city and form a centralized priestly administration to support the political power of their culture in Babel. They bolster that nexus by means of the construction of a great tower or temple. God dislikes this monopoly of political and religious power and scatters the people abroad into numerous decentralized cultures with their own languages, and presumably their own separate religions. What the story doesn't say, but implies, is that minority groups migrate away from the center to relieve themselves of its oppressions. This action presumably reduces the immediate problem of internal socio-political oppression of the people living in and around Babel, but ultimately subjects the world to the temptation toward petty rivalries across nations and peoples and to the temptation toward promiscuous pluralism (too broad a range of religious and political diversity). A passage in Deuteronomy suggests the result much later on of this licentiousness. The nations outside Israel are appointed (perhaps self-appointed) to worship the sun and moon and the heavens, using the primitive sexual and social rituals associated with such worship, but Israel is ordained to worship the God who frees peoples from the iron furnace of oppression and stabilizes families and communities. (Deut 4:19–20)

In the Bible, the solution to the problem of political and religious rivalry, over and over in the patriarchal narratives, and in the permanent settlement histories, is to find a place for the rivals without resorting to violence. The answer is the same in every case. The ethically superior party is to give way to the ethically inferior one, while at the same time the ethically inferior party ultimately suffers some tangible loss as well. In other words, the solution must be both just and merciful, reasonable and effective.

When Abraham arrives in Egypt there is socio-political rivalry between he and Pharaoh around Sarah's beauty. Abraham believes Pharaoh will be tempted to use his power to dominate the visitor and his wife. (Gen 12) Abraham submits to Pharaoh's political authority, essentially agreeing to give up his wife in order to keep peace. We will examine this story in greater detail in the next section.

Abraham applies a similar solution to the problem of cultural aggression in his day when he recognizes conflict among his own

Falling Into Captivity and Rising Out of It: The Foundational Stories

herdsmen and those of Lot. He chooses peaceful spreading out of the retinues of the two powerful pastoralists rather than confrontation and imposition of his own will. He further emulates God's method of deference to the agency of man by suggesting Lot choose his own favored place for pasturage and for settlement. Lot chooses land east of the Jordan River. Abraham accepts what is left over. This recalls the fact that God offered Adam and Eve a similar choice of habitats as well—life within the garden or life outside of it. What remained after their decision was left to God.

In Canaan, Abraham and Lot live a tenuous existence on the margins of Canaanite city-states, and are treated with suspicion by kings in the area and with outright contempt by kings outside of Canaan. The family interact with monarchies in the polities of Sodom, Salem, Gerar, Shechem, and Adullam.[7] There is tension, stratagem, and misunderstanding between Abraham and King Abimelech of Gerar, for example, based on the reasonable expectation of social dominance exhibited by tribal kings over families in their societies (see section 2 below). Abraham and his group are especially vulnerable, since they have wandered away from the protective wings of the larger clan in Harran. (Gen 20:11–13) Ultimately, Abimelech recognizes Abraham as an ethical "prophet" and seems willing to deal with the couple on the basis of common law propriety or international law.[8] (Gen 20:7)

Within Abraham's own family, there also arises religious tension. Abraham's son Ishmael "played" (Gen. 21.9 NRSV) or "laughed"[9] with (at) Isaac, the other son. The significance of this wording is often overlooked at first by readers of the English Bible, and the passage is unfortunately depoliticized thereby. But the Hebrew word translated into English here more particularly means "mocked" (KJV) or "persecuted," and it is this meaning the apostle Paul sees in the incident. (Gal 4:28–29) Here the incipient religious contention is solved in the same way. Abraham defers to the wishes of his wife, who wishes to maintain a comfortable distance between her son and Hagar's son, so that Isaac is secure as Abraham's heir. (Gen. 21.10, 12) Hagar and Ishmael move to Beersheba and Paran, where Ishmael's lineage become capable and independent, like those scattered from Babel long before. But, at root,

---

7. Gottwald, *Politics*, 36.
8. Gottwald, *Kingdoms*, 10, 12.
9. Smith-Christopher, *Theology of Exile*, 187.

Biblical Captivity

the story is one of religious conflict between the two women. Hagar has a deeply spiritual-ethical bent, as we learn shortly when she experiences a theophany. Sarah, the lesser of the two, is jealous of her and engineers the abdication based, apparently, on notions of ancient Near East socio-legal propriety.[10]

The tendency to overlook the political content of words translated into English can be found elsewhere as well. In the apocryphal book Bel and the Dragon, also called Bel and the snake, included in the Septuagint version of the Hebrew scripture and in some versions of the Protestant Bible (such as the New English Bible), Daniel "laughs" when the King believes that an idol of the god Bel has eaten the food left out for him in the temple. Daniel points out that the priests have entered the locked room through a hole in the floor and taken the food for themselves.[11] But the import of this innocence is more consequential for people than in the case when a modern parent laughs when a child finds the cookie left out for Santa is gone in the morning. Such laughter in the Bible is associated with scorning or mockery, and thus disbelief and resistance, as when Sarah "laughed," mocking God for asserting he would bring her a child.[12] (Gen. 18:11–15) Here Daniel successfully badgers the king into realizing the priestly system of his administration is based on primitive notions, and that Daniel's understanding of law and progress is more fitting for his rule.[13] (Bel and the Snake: 21–22)

As a result of several episodes of youthful mischief, which implicate Jacob as a misbehaving sibling, Esau develops considerable animus toward Jacob, especially after his brother obtains the blessing reserved for the elder child. (Gen 27) Jacob flees Palestine, sensing the intensity of Esau's hatred toward him. (Gen. 27:41—28:2) Both boys mature considerably in the interim, yet considerable deference, skill, and gifts are required by Jacob to secure Esau's forgiveness. (Gen 32) However, the story ends well, without violence and the rivalry is thus resolved in true, constructive Biblical fashion. (Gen 33)

The story of Jacob's sons in Shechem, on the other hand, is an example of how socio-religious difference can lead to considerable political aggression. Jacob's clan holds to a different standard of pre-marital

---

10. Trible, *Texts of Terror*, 9–35.
11. Daniel, *Bel and the Snake*:14–22.
12. Smith-Christopher, *Theology of Exile*, 187.
13. Daniel, *Bel and the Snake*:21–22.

Falling Into Captivity and Rising Out of It: The Foundational Stories

sexual conduct than one of the heathen townsmen apparently does. The young townsman sleeps with Dinah, the daughter of Jacob, and then proposes to take her as his wife. The father of the impudent young man proposes that Jacob's clan should settle among the Shechemites and intermarry. The sons of Jacob propose, deceitfully, to do so, as long as the Shechemites take care of a "ritual" public health matter—the circumcision of the males of the tribe. While the townsmen are recovering from the procedures, the brothers Simeon and Levi kill the males of the city and confiscate their flocks in retaliation for the liberty Shechem has taken with their sister Dinah. (Gen. 34:25) This episode of culture - or religion-swaddled political rivalry distresses their father Jacob, who believes his clan is at fault. Jacob then removes the family out of the area into a self-imposed exile of shame in Bethel, where the people are presumably a bit more hospitable to Israel's brand of civic sexual rectitude. (Gen 35:1–7)

Jacob's problems with his sons do not end there. A number of Jacob's sons are jealous of the youngest son Joseph's self-proclaimed ethical and religious superiority, and they mimic God's method of resolution in an ignorant fashion by creating geographic space for the exercise of their own divergent modes of expression. They remove Joseph from the land of his birth.[14] (Gen 37) In Egypt, Joseph prospers and finds a degree of acceptance for his ethical proclivities and administrative abilities, and the family later resolve the rivalry in a mature way.

In sum, God, together with Adam and Eve, give way and place to Cain. Abraham gives (another) place to Hagar and Ishmael so they can develop a powerful ancestral legacy in their own right. Abraham gives the best land to Lot when economic conflict arises. Jacob leaves his homeland for decades in deference to Esau, and later removes himself from his settlement at Shechem when friction develops between his family and the locals. Joseph lives outside his clan territory and without enmity toward his brothers after they sell him into servitude in Egypt.

This pattern of socio-political deference continues on throughout the Bible narrative. Much later, Moses forgives his brother Aaron, who tries to usurp power from him during the Golden Calf incident, and instead shares power with him. Moses later gives the glory of leading the settlement effort to Joshua at the time of the Jordan crossing. He stays completely away from the land so Joshua can have command of the

---

14. Ironically, this action also diminishes the temptation to further persecution.

operation. Job and the Psalmists continue to embrace ethical behavior even when they are not rewarded for it, and when their rivals, who behave poorly, seem to be rewarded instead. David repeatedly gives right of way to Saul and lives for extended periods of time to the west and south of his home territory, even when Saul behaves badly. The literary prophets protest that there are others more capable than themselves, and use the sword of truth and knowledge rather than of violence to achieve an effect on the populace.

Prophets like Job, Second Isaiah, and Jesus are suffering servants, proponents of the deference to others modeled during the patriarchal age. They are peaceful exemplars of support for the common good rather than support for partiality and privilege extended to the educated, wealthy, and influential. Jesus carries his socio-political protest right into the precincts of illegitimate political power in Jerusalem, and in effect, to Rome itself, with a boisterous, individualized protest devoid of corporate violence and violence against persons, in the Temple. He teaches in a parable that the prodigal son, like Cain or Ishmael, when given time and place, can mature and ultimately be given a respectable title in the family, a seat like Mephibosheth was given at the table at David.

In sum, the Genesis narrative, together with others following it, suggest the great problem of human civilization is politico-religious tension, and chronicles a variety of solutions ranging from patience, negotiation, and deference (God and serpent; Adam and Eve); to sharing the land (Abraham and Lot), exile (Cain; Ishmael; Jacob; Joseph), and migration (Babel; Abraham; Isaac; children of Israel in Egypt). The rationale for these policies and activities is to provide opportunity for growth, enact justice, provide peace, and establish holiness (responsible liberty/trustworthiness).

In the next section, we will review in a bit more detail the problem of the socio-sexual licentiousness of kings in the ancient world, and then evaluate the political dominance of the people of Jacob in Egypt by a particularly absolutist king. The political secession story that plays out in the Book of Exodus and the entire Pentateuch is a story of internal captivity leading to a negotiated religio-political schism or secession and unanimous consent to a new constitutional law for a new people hammered out at Sinai. Once in the wilderness, the prophetic leadership of the group experience an anarchist-oriented rebellion—a coup attempt to overthrow the Decalogue and the community's legally constituted political prophet-leader. This story of Korah underscores the age-old tendency in the Near East for local government to be jettisoned in favor of fanaticism or absolutism. But before we proceed to these stories, we look at the extra-biblical story of another Egyptian Moses-type figure, whose story resembles that of those in the Bible narrative who serve as advisers at the court of government.

THE ANCIENT COURT OF FEAR—SINUHE AND HIS BIBLICAL COUNTERPARTS

It has been suggested that the ancient Egyptian story of Sinuhe parallels some aspects of the lives of Abraham, Jacob, and even Moses.[15] Sinuhe is an official in the court of the Middle Kingdom Pharaoh Amenmhet I, who rules from 1991 to 1962 BCE. While Amenmhet's son is involved in "extending the frontiers" of Egypt in Lybia, Sinuhe back at home accidentally witnesses a successful plot to assassinate Amenemhet.[16] Although there is not even a faint hint of his involvement in the crime, the god of Thebes nevertheless cautions Sinuhe in a dream revelation that the best course of action is to flee the country anyway.[17] Sinuhe runs to Syro-Palestine because he believes the conspirators will try to kill him to keep him quiet. He is only able to return home when Pharaoh's son Senwosret, now on the throne for some time, hears he is alive and summons him back to court.

Abraham and Jacob are each injected multiple times into the tenuous world of royalist or aristocratic intrigue as well. Abraham essentially flees Egypt to avoid the mischief that appears to surround him there in the house of Pharaoh. (Gen 12) He also rubs up against court intrigue in Gerar of Canaan. (Gen 20) Jacob flees the environs of Laban in Padan-aram (Gen. 28-31) after wrongfully being implicated in the theft of household idols. Both men find refuge in the hill country of Canaan. Sinuhe, too, is sheltered and essentially adopted by kind herders for a lengthy period of time. This aspect of his story recalls the life of Moses, who takes flight to Midian after committing manslaughter,

---

15. Matthews and Benjamin, *Old Testament Parallels*, 137–141.
16. "The Story of Si-Nuhe," *ANET*, 18–22.
17. Ibid, 19, 21.

fearing he will not be given procedural rights under the Ramesid regime. (Exod 2:11–22)

All of these incidents demonstrate the all-too-ready environment of royal court terror and capricious justice in the ancient Near East, and the desperate measures that must often be taken, even by those of noble reputation, to avoid being consumed by it. More than any other, perhaps, the story of Sinuhe resembles that of David, trying to survive in the shadow of the jealous and rapacious Saul, the first king of Israel. Sinuhe, who works his way into leadership in the military in the tribe he is taken in by, is later challenged to a duel by a strong warrior in large measure, it seems, because Sinuhe evidences loyalty to the political authorities. Thousands gather to watch the event and Sinuhe amazingly prevails, just as David does against Goliath.

Beyond the war story connection, there is another even more interesting parallel. Sinuhe, much like David, is ultimately exiled for a couple decades by the machinations of a royal clique out to kill him. He lives a disguised life in devotion to a foreign king until it is safe for him to return to his homeland. David, too, is famously exiled for almost as long a period, and finds quarter in the foreign land of Philistia, where he demonstrates skill as a mercenary warrior and remains on the lam while Saul is still alive. Like Sinuhe, David finally returns to the court to re-enter the lifestyle of a royal and lives out a distinguished career writing psalms of praise to the God who delivered him.

THE SISTER RUSE

There is a patriarchal period narrative which further illuminates the pervasive fear of monarchic oppression and conquest that we examined in the vocabulary section of chapter 1. A beautiful woman traveling in the retinue of the patriarch is presented to the king as one's sister rather than as one's wife. Abraham uses this protective device twice (Gen 12:12–20, 20:1–18) and Isaac uses it once. (Gen 26:7–11) We see this "sister" ruse as a method to prevent the all-too-normal socio-sexual depredations of kingship in the ancient world and also the retribution which can ensue after such depredation, such as can be seen, for example, in the story of the violation of Dinah, and the retribution by her brothers against Shechem. (Gen 34)

Falling Into Captivity and Rising Out of It: The Foundational Stories

In each use of the sister ruse, the Bible gives as the reason for the ruse the potential victim's fear of death at the hands of the king. Given the history of royal violence in the ancient Near East (chapter 2), we have no reason to view the existence of this intense fear with any suspicion. From earliest times in recorded history, through biblical times, down through the medieval era, and even to modern times, powerful kings manifest their omnipotence by means of an outrageous sexual tradition that plays out at the expense of individual victims, their spouses, and families. In some European feudal contexts, for example, it was the right of the feudal baron to take the virginity of his serf's maiden daughters, a practice known as "droit de seigneur" (right of the Lord) or "ius primae noctis" (law/right of the first night).

In the Epic of Gilgamesh, written in Mesopotamia around 2000 BCE, the king "leaves no girl to her mother" in his sexual demands once he achieves a good degree of power. The Esther story in the Bible describes a somewhat more benign version of a monarch's sexual ritual during the time of the Persian Empire. The most beautiful women of the realm are assembled for the king to choose among. (Esther 2:1–4) The Greek historian Herodotus suggests that the kings of ancient Libya chose many wives this way, not just one.[18] As late as the twentieth century, Kurdish kings (khafirs) in Western Armenia maintained the right to deflower maidens on their wedding night.

Abraham and his family are vulnerable in the presence of any rapacious king in Egypt or Canaan on several accounts. First, a despotic king may easily do whatever he wants to both person and property to virtually anyone in his realm. This is evident even in the Bible context in the story of Naboth. (1 Kgs 21) Secondly, Abraham and Sarah are especially vulnerable in Egypt because they are "sojourners," that is, resident aliens. They lack the protections of law and custom given to natives. They also lack the protection of a nearby clan presence. Thirdly, Abraham represents a minority, and very likely dissident, religious faith (ethical monotheism) that almost by definition poses a threat to the king in somewhat the same way Moses and his fellow monotheistic followers posed a threat to Pharaoh much later, and the same way Ahkenaten's monotheist faith threatened the religious traditions of his political rivals in Egypt before Moses. This is due to the fact that new oracular revelation promotes local charismatic prophetic leadership of

---

18. Strassler, *Landmark Herodotus*, 4:168.

faith and civic activity rather than traditional national monarchic leadership of culture. At the very least, the new faith would draw converts away from the old.

Some interpreters suggest that Abraham is unethical, self-serving, and patriarchal in the worst sense of the term because he lies to save his own skin, while sacrificing the interests of his wife Sarah, who is taken abruptly into the harem of the king. Abraham seems even to come out quite well economically as a result of this strategy, since he is given a sort of bride price by Pharaoh. (Gen 12:16, 20) But the story is a bit more complicated than this simple interpretation would suggest. Sarah is, in fact, actually his step sister, as well as his wife, so the presentation of the scenario is not really a lie. In the end the strategy works out well for both Abraham and Sarah as individuals, and for their relationship as a couple as well. The couple survive the famine that compelled them to Egypt in the first place, and are re-united as a married couple. Sarah is not violently abducted, as was possible or even probable without the ruse. Pharaoh agrees to let the couple go off with the bride-price as a sort of restitution for his near-adultery with Sarah. The strategy seems also to have carried some long-term advantage for Sarah, since her husband's assertion of legal status as a brother to her assured that she would have more protection and benefaction from his family in the event of his death, in the ancient Near East legal tradition. A widow was much more vulnerable. In Hurrian legal texts uncovered at Nuzi, there is evidence of a social practice whereby the husband might not only marry a woman, but adopt her as a sister in addition, so as to confer this further legal benefit on her.[19]

There is also a distinct possibility that Abraham is merely exercising an early form of international law by negotiating a treaty for the placement of a female family member from his retinue into marriage with a political rival. He may have been cementing a treaty of friendship between the two parties through marriage, by sacrificing his own interest in Sarah, thus making the prospect of violence between the two parties less likely. This happened in the case of Solomon, who accepted a daughter of the King of Egypt in marriage, in order to forestall the kind of warfare between Egypt and Israel that later nearly ended Israel's existence in the time of Pharaoh Shishak and Solomon's son Rehoboam. (1 Kgs 3:1; 2 Chron 12) In point of fact, neither Hebrew prince, Abraham

---

19. Speiser, *Genesis*, 92.

Falling Into Captivity and Rising Out of It: The Foundational Stories

or Isaac, had an unmarried female relative to use for this purpose, and thus did the best they could under the circumstances.[20]

MOSES'S SECULAR MISSION

Above we briefly touched on the relevance of Moses' story in the context of court politics of the ancient Near East, and in particular noted its parallels with the story of the Egyptian courtier Sinuhe. In this section we will review the story of Moses in a bit more depth, in order to demonstrate the Bible writers' interest in setting up the Decalogue as the solution to the problems of life experienced by the Hebrews in Egypt. The story of a Hebrew people in Egypt is complicated, many scholars note, by lack of direct independent evidence for their sojourn there in the late Bronze period. Indeed, many scholars were skeptical of the historical basis for a Davidic dynasty in Syro-Palestine, until an artifact was found mentioning it explicitly. Patience may well pay off for those interested in the Exodus story.[21] In fact, indirect corroboration of the Biblical story has been found in extra-Biblical evidence of the use of straw in brick-making, the presence of foreign children raised at the court of the Pharoah, foreign captives used in building projects, and slave groups escaping from Egypt.[22] In our review of the Bible account of Moses, we will follow the story line as it unfolds in the text the compilers and editors prepared for us.

The story of the lineages of Jacob's sons is lost for several hundred years after their descent into Egypt, but we learn that that many of them continue to reside in the Delta region after the burial of Jacob. They multiply and prosper there and eventually come to pose a threat to a culturally xenophobic Pharaoh of the thirteenth century, likely Ramses II. Pharaoh denies them economic and religious freedom, which one scion of Jacob then proposes to remedy. Moses, after receiving a word from God, acts with incredible yet deferential persistence in petitioning Pharaoh for religious freedom. Ten times he asks and is rebuffed. At no time does he use violent means, nor does he encourage it among Israelites. He does, however, predict differential outcomes for Egyptians and

---

20. Millard, "Abraham," 40.
21. See, for example, Hoffmeier, *Israel in Egypt*.
22. Kitchen, "The Exodus," 704.

Biblical Captivity

Israelites caught in the throes of a variety of seasonal natural events, acts of God, which seem clearly to indicate God's favor for a people petitioning for free exercise of religious belief.

The crux of the story of Moses in Egypt is the rise of a freedom-seeking political movement with a broad new church/state focus, goaded on by the unwillingness of Pharaoh to extend the kind of tolerance to the middle-aged prophet and his followers that an earlier Pharaoh extended to the aging prophet Jacob. Moses' understanding of the great Mesopotamian and Egyptian traditions of religious freedom may have been passed along among the Israelites through their cultural memory in Egypt. Moses seems to have obtained a sense of the importance of fighting for it long before the burning bush incident. His first attempt at rebellion involved attacking an Egyptian taskmaster (Exod 2:11–15), but the Hebrews did not see wisdom in what appeared to be a violent approach to solution of the problem.[23] (Exod 2:11–14; Acts 7:23–29)

As he fled to Midian, Moses must have contemplated whether there existed any effective means whatsoever to counter the daily violence meted out by the taskmasters against the Hebrew people. (Exod 1:11–14; Exod 3:11) The story of his encounter with a woman of Midian underscores his ready acceptance into the house of Jethro, but leaves out details of his engagement in the larger Midianite society. One wonders which society he refers to when we learn that Moses names his son Gershom, which means "I have been an alien residing in a foreign land." Is the alien land Egypt, or Midian? Likely both, for while his ancestors have long been treated like a foreign minority in Egypt, Moses lived his entire lifetime in Egyptian society, and was now an exile on the foreign soil of Midian.

But while outsiders are treated poorly by the priestly Pharaoh in Egypt, it is hard to miss the fact that the Midianite priest who is Moses' father-in-law does not discriminate against him after he has his encounter with God, but allows him full freedom not only to practice his new prophet-based religion in Midian, but also to take his family to Egypt to investigate the situation of his people there. (Exod 4:18–20) This is the way an alien should be treated by the mainstream religion of a nation. Moses also understands that his ancestors once had land and freedom of conscience in the early days of Egypt, and of Canaan as well. (Exod 6:1–4)

23. Albertz, *Israelite Religion*, 46.

Falling Into Captivity and Rising Out of It: The Foundational Stories

The God Moses encounters at the burning bush identifies himself with the culture of independence of those ancestors. (Exod 3:6) Moses may also have known that relatives still living in Canaan were involved in freedom projects at this time as well, which may have provided additional motivation for a venture whose object was to install a new nation there. Yahweh says, "I am sending you to lead my people out." (Exod 3:10) In fact, the very name of the God he has encountered is linked to the project at hand. The God reveals his name as "I am who I am." The connotation of the name may be rendered variously as "I live and create anew," "I live and will be what I wish," and "I will be with you in reality."[24] (Exod 3:14) In essence, this is a God with power to act in history in behalf of ordinary and even dispossessed people. This God is real and effective, and seeks a people willing to be so as well.

Thus, the first revelation to Moses relates to political organization: "Go and gather the elders of Israel together . . ." (Exod 3:16) The "elders" in the Bible context are local civic officials who deliberate on secular matters, while priests and Levites handle sacred matters and a few secular matters too. Moses must stir up the civic and cultural leaders of the people with a specific policy proposal. From Yahweh's perspective, the goal is complete political enfranchisement and nation building. That is the real, yet hidden, agenda. But the agenda to be put on the table initially before the people and before Pharaoh is to be a more limited one, a partial political enfranchisement, and even that is a hard one to sell to the people. (Exod 4:29; 6:9) The second oracle is one directly related to the First Commandment.[25] Moses is to tell Pharaoh that the Hebrews have a God and have need of free worship: "The Lord God of the Hebrews hath met with us: and now let us go, we beseech thee, three days' journey into the wilderness, that we may sacrifice to the Lord our God." (Exod 3:18) Yahweh's specific directive to Moses is to request of Pharaoh that he "Let (Israel) go, that he may serve me." (Exod 4:23) Here Moses asks for simple rights of citizenship—the right to conscience like other worshipers in Egypt.

But there is something of the larger agenda made clear in the message to be delivered to Pharaoh. He is to announce an epiphany directed toward a particular sub-population of Egypt. This epiphany constitutes a claim for special treatment and a degree of autonomy for this group

---

24. Albright, *Stone Age*, 198; Terrien, *Elusive Presence*, 119.
25. Shinkoskey, *Do My Prophets No Harm*, 81–117.

of people, based on a mandate from a heavenly god. This new light announcement is no trivial matter, as it constitutes a contradictory and dissenting position with respect not only to Pharaoh's religion, but to the several other mainstream cults current in Egypt at that time. There is a hint of political, or at least religious, self-government, in the request for a sort of pilgrimage-type travel away from their dwellings (toward Mt. Sinai?). This is not lost on Pharaoh. In fact, the request for sacrifice, in the ancient context, carries with it an unmistakable hint of political secession, since, as we shall see below, sacrifice can be an act of nation creation.

From the beginning, then, Yahweh is a God of a people who wish to grow politically, not the god of an established political party or of a specific denominational priesthood, or even of a geographic place like a city. His presence is mobile and universal, having roots in many nations and climes. For example, there is no command to gather the priests together, or assemble an ecumenical council or a tent revival, or to build a city. Type of worship and place of divine dwelling is a secondary concern. Ability to worship and opportunity to govern is a primary concern. From the outset, then, the story of Exodus is religious only in the broadest sense that freedom of religious worship is a major concern. It is not about partisan worship. It is about civic religion/political ethics/constitutional culture. It is about a people who wish to be governed by law, and not by despots. Moses' first concern is to organize the state, and only after that is done will he deign to even think about organizing a religion. In fact, as we will see below, it can be argued that Aaron, rather than Moses, is the founding leader of Israelite religion.[26]

Moses' discussion with Yahweh at the time of the burning bush establishes the notion that the name given to God by the ancestors is but an artifact. (Exod 6:2–3) It is not particularly problematic for Israel to speak of or even acknowledge a variety of gods, or god-names, in addition to the one given to Moses, since it is clear in ancient times that a god identified by a specific interest or function in one culture was known by a different name in another culture. A god devoted to oracular revelation of a political nature was known by a variety of local names throughout the Near East. A god devoted to war-making was known by a similar variety of names. A healing god was known by another range of names. An example would be the rather exact correspondence

---

26. Albright, *Stone Age*, 48.

Falling Into Captivity and Rising Out of It: The Foundational Stories

between the gods of Greece and Rome. One culture knows without question the equivalent god in the other culture and respects that god accordingly, or at least understands it.

Many of the ancients shunned popular polytheism and held to a "high god" tradition that suggested one or another god was actually pre-eminent above all others. Could not a high God who acts like Yahweh be called by the name of El, or Marduk, or something else? After all, Abraham, Isaac and Jacob all used different names for God. (Exod 3:13,15; 6:2-3) Many other god names were used for the ethical religions of the area too. (Gen 14:18-22, 16:13, 21:33, 31:13; Exod 12:41, Judg 9:46; 1 Sam 11:7) But this god was a tolerant god. Indeed, it has been said that the patriarchal narratives are remarkable for the lack of polemics directed against other denominations or in support of their own, precisely because there seemed to be several other ethical religions in Canaan. It was common for a nation to follow a high or national tutelary god, but also to give safe haven to a number of minority or newer gods as well. This Egypt did as well. But Ramses, protective of several religions besides the denomination devoted to Seth and after whom his own dynasty was named, drew the line at Israel and Yahweh, since their god was so clearly democratic and his god was identified so clearly as monarchic.

The patriarchs seem to acknowledge, on the other hand, as does Moses, that while there are many objects of legitimate devotion in the ancient world, the Hebrew high God of ethical living in Canaan begs for attention above all these, since he has all the best interests rolled together into one. He is, by turns, an oracle god, a god of war, a god of healing... in fact, a god heralding all good uses of power and all good things.

Also, Israel's God is first and foremost interested in secular affairs, the mode of government used by the creatures he has created. He is not concerned about liturgy or denominational factionalism. He is a generic God, though the true one in Israel's view. The God of the ancestors, Yahweh suggests, is characterized more by his ethico-political aspirations for his people—his desire that they have land and freedom of conscience—than by ecclesiastical doctrine or place of worship. Unfortunately, this enlightened view of religion held by Moses and his people is a far cry from the political and religious absolutism of Pharaoh and his party in Egypt.

ABOMINATION THEORY

In Egypt a group of the descendants of Jacob experienced ethnic, economic and religious oppression. According to the Bible record, the new culture specified by the God of Moses included a type of sacrificial worship considered "an abomination" (KJV) to the Egyptians. Other Bible translations use terms like "abhorrent," "offensive," or "extremely disgusting" to render this word. In fact, we learn they were unable to participate freely in the new religious culture brought to them by Moses without threat of violence. (Exod 8:25–26) Even in the early days of Joseph, the tradition recalls it was "an abomination" for Egyptians to eat with Hebrews. (Gen 43:32) Thus, they had to be seated separately from their hosts in a sort of Egyptian caste system. Apparently the agricultural people of the Nile Delta had an historical dislike for nomadic shepherd people. (Gen 46:34)

A hint of what the new form of worship might entail is given in conversation between Moses and Pharoah. Pharoah believes only men should participate. (Exod 10:11) Moses wants women and children to be involved in the festival worship. Aside from the risk of full flight that it poses, this egalitarian approach to worship apparently offends Egyptian social and religious sensibility.

The history of the Hebrews as a people also explains some of the antipathy. There are a number of possibilities of connection with historically demonstrable peoples of the day and locale. Language specialists believe the nominal word "Hebrew" ("ibri") may be related to the verb "to crossover," bringing to mind their ancestors who crossed the Euphrates and came into Palestine.[27] Thus they are reportedly not a people native even to the neighboring area of Syro-Palestine, but hail from the land of Egypt's rival, Mesopotamia. The Bible's two major genealogies indicate the Egyptians descended through Noah's son Ham, whose offspring settled in Africa and Arabia. But Israelites descended from Noah's son Shem, whose lineage settled in the far north and far east, in the areas of Assyria and Elam. Abraham's specific descent in the genealogy of Genesis and Chronicles is through Shem's son Eber, a people called "Eberites," which some scholars believe is close to "Hebrew." (Gen 10:21, 24–25; Gen 11:14–17; 1 Chron 1:18—19, 25) Interestingly, the Hebrews, as they are known in the eastern Mediterranean

---

27. Knight, "Hebrews," 273.

Falling Into Captivity and Rising Out of It: The Foundational Stories

as they leave Egypt, seem to have more of a socio-political identification than a strictly ethnic identification.[28] This comports with the idea they may have had a long and an-iconic, that is, democratic, tradition in the pastoral locations where they moved about, much as outlined in the patriarchal narratives.

In a more proximate sense, the Egyptian mind may associate Jacob's people with a group of gypsy-like nomads who for centuries lived along the margins of mid-East civilization, and in particular in Canaan, called the "apiru" or "Hapiru." These were known at times as fugitives, bandits, or refugees[29] and were sometimes hired as mercenaries, worked as migrant workers, or purchased like Joseph as indentured servants, as the Nuzi tablets demonstrate.[30] Their earlier treatment as servants may explain Ramses' willingness to revert to such treatment of them. Their reputation as highland or wilderness political bandits may have descended into Egypt with them, or may have been noticed as Egyptian-based Hebrews maintained connections with Canaanite branches of their families. During the century or two before the Exodus, Egypt made a garrison at Manhatu in Canaan to defend against what the Amarna tablets called "the hostility from the mountains."[31]

The "Shasu" are a semi-nomadic people noted in Egyptian records. They seem to have had a democratic political organization in evidence in Central and southern Transjordan (east of Jordan) and in southern Palestine and Sinai, where Moses may have come in contact with them upon first running from Egypt.[32] Also, the Kenites of the Bible are known to use Yahweh names for their children and are known to have joined with the Israelites during the settlement period, and some theorize they may have been the first to worship Yahweh.[33] (Judg 4:11) All these groups—ibri, Eberites, apiru, Shasu, and Kenites—are candidates for the political ancestors of Moses and his followers.

According to a number of scholars, the Hebrews in Egypt are additionally associated at least schematically with the hated Hyksos, who migrated south in the eighteenth century out of Hittite (Asia Minor),

---

28. Meyers, *Exodus*, 37.
29. Ibid, 36; Albertz, *Israelite Religion*, 45.
30. Anderson, *Old Testament*, 33; Eichler, "Nuzi Tablets," 563.
31. Knauf, "Manahath," 493.
32. Zevit, *Religions*, 91, 118.
33. Vaux, *Ancient Israel*, 15.

Biblical Captivity

Hurrian (northern Mesopotamia, Caucasus, Armenia, Syria), and eastern territories.[34] These groups seem to have settled in Syro-Palestine,[35] where they constituted a political coalition of Semites, particularly Western Semite Amorites/Phoenicians,[36] with Horites (Hurrians) and Indo-Iranians.[37] The amplitude of their political strength seems to have exceeded even that of the political coalition the biblical David assembled 800 years later in the same area. They managed to occupy Egypt in the period roughly 1700 to 1600 BCE, perhaps about the time Jacob's family descended into Egypt, making their capital at Avaris, at the far eastern margin of the Delta. They extended their sway well into Palestine and Syria and the cultures of this whole area came into close communication with Egypt as a result.

Since some of the Hyksos seem to have been of Semitic origin, it seems plausible that one of their kings may have used a talented Semite like Joseph in the affairs of state. In fact, the period of their reign in Egypt seems to be associated with the religious liberty notable in the Abraham tradition, since they accommodated the worship of the Egyptian sun god Re, in addition to their more favored deity, the syncretistic Baal/Seth construct of god.[38] Egypt made many military forays into Palestine and its coastal area, bringing back slaves during the last half of the second millennium.[39] The fact that the Hyksos capital was moved from Thebes to Avaris in the Nile Delta, and the Bible story places its Pharaoh there rather than Thebes, helps this theory.

The point we are making here is that Moses' Hebrews are different from Egyptians, Phoenicians, Mesopotamians, Arabs, and the people of Asia Minor in one important respect. They are not settled, like those peoples, in a land of their own. And because of this they often lack citizenship and citizen rights in the places of their transient dwelling. They are small in number and deemed to be of inferior socio-economic status.

This minority status alone assures discrimination against them in Egypt. But then, their leader Moses, rather than assenting to the

---

34. Anderson, *Old Testament*, 39; Herzog and Gichon, *Battles of the Bible*, 33.
35. Garnsey and Whittaker, *Imperialism in the Ancient World*, 21.
36. Redford, "Hyksos," 341.
37. Herzog and Gichon, *Battles of the Bible*, 33–34.
38. Redford, "Hyksos," 343.
39. Meyers, *Exodus*, 8.

Falling Into Captivity and Rising Out of It: The Foundational Stories

general perception of his people as foreign and marginal, champions their goodness and assigns them a great destiny. (Exod 6:2-9) He even elevates his own spiritual connection with God above that of Pharaoh and his priests, thus challenging the cultural expression of Pharaoh's political power. A hint of the attitude that Moses brought to Pharaoh's court is seen in the passage "and the Lord said unto Moses, See, I have made thee a god to Pharaoh . . ." (Exod 7:1) Even before he obtains an audience with Pharaoh, Moses complains to the Lord that he has "uncircumcised lips." (Exod 6:12) He believes inalterably in free speech. He wonders how Pharaoh will listen to one who has a tendency to speak his mind, and promote ideas that are not politically correct.

For example, Ramses II seems to have worshiped the Egyptian version of the Canaanite deity Baal, whom the Egyptians called Seth.[40] Moses' anticipation of and antipathy to Baal worship in Canaan thus may have been learned first hand, observing the religion of Egypt. Moses wonders how it will go for him once he proposes a religion for some of Pharaoh's subjects so far removed from that favored by Pharoah. Ramses' religious convictions place Moses and his people in the unenviable position of trying to extricate themselves from nature worship[41] in Egypt in one land, only to face it once again in the land they intend to make their home. If Moses is able to extricate his people from political violence in Egypt without use of the sword, it will be more difficult to do it against the Baalists in Canaan, because here they will be moving into their territory rather than moving out of it.

The experience of continual petitioning of Pharaoh to allow them to practice their new religion (Exod 7-12)—ten times they request this freedom—becomes indelibly etched in their minds. Once they leave, they determine to tolerate reasonable religion among their neighbors and among themselves, wherever it is they go. At Sinai they make a grand promise or covenant to this effect. Moses proposes the First Commandment, which we understand as a law for religious and political freedom[42], and the people respond to it "with one voice." (Exod 24:3)

---

40. Albright, *Stone Age*, 224; Bauer, *History*, 67.

41. Nature worship may be defined as polytheistic worship of a variety of gods related to elements of nature, including rivers, mountains, forests, animals, and objects in the heavens, such as sun, moon and stars.

42. Shinkoskey, *Do My Prophets No Harm*, 81-117.

THE EXODUS EVENT: JUST ANOTHER ANCIENT NEAR EAST CATCH AND RELEASE STORY?

The immediate and perhaps best contexts for our understanding of Moses' political orientation toward religion are the personality and behavior of Pharaoh, and the first revelation given to Moses from Yahweh. As we mentioned, that first oracle encouraged Moses to meet on a political basis with the leaders of Goshen: "Go and gather the elders of Israel together." (Exod 3:16) From the beginning the story of nascent Israel is a story of the organization of political power among a largely impotent people.

Moses' dealings with Ramses II must be understood in the context of the expansionist 19th Dynasty of Ramses' father Seti I.[43] A number of scholars believe that Seti I is the genocidal Pharaoh of Moses' birth, and that the insatiable Ramses II is Moses' nemesis at the time of his return to Egypt. Ramses had excellent credentials for the kind of tireless tyranny that could inspire separatist or secessionist political ideology in a relentlessly oppressed people. He made imperialist incursions to the north into Palestine and Syria, which could explain his antipathy for a minority group within his own borders who hailed from there. He also had a penchant for massive public works projects for his capital of Thebes and for his temples in Nubia, which could explain the excessive objectives of the Israelite brick-making foundries in Goshen. His was a totalitarian grip on his people, and potentially an especially complete grip on minorities inhospitable to his personal needs.[44]

Rulers who demonstrate such great emotional insecurity and compensatory control over the objects of their insecure affection are wont to waffle in decision-making. They flip-flop back and forth between what is obvious, best, and right, and irrational and spiteful reaction against that initial inclination. Thus was Pharaoh. He promised again and again to let Israel go to worship freely. Then, in a rage, he would rescind his announced intention each time. A generation before Moses, Ramses' father, insecure over the rapidly growing sub-population of Hebrews in the delta area, tried to thwart their culture by having Hebrew midwives strangle baby boys born to Hebrew mothers.[45] (Exod 1:15–22)

---

43. Plumley, "Egypt," 181.
44. Noss, *Man's Religions*, 359.
45. Meyers, *Exodus*, 37.

Falling Into Captivity and Rising Out of It: The Foundational Stories

We have mentioned that Moses' experience with Yahweh in Midian may have involved some exposure to the democratic ways of the Shasu pastoralists who inhabited that area.[46] His subsequent efforts to convert Hebrews in Goshen to his new culture of empowered citizenship placed extreme political pressure on Pharaoh. Ultimately, Ramses seems to have temporarily lost even the confidence of his native people (Exod 3:21; 11:3), and thus agreed to allow the motley band of Israelites a short pilgrimage away from work and home so they might worship in a safe environment, and more to the point, so that he could earn back the trust of his people.[47] Those among the departing multitude who may have intended to return to Goshen after the three day holiday apparently changed their minds when they saw Pharaoh descend upon them with his legions, convincing them they had best lay their hopes for survival as a people with Moses, rather than with the mad ruler of Egypt.

Pharaoh asks a question of Moses that is pertinent to our discussion here: "Who are they that shall go?" (Exod 10:8) Just who left Egypt with Moses? Was it one perfectly homogeneous ethnic group with one set of beliefs and one church affiliation? Were all the Exodus crowd faithful followers of some pure strain of the religion of Abraham, which they, along with Moses, understood implicitly?

In fact, it is clear that the Exodus crowd that affiliated with Moses were much more divergent than that. One important king of Israel understood that the Exodus group included a multiplicity of religious views. He mentions "thy gods, O Israel, which brought thee up out of the land of Egypt." (1 Kings 12:28; cf. Exod 32:4) Moses was leading a political movement for religious freedom, for an end to slavery, and for the distribution of land to those who had lived long without these social amenities. Accordingly, any religionists who chaffed under the cult of captive religion prescribed by this particularly intolerant Pharaoh might be tempted to join in. So might any worker who longed for freedom from state-directed labor. So too would any ordinary human being who longed for more than a crowded hut, or an end to the disease-ridden life on the Nile Delta. All these might easily be lured by the vision of the wide-open hill country of Canaan.

---

46. Ibid, 45.

47. One theory has it that the jewelry they gave the departing Hebrews was a reparation payment for the disrespect Pharaoah was showing their God.

Ethnicity is an important factor in determining religious affiliation. If the group leaving Egypt were ethnically uniform, we might imagine one heavily predominant worship tradition. If, on the other hand, there was ethnic diversity among the migrants, it can safely be assumed that a good measure of tolerance was required in sacral matters, since variety in culture presupposes variety in religious ideas and worship traditions. In fact, the scripture says, "A mixed multitude went up also with them." (Exod 12:38) Another source renders the verse, "People of various sorts joined them in great numbers."[48]

There are two requirements for Egyptians and Israelites who wish to accompany Moses on his pilgrimage journey outside of Goshen. These are mentioned in Exodus 12 in conjunction with the account of the beginning of the Exodus. Such a traveler must pledge to keep the Passover celebrating release from religious and economic oppression. In some ways this is analogous to a day of remembrance for deliverance from a major threat at the start of other new political society, such as America's own day of thanksgiving. The other requirement is that males be circumcised. (Exod 12:11) In the minds of many, however, it is not clear whether these two provisions constitute a requirement for church membership or a test for (temporary) citizenship, since the Israelites do not enact an actual national government until two months later at Sinai. Likely they are a foreshadowing of the kinds of remembrances that will long be associated with both cultural associations, a beginning point from which state and church both derive, prior to the definitive separation of those two agencies at Sinai.[49] Many Egyptians and many Semitic people throughout the mid-East, such as the tribes of the Arabian peninsula, routinely practice circumcision by virtue of their own civic or religious traditions. Thus it was probably easy enough to become a member of the cultural revolution of the Exodus.

It would be hard to imagine such a large group of people giving unanimous assent to a law restricting the varieties of religious worship among their own diverse company. Yet, this is how the interpretation of the Sinai First Commandment often goes. This interpretation persists

---

48. Riley, *Civilizing Sex*, 66.

49. We argue in a forthcoming essay that First Commandment religious liberty necessitates separation of cult and state, which is duly performed in the allocation of secular government responsibilities to Moses, and priestly responsibilities to Aaron, and then strictly observed in subsequent Israelite history down to the time of exile.

Falling Into Captivity and Rising Out of It: The Foundational Stories

even in view of the fact that Bible compilers down through the centuries gather and edit accounts such as Job, Ruth, Jonah, Esther and even Daniel, and insert them in their collections as expressions of the willingness of Mosaic people to tolerate religious and cultural difference across boundaries with neighboring nations, and those nations' willingness to tolerate the people of Moses.[50] The Bible compilers and editors also take great pains to describe the consistent effort made by judges, kings, prophets, priests, scribes and common people to exercise and assure religious and political freedom within the bounds of the Israelite polities. These accounts and efforts are the subject of a section of chapter 5, and will be developed in a more detailed fashion in an upcoming essay.

If the people were not religiously "of one voice," they seemed to be so politically. This political unanimity meant that the group leaving Egypt were self-selected in terms of their antipathy to kingship as much as by any other factor, including economic class, nationality, or ethnicity. Once the people begin to deal with the issues of governmental organization (that is, after the scurrilous golden calf incident), there is little hint of a desire to return to kingship. On the other hand, there is much talk of varieties of democracy with which to dabble, and some even push for extreme libertarianism or collectivism. (Num 12–14, 16) In sum, it seems that only those who were willing to experiment with an alternative form of civic organization granting broad human rights to its members, cared to or dared to join the group, since the Exodus required giving up so much in terms of sumptuary culture. (Num 11:5)

CANAAN: DESTINATION OF DISSIDENTS AND WILDERNESS OF HOSPITALITY

The fact that Canaan is historically a buffer zone between large and competing Near East cultures means its indigenous populations must frequently play host to political, military, economic and religious

---

50. In fact, there are many recorded instances of kings and reformers in the broader Mediterranean world granting or restoring rights programs at the time of coronation or election, much like the program enacted at Sinai. See, for example, Shinkoskey, *Do My Prophets No Harm*, 111–113. The story of Moses, of course, is not so much one of a benevolent ruler deciding on his own to free slaves, but of one outside the political power structure leveraging the liberation event on behalf of the people.

Biblical Captivity

parties, influences, and intruders penetrating that small land bridge. Moses and his group exiting Egypt propose to be one such party of intruders. At least, that is the view from some of the city-states already resident there. On the other hand, the hill country of Ephraim and Judea is located away from the great river cultures of Mesopotamia and Egypt, and thus it is less well settled than those areas for long stretches of time and provides a place of refuge for migrants dissatisfied with those cultures. That is the view of the migrants in Moses' party.

The highways running north and south, east and west through Canaan join Egypt with Phoenicia, Syria, and Babylon. The land bridge also provides a route from Arabia and the Persian Gulf to the ports of the Mediterranean, which lay to the northwest of Canaan.[51] Thus, Palestine is a bridge that funnels unceasing transitory traffic and culture back and forth between Africa, the Mediterranean, Asia Minor and Mesopotamia.

The great highways through Palestine were noted by Biblical writers. For example, the Bible mentions a coastal passage from Goshen to Canaan called "The Way to the Land of the Philistines." It also mentions an inland passage through the wilderness of Shur called "The Way to Shur." This is the postulated northern Exodus route. This goes through northern Sinai, through the Negeb region to Beersheba, at the southern border of Israel, and north to Hebron, Jerusalem, and Bethel. The Bible also mentions a great highway east of the Jordan River called "The King's Highway." It runs just west of a line of border fortresses meant to discourage invaders from the Arabian east. This national highway connects Ezion-geber at the northern tip of the Red Sea through Edom, Moab, Reuben and Ammon. For millennia, travelers used donkeys, oxen, camels, carts and human porters to carry goods across their shoulders along these roads.[52]

Over the millennia enveloping the Biblical era, international trade brings complex, variegated, and disruptive religious and cultural patterns to the well-traveled low land routes. Imported goods are found in Canaan from the Neolithic period, starting in 3200 BCE and onward, and we see varieties of religious culture alongside each other from early times as well. On the other hand, the semi-isolated hill country above and beside those highways inspires independent local living and trade,

---

51. Dorsey, *Roads and Highways*.
52. See, for example, Matt 11:30.

Falling Into Captivity and Rising Out of It: The Foundational Stories

which militates in favor of settled religion and culture. The people of the highlands must learn to deal with and accommodate international traffic and culture.[53]

The hills, ridges, and valleys of Canaan afforded a mixed vulnerability to threats from external forces. Those who lived in the valleys were vulnerable to the chariot-based forces of the Philistines, for example, but could retreat to the hills if need be and hang out there for a time. But, in fact, Israelites of hills and valleys alike could not easily preserve a coherent political culture unless that culture was based on an ethic of civic hospitality which entertained pluralism in both faith and government matters locally, and extended courtesies to governments and their faiths from abroad. For example, over the long pre-exile history of Israel in Canaan, the polities had to entertain many foreign trade outposts, garrisons, and embassies representing economic and political powers with an interest in the area. Archeology shows foreign settlements along the coast in the eighth century BCE, so there was clearly pressure on the hill country from the coast eastward.[54] Manufacturing in the pre-exile period produced Greek-style goods, indicating contact and commerce with that section of the Mediterranean. Manufacturing in the post-exile period understandably produced Persian-style goods. The prophet Joel complained of the high frequency of foreigners passing through Jerusalem. (Joel 4.17 JPS; 3.17 GNB) He wishes that "Never more shall strangers pass through it." This statement reflects the tension in a culture committed to constitutional uniformity of politico-ethical values, one of which, ironically, is a degree of tolerance that invites departures from those same values. Pottery, coinage, seals, bullae, engravings on gems, all show great diversity of cultural influence, from Greek, Egyptian, and Persian religious culture.[55]

One point we wish to make here is that any period of secure political life, let alone any period of unification of Palestine under single independent rule (the Davidic united monarchy) was very brief in overall terms of Bible time. Most of the time, Palestine was subject to temporary overrunning (land on its periphery falling in and out of its political control), division in and disunity across its regional polities, spheres of influence conditioned by treaties of friendship or vassalage,

53. Bailey, "Trade and Transport," 748.
54. Smith, *Palestinian Parties*, 61.
55. Smith, *Palestinian Parties*, 62.

and conquest and colonization by superior powers. It was this very political instability that spoke opportunity to the Moses group, and that also bedeviled them for the 1,200 years they occupied its terrain. It was the same opportunity, apparently, that had been presented to Abraham and his group some 500-600 years before.

Abraham's father Terah left Ur where worship of the moon god Sin was essentially the established religion. The family's original destination was Canaan, but they ended up in Harran to the northwest for a time. (Gen 11:31) In Harran the family came up against a state-enforced cult of worship of the moon god once again. Abraham, a political and religious dissident in both Ur and Harran, eventually left Harran looking for a land that would give free reign to his political belief system, undergirded as it was by the anti-establishment, progressive, religio-scientific worldview we now know as ethical monotheism. He brought with him in his migrating party a culture that he was eventually able to turn at least part way away from primitive notions of science such as human sacrifice. He seems to have valued the political freedom to govern his own family and clan free of central state control. He is at first suspicious of the political ethics of Canaanite leaders like Abimelech, but learns that this leader of Gerar is a moral and civic-oriented monarch willing to accord religious and political freedom to others. He interacts freely and happily with the apparently ethical priestly state of Melchizedek during his time in Canaan as well.

Both the Bible account and archeological finds reveal plenty of unsettled space in Palestine in Abraham's day, just as later in Moses' day. This allowed sojourners there to spread out. Thus, when Abraham and Lot experienced conflict, the two were simply able to divide the land and resolve differences by spreading out. (Gen 13) The same scenario plays out, it can be said, when religious jealousy arose between Isaac and Ishmael. Their clans settled in different regions of Canaan, with Ishmael and later Jacob's brother Esau settling to the southeast in Edom.

Abraham's family apparently could not countenance an immediate move from Ur into an uncharted area peopled by fiercely independent groups, just as Moses' people could not either. But both seemed to know that their best chance to live outside the reach of monarchic government and established religion was precisely this place. Here they could devote themselves to pastoral living, and develop agricultural proficiency at the same time, in a semi-wilderness setting.

Falling Into Captivity and Rising Out of It: The Foundational Stories

On the one hand, the new nation of Israel settling in Canaan after the Exodus are still a nomadic people after forty years of wandering. They have a nomadic perspective on engagement with and tolerance of other cultures. At first act of offering to God in the new land of Canaan, they were asked to remember their roots as nomads, and to repeat, "A wandering Aramean was my father." (Deut 26:5) Jacob indeed wandered from Palestine to Harran to obtain brides, and back to Canaan, where he moved regularly and depended heavily upon the tolerance of his hosts. Jacob and his sons finally wandered into Egypt where it was necessary to obtain the largesse of a large centralist river power. His descendants in Egypt, after their liberation, wandered in the wilderness and then continued as nomads in their own settled land as they moved their flocks from one pasturage to another.

But despite this nomadic heritage and its long-standing ethic of friendly treatment of travelers and resident aliens, they, on the other hand, were determined to protect their political culture from the kind of degradation that was clearly possible in the event of too great syncretism of their political culture with the native Canaanite cultures. The affair of the ancestors between Dinah and the culture of Shechem demonstrated that clearly, (Gen 34) as did the affair of their friendliness with the people of Peor before entering Canaan. (Num 25) Much too often, their wandering was a sort of voluntary exile to remove themselves from sources of local aggression or oppression, as in the case of Isaac putting distance between himself and Abimelech, who sought to confiscate a well he had built, and Jacob, who needed to get away from a conflict in Shechem that was destroying both his clan and the clans of the Shechemites.

Indeed, during that time of the Judges, some foreigners, less hospitable than others, pushed up against their villages and lands from the outside and forced defensive military action in order to recover lands and freedoms. Kings Jeroboam, Jehu, and Josiah lead politico-cultural revolutions to recover what they understood to be constitutional law boundaries which had been frittered away from within or taken from them from without. During Greek colonial times, Judas Maccabee and his family, and Jesus and the many other dissident parties in Judea during Roman times also led revolutionary movements. All of these protest activities required geographic terrain which provided enough physical security to allow the dissident parties some breathing room

Biblical Captivity

from political oppression, as David demonstrated so often when he regularly skirted Saul's political depredations. Such physical movements amounted to mini-migrations, temporary relocations of a type familiar to a nomadic people.

Images of migration abound in the Bible.[56] The Hebrews were apparently a particularly independent and mobile group of Semites. The parties of Abraham, Isaac, Jacob, and Moses made long, often painstaking migrations, and a variety of smaller relocations as well. Israel as a nation fled from aggressors and then returned to their villages countless times. They went into long exile, and returned from exile. They made regular pilgrimages to sacred civic and religious sites. They often lived in tents, and kept tents available even when they were not involved in migratory or nomadic travel. Some of their number, like the Rechabites (Jer 35), consciously continued to live like the ancestors, refusing new technological advances like some of our Amish and Mennonites today. The opportunity provided by migration carried over into Christian thought and practice, and motivated the settlement of America by the Puritans, and South Africa by the Afrikaners.

The biblical "wilderness" is either a desert region, a pastoral terrain, or a marginally fruitful agricultural place. But the wilderness is also a place where people are forced to rely on God. (Exod 16,17; Num 11; Deut 8; Ps 78; 1 Cor 10) It is a place where they might meet God "face to face," as Moses and Jesus each did. It is a crucible for testing, and for testing of tolerance as well, as the incidents of Miriam and Korah demonstrate. The wilderness is associated with new light renewals and purification ceremonies, as indicated in Hosea, Jeremiah, and John the Baptist, and the Essene community.[57]

The Israelites, whether as a people who are nomads living in such wilderness, or as a settled people constantly remembering those nomads who came before them, also try to hold on to the pastoralist mentality of fierce independence and peerless hospitality and tolerance. Nomads are generally in some sort of physical want. They learn to be skillful traders, diplomats, and negotiators to supply for those wants.

Hospitality is important among semi-nomadic people who make pilgrimages and trade trips, and who frequently maneuver to defend their lands and families in time of war. This theme is reported by

56. Barr, "Politics and the Bible," 600.
57. Propp, "Wilderness," 798–799.

scholars who find that it serves as a framework to understand Judaic ethics.[58] A reputation for hospitality is so well known among the tribes that when hospitality standards are neglected a major political issue develops among peoples living in the area. The story is told in Judges 19 of a northern Levite traveling through the land of Benjamin, returning from Judah to his home in Ephraim. When Benjamites refuse to extend the courtesy of the comforts of home and social protections to travelers, and neglect to punish offenders against the hospitality and sexual ethics laws (and decline to extradite the criminals[59]), their outrageous behavior inspires war between the northern tribes and Benjamin.

The requesting and offering of "shalom" extends to all individuals and religious denominations of an ethical bent in Israel. Hospitality extends in this way from Boaz to Naomi's daughter-in-law Ruth, who is a Moabitess. It is also seen in Abraham's tolerance of Lot, in offering him the choicest portion of the land. It is seen later in the First Commandment-conscious Christ, who tolerates the Samaritans, Romans, publicans, and criminal sinners in a way unthinkable by the narrow-minded in his culture.

Israel's entire system of social, ecclesiastic, and political law dispenses a stranger/alien-sensitive system of justice. The law treats visitors like one of their own, extending full political rights, and demanding ethical conduct only, in return.[60]

Such a tradition of religious and cultural freedom and independence is exactly what rulers all about Israel complain about with respect to the hill country of Ephraim. They desire to impose a restriction of conscience and action upon those people more in line with their own great nation dictates, but have great difficulty in doing so. The Egyptian Mernepta complains, the Assyrian Tiglath-pileser complains, and the Babylonian Nebuchadrezzar learns first hand[61], as they are rebuffed by this rebellious people time and time again. Even Alexander the Great and the Emperors of Rome cannot secure the area very long before uprisings break out in pursuit of freedom.

58. Janzen, *Old Testament Ethics*, 36–44.
59. Westbrook and Wells, *Everyday Law*, 38.
60. Kent, *Israel's Laws*, ix, xvii.
61. The apocryphal book of Judith is a story of an uprising brokered by Judith against Nebuchadnezzar's general Holopernes, and emphasizes the quasi-historical lore handed down from this period.

Biblical Captivity

The entire Biblical history of settled Israel is the story of a riot of new priestly religious cults and prophet-led political movements taking the opportunity given them to incorporate and operate in the territory. The broken geographic terrain of the hill country from the north in Galilee, through the central hill territory of Ephraim, down through the southern hills of Judea, is historically poorly suited for the kind of controlled culture found in the plains areas. In fact, it is a perfect place for a people devoted to local home-rule in political and religious matters. It provides freedom fighters with the kind of guerilla hiding places from which to descend and attack their frequent political oppressors, and provided the likes of Joshua with the cover and heights necessary to prevail during the conquest.[62] In this respect, Canaan is much like the Kurdish highlands fronting Turkey in northern Iraq today, and the badlands of northwestern Pakistan on the Afghanistan border, where even American military forces and Pakistani military are unable to corral the Taliban rebels operating there. This is exactly the environmental milieu that Deborah, Gideon and Sampson used to challenge adversaries and restore freedom in the days of the Judges. It is the strategy Elijah and Jehu used to conduct their revolutionary activities against the Phoenician-dominated coastal culture of Ahab in ninth century BCE. It is the geography that the sons of Mattathias manipulated against the Syrian overlords in Palestine during the time of Maccabees in the second century BCE. And it is the modus operandi for the Zealots and other revolutionaries in their attempts against the Romans shortly after Christ's day in the first and second centuries of the Common Era.

In point of fact, archaeologists see little settlement in the hill country of Ephraim before the Israelite migration into Canaan. The civilization mostly is confined to the coastal area. But then dozens, even hundreds of village sites yielding up relics can be uncovered dating to the period of the settlement. The material remains demonstrate a tremendous variety of political, economic, and religious organization throughout the period of Kings, within the overall framework of northern and southern citizenries living as independent political cultures for about 300 years, from 1000 to 700 BCE.

After the fall of the northern kingdom in 721 BCE, Assyria transplanted people from Syria and Mesopotamia into the area, and they

---

62. Herzog and Gichon, *Battles of the Bible*, 57–63.

brought their native religious cults and political ethics with them.[63] After the fall of the southern kingdom, neighboring cultures such as Edom moved into the vacuum left by their deportation, as Obadiah complains of in his gospel.[64] There are many reports of syncretistic intermarriage of the Jews with other peoples in the area upon the return of some of the deportees from Babylon. (Ezra 9-10; Neh 6:18; 10:31; 13:1-3, 23-30; Mal 2:11) Slaves living in Palestine and sporting a variety of cultural traditions married Jews in order to gain their freedom.[65] Whichever kingdom rose into power in the area built entirely new cities, agricultural colonies, and private estates for the use of patrons.[66] All of this assured a continuation and even expansion of cultural and political pluralism managed so well by the ancestors for so long.

Indeed, Palestine served early on as a tourist center, because of its great temple and constitutional tradition and great cities of antiquity: Hebron, Jerusalem, Damascus, Shechem. Palestine also served as a center for lines of military supplies and communication between empires and provinces. It was a place for provincial military garrisons and a home for mercenary soldiers, a front line embarkation point for battles and wars between mid-East powers. In the Ptolemaic period from 323-198, Jerusalem was captured 10-12 times during its wars with the northern Seleucids.[67] Foreign troops were frequently billeted in villages inland.[68] In the 260 years from Alexander's death to Pompey's conquest of Jerusalem in 66 BCE, no less than 200 military campaigns raged across the land of Palestine. All of this is to say, there was constant challenge to existing political and religious culture, and constant negotiation and change over the broad expanse of Biblical time.

Moses himself seems to have had an understanding of the prior history of the land of Canaan as handed down in oral and written form to him in Egypt and Midian. He thus seems to have had an inkling of the potential both for freedom and for political tension that could be expected there in the future. These kinds of thoughts must have weighed heavily on his mind as he camped his people at the base of

63. Smith, *Palestinian Parties*, 84.
64. Ibid, 85.
65. Ibid, 238.
66. Ibid, 87.
67. Ibid, 63.
68. Ibid, 64.

Biblical Captivity

Mt. Sinai, in preparation for guiding his people toward this promisingly diverse and tolerant land. After laying down the law at Sinai, he still had to tutor them for 40 years not only in the possibility but the necessity of political and religious freedom as a base for achieving economic and social happiness in Canaan. The fact that they so quickly embrace the variety of cultures available to them in Canaan (Judg 2:10–15) shows how well he tutored them in independent and individual thinking and decision-making. And it also shows how deeply the nature culture of the period tugged on the flesh, even after 40 years of politico-spiritual indoctrination. Later, when Solomon welcomes a wide variety of international cultures and religious denominations to reside in Jerusalem as a diplomatic courtesy, we understand this tradition of hospitality is not lost in the monarchic period either, and in fact is only just beginning to develop. In course of time, Jeremiah reports that there was a separate religious denomination for every city in Judah, and distinctive altars for every street in Jerusalem. (Jer 11:13)

We will next turn our attention to the legal framework for religious and political freedom attributed to the Sinai event (chapter 4), and to a brief discussion of the constitutional framework of cursing and blessing used to track the ensuing 600 year national history down to the time of exile in Babylon. In chapter 5 we will review the political history of external and internal captivity in Israel after the sojourners political compact at Sinai. The sojourn at Sinai and Kadesh explains much of the tension that later, in Judges and Kings, ultimately leads to political decline, captivity, and destruction.

4

The Constitutional Tradition of Ancient Israel

THE SECULAR LAW

THE INTRACTABLE SITUATION OF life un-productive of intellectual freedom in Egypt is remedied when the Hebrew tribes, freed for a three-day holiday pilgrimage, flee Pharaoh by crossing the Reed Sea, camping two months later at the foot of Mt. Sinai. They unanimously accept a foundational charter protective of human rights, the first provision of which requires citizens to enthrone human political freedom in the new society (first commandment), and the second provision of which requires the citizenry to re-enthrone this God when his human rights program is frittered away down the road (second commandment).[1] Freedom for God to reappear in society—really, freedom for an individual prophet to report such an occurrence of God's reappearance and for people to organize religious or political belief systems around such a report—thus requires a very civic sector-oriented freedom of political action.

It is the view of this author, then, that the best framework for viewing the Decalogue is a starkly political and secular one. The Decalogue

---

1. Shinkoskey, *Do My Prophets No Harm*, 60–80.

is a statement of political science so far-reaching in its ramifications that it is virtually a charter for the advancement of regional Semitic civilization from a primitive, semi-literate stage to a "modern" (in its day, and even today) stage of mass literacy (Deut 6:6–8), political rights, and historical consciousness.[2] The charter activates progress not only in government and education science, but in economic, social, health, and ecclesiastic science.

Migrating Israel is a deeply socio-politico-economic event that is, for better or worse, cast enduringly and endearingly in religious garb. That clothing, however, does not ultimately disguise the revolutionary, popular politics of the historical man Moses. His, and theirs, and ours, is a story of the formation of an autonomous ethnic republic, in some ways like the break-away states of the former Soviet Union. But Moses' particular bent is less that of a radical, and more that of a conservative liberation theologian, leading his people not so much in the direction of a post-monarchist Russia, a post-communist Georgia or Azerbaijan, or even a nineteenth century Latin American revolutionary nation, as toward the ethics-inspired, Spirit-moved planting of America in the seventeenth and eighteenth centuries.

After the plague-riddled confrontations with Pharaoh, the Israelites cross the Red Sea into physical safety. Immediately the Israelites treat Moses like a political leader, and not a religious one. In the narratives about these events, he is never spoken of as priest. In fact, the first event of religious sacrifice for the travelers is performed by a priest of Midian, Moses' father in law. (Exod 18:12) This event seems to be as much a civic ritual of public safety as a religious one. It is traditional that at key political events—the founding of a nation, its renewal at the time of coronation—that a national sacrifice of well-being or thanksgiving be offered, essentially celebrating freedom from captivity and fullness of socio-political hope.[3] This, for example, is accomplished when society is re-generated after the great flood by Noah, (Gen 8:20) and also by the Mesopotamian version of Noah, Utnapishtim.[4] As politician, Moses seems to promise much but deliver little. The people complain about food, drink, shelter, all the creature comforts of home. (Exod 17:7) Part

---

2. Halpern, *First Historians*.
3. Milgrom, *Leviticus*, 28–29.
4. Coogan, *The Old Testament*, 16.

The Constitutional Tradition of Ancient Israel

of the problem is that they do not yet have a set of laws to guide their new society, not the least of which is their economy.

While Moses is clearly the leader of the migrating society, the people petition Moses regularly to respect the majority's wish, even when it differs from his clear direction for them. As Moses reminds his readers, "ten times" the people "murmured" and overruled him. (Num 14:22) The people seem dead set upon participatory government. If God inspires Moses with plans for action, the people temper those inclinations with their own notions.

One of the evidences of the idea that at the foot of Sinai Moses, Yahweh, and the Israelite people self-consciously constructed a secular constitution for the civil government of several hundred thousand pilgrims was simply that they needed one at that moment in time. In addition to a law to regulate property, they needed a way to organize government, and a way to define acceptable political and religious murmuring versus unacceptable murmuring. They needed both to promote and limit speech and action in the new nation. They intended to set that boundary quite far to "the left," i.e., in favor of liberality, since their "god" was one who gave "uncircumcised lips" (Exod 6:12) to their first citizen, Moses, and allowed much political conversation, or murmuring. (Exod 15:24; Num 14:2) But the law still needed to provide a line past which citizens could not pass without repercussions. Thus, they needed a definition for sedition and treason against the government. That law was set in the Decalogue by means of the Second Commandment. A law against idolatry prohibits the development of despotism, and thus, efforts to usurp power or subvert the democratic provisions of the constitution, are treasonous.[5] The law was tested and defined in the earliest days after Sinai at Kadesh, as we shall see in chapter 5 below.

The secessionists also needed a law protecting the practice of ethical religion, and a law setting boundaries on the practice of religion in their communities—a law differentiating legitimate religion from illegitimate religion. The first would be handled by a law on blasphemy, or blasphemous libel, and could be found in the First Commandment, since the freedom for prophets to promote the interests of the poor and promote the God of the Exodus was enshrined therein.[6] Any effort to

---

5. We use the Protestant numbering of the Decalogue here, and acknowledge a slightly different numbering system for Catholics/Lutherans and Jews.

6. Shinkoskey, *Do My Prophets No Harm*, 81–117.

Biblical Captivity

limit the political or religious speech of prophets, or denigrate such speech, was thus blasphemous or libelous. The second was handled by a law or laws relating to socio-political and socio-sexual behavior. Those boundaries were provided roughly by the Second and Seventh Commandments of the Decalogue (against idolatry and adultery, respectively), and the policies were tested soon after Sinai as well (see chapter 5 for more on this). After governing themselves at first by following Moses as an emergency civil, and at times military commander (Exod 14–17), and next by means of a hierarchical system of judges (Exod 18), the camp of Israel was ready for a law document which institutionalized and extended these arrangements. (Exod 20:1–17) They also needed a process that would provide for official consent of the people to those governing parameters and definitions. (Exod 19:8–9)

They were not about to use the laws of Ramses, but they may have had access to libraries containing the kinder or gentler codes from earlier rulers or dynasties in Egypt, Syria or Mesopotamia.[7] There may also have been a common law tradition extant among nomadic tribes like the Midian group Moses lived with. In fact, there is evidence of an aniconic (anti-idolatry) tradition there.[8] They needed a simple, broad law for government of a people in a migratory mode, until such time as that law could be further elaborated to meet the specific settlement situations that would arise in the new land. This they found in the Ten Commandments (Ex. 20; Dt. 5), or possibly an abbreviated or pastoral version of these laws, modified or polished by the time of the writing of the Deuteronomist history. One possibility for an early, or alternative, Decalogue, although it, too, seems to reflect a more settled society, is the so-called "ritual" Decalogue found in Exodus 34. (Exod 34:11–26) Some authors have tried to reconstruct the content of the earliest form of the Decalogue.[9] These early precepts were necessarily couched in the form of apodictic or categorical principles—like treaty provisions—which allowed for later snippets of case law meant to interpret the great legislation. The Decalogue may have given support to law

---

7. Westbrook and Wells, *Everyday Law in Biblical Israel,* 9–33; Wright, *Inventing God's Law.*

8. Weinfeld, "Deuteronomy," 292.

9. Nielsen, "An Attempted Reconstruction of the Primitive Decalogue," 78; see also Weinfeld's reconstruction in *The Ten Commandments,* Segal and Levi, eds., 6–7.

statements like the "mishpatim" of the so-called Covenant Code[10] (Exod 20:18–23:33), which were "casuistic," hypothetical (if... then), or case law-type instructional guides, summarizing the secular common law handed down to them from Mesopotamia.[11] This two-step legal process of grand proclamation of foundational values (Exod 24:3–8), followed chronologically by elaboration of casuistic law, is found throughout the ancient Middle East.[12] The opening text of Hammurabi's laws, for example, also elaborates broad statements of political values which are meant to guide the legislation that follows.

Because the Decalogue constitutes the political constitution of democratic-oriented ancient Israel, it contains summary provisions much like the several Articles and Amendments of the democratic constitution of the United States. From the intent language surrounding them,[13] it can be seen that the laws are intended to reach to all living within the bounds of the nation. They apply to individuals and families adhering to the predominant culture, all those indifferent to or outside that culture, and also to corporate interests like government, the military, trading and transportation enterprises. The commandment against theft, for example, prohibits stealing by individuals, but also prohibits theft by institutional agencies, including the government, as well. The fourth commandment against profaning the day of rest is aimed at curbing the tendency of both commercial and governmental enterprises to extend their reach too far into the private realms of family function, worship activity, and scribal/study/learning activity. Thus a day is appointed during which those generally authoritative agencies are disabled from pursuing their constitutional objectives and allows the people time to pursue their own constitutional objectives. The sixth commandment against killing is aimed at curbing government's power over life and death (principally the waging of war and domestic political killings) as much as curbing private killing. The "thou" of the "thou shalt nots" thus points as much to the high and mighty in governing circles in Shechem and Shiloh (and later Jerusalem) as to the untitled, servile field hands and shepherds of Gilead and Galilee. Without

---

10. Meyers, *Exodus*, 179.
11. Westbrook and Wells, *Everyday Law*, 24.
12. Weinfeld, *Social Justice*, 9, 175.
13. See, for example, Num 9:14.

Biblical Captivity

regulation of institutional interests, regulation of individual interests is rendered hypocritical and meaningless.

As we will discuss in an upcoming essay, these early constitutional provisions tend to elaborate a conscious tension and demarcation between the functions of church and state, private and public activity, the freedoms of people and the responsibilities of government. For example, if the first commandment protects religious liberty, and the second commandment protects against despotism, the two together necessarily require separation of church and state. They also constitute a demarcation between the separate executive/judicial and legislative powers at both central and local levels.[14] For example, the second commandment and tenth commandments together outline the function of the local legislatures, while the first commandment enacts a charismatic executive or "judge" (later elective, constitutional kingship) for the nation, both enfranchised by the constitution.

It is also true that the statutes are general and summary. This allows adaptability to a variety of forms of government. In the Bible land this included, over time, confederate republican (Judges), elective monarchic (northern kingdom), herediary monarchic (southern kingdom), land-grant colonial (Persian), self-governing protectorate (Greek and Roman), and provincial tetrarchy (Roman) forms of government. In several of these early and later forms, the people managed to enforce a brand of the original constitutional law, along with the local legislation and case law which bolstered it.[15]

The Ten Commandments in roughly equivalent form are found in Exodus 20 and Deuteronomy 5. The oldest collection of subsequent laws, likely the first result of Decalogue-based legislation or adjudication, is the so-called Book of the Covenant. (Exod 20:22–23:19) The Laws of Deuteronomy (Deut 12–26) are a much later codification, likely from King Josiah's day, rearranging and editing laws which likely had currency at various times throughout the history of Israel. Chronologically, the last biblical collection, which seems to spring from a priestly

---

14. Shinkoskey, *Do My Prophets No Harm*, 94.

15. For example, when Josiah was presented with an old law document, he made it the basis of reforms (2 Kgs 22–23), and two hundred years later Ezra presented another such reformulation to the people returning from Babylon to Judea. (Ezra 7:25–26, Neh 8) Jesus, indeed, announced his intention to focus on the human rights provisions of the original constitutional law of Israel, as well. (Luke 4:18).

group of legal scholars, perhaps working in exile, is called the Holiness Code. (Lev 17–26)

It is relevant to our argument here that the first law of the Covenant Code (Exod 21:1–11), relating to manumission from indentured labor captivity for the citizenry of Israel, directly recalls the Decalogue's prologue/first commandment ethic of liberation from bondage. (Exod 20:2) Textual sequence in legal materials of both the Bible and the ancient Near East is known to assert the priority of the legislation for the legal system. Because the constitutional law outlines release from physical and intellectual confinement as the highest priority and preferred political ethic for the new nation (Prologue and First Commandment), legislators who made policy based upon that formative law saw fit to maintain this same priority in the laws governing the communities of Israel upon settlement in Canaan (the first law of the Covenant Code).

Israel's society, though, for the time being was to be a military and pastoral society, and not until "40 years" later would it become a truly agricultural society, although it is likely they engaged in agriculture previously during their lengthy stay at Kadesh, for example. They needed rules to aid them in side-stepping regional cultural practices which were inimical to their new way of life, and which tempted them in their travels and temporary settlements. And above all, as we mentioned above, they needed guidelines for religious and political exercise, a structure for civil government, a set of ethics to guide local civil and criminal law, and an outline for foreign policy. These were fulfilled, remarkably, in the brief categorical pronouncements of the Ten Commandments, and in the policy statements/legislation elaborated during the wilderness period pursuant to those laws. For example, foreign policy objectives were conditioned by the commandment against killing, which apparently referred both to domestic and international killing. The policy legislation laid down during the wilderness period about avoiding contentious contact with Edom and Moab served to guide international policy for hundreds of years into the period of settlement. (Deut 2:5, 9)

A governing charter or constitution must perform two broad functions. First, it must formalize the organization and operation of the government. Second, it must protect the citizens of that nation *from* the government. The document itself contained both the organizational and operational principle in its First Commandment. The law prohibits the elevation of any other governing principle or "god" above that of the principle "god," or "God" of freedom.[16] The commandment thus encourages a society allowing for free political and religious opinion, which free opinion will enable the citizenry to avoid the sad history encapsulated by the prologue to the first commandment, the reminder of the captivity in Egypt. The first commandment necessitates that the government be run by a charismatic, elected, populist prophet, a sentient, highly ethical political theorist and practitioner like Moses (Deut 18:15), whose term of election is based on the consent of the electorate.[17]

Because the plural and even dissident voices of the people are perpetually enfranchised as against prevailing conventional opinion, the consent of the people is rarely universal and never static. It is always voluble and subject to cross currents, and the political scene soon after acceptance of the constitution at Sinai is dominated by changing coalitions of power. Moses himself presents the rights-and-responsibilities-laden Decalogue—a proclamation of freedom for all who dwell in the camp of Israel—at a large gathering, so that all may indicate approval or disapproval. (Exod 19:7–8, 24:7; Deut 4:9–14) While there is reported unanimity on this historic occasion, universal consensus for government policy and political ethics is difficult to apprehend as time goes on. But the nation, and its offspring polities, try to find leaders "like Moses" (Deut 18:15) who imitate the nurturing instruction and political example of the original populist political leader. These turn out to be a mixture of those in, or close to, or pounding upon the government from far outside of it—the likes of Deborah, Samuel, David, Elijah, the literary prophets, Hezekiah, Josiah, Daniel, and in New Testament times, John the Baptist, Jesus, Paul, and John of Patmos.

Many generations after Moses, the people of the northern communities of Israel re-enact a similar episode of political secession and reconstruction of government, apparently based upon the authority of the Decalogue interpretation we give here. The northern provinces of

---

16. By this I do not wish to demean the source of inspiration for the law which Moses claimed and the people believed. I simply mean to say that this God, real enough to many then and now, is unswervingly devoted to secular rights, and seems to not be threatened by giving the people freedom to believe religiously as they wish. This God trusts that by means of free religious, and political and scientific-academic inquiry, the people will ultimately have an adequate respect for his Spirit and personality.

17. David, for example, was rejected as to a continuing term of office in favor of Absalom. (2 Sam 15:1–12). Also, Rehoboam was rejected as to continuation as king in favor of Jeroboam. (1 Kgs 12)

David's united kingdom experience economic and religious oppression at the hand of Rehoboam, Solomon's son. Jeroboam's rebellion is encouraged by the prophet Ahijah and has at its root a desire for local/regional independence in matters of religious conscience, and relief from the onerous burden of labor taxation imposed by the king, who would normally be expected to ease the burden of taxation upon coronation rather than escalate it.[18] (1 Kgs 12) Some generations after that, Josiah frees the people of the southern kingdom from the level of forced labor of his predecessor, who used "his neighbor's service without wages." (Jer 22:13) Zedekiah, Josiah's son, also released laborers from servitude as well. (Jer 34:8–17) These political acts can be said to enact as well either the spirit or the letter of the secondary commandments relating to liberation from economic oppression gathered together in Leviticus and Deuteronomy, and the law precept against idolatry contained in the second constitutional commandment.[19] (Lev 25; Deut 15; Exod 20:4–6)

In other ancient communities of the Near East, too, it was thought to be incumbent upon sentient politicians like Jeroboam to respond to political injustice perpetrated within the society. At Mari, for example, a prophet advised a ruler, "When an oppressed man or woman cries out to you, rise up and do him justice."[20] In Egypt, Ptolemy V (200 B.C.E.) made a proclamation of liberty for a group of people which read, "Each of you shall return to his holding and each of you shall return to his family."[21] This mirrors very closely the language of manumission found in the Jubilee law of Leviticus 25:10, and speaks to the idea of liberation from financial debt. Similar language is found in the writings of the Greek political historian Xenophon. Language like this is reported in the Jewish apocryphal book of Maccabees (3 Macc 7:8) relative to a proclamation by Ptolemy Philopator (163 BCE). Ptolemy VIII (118 BCE) made an amnesty of arrears of civic labor as well.[22]

The Bible's days of "judgment" (defined roughly as days of either remarkably positive or notably negative civic activity, or as days

---

18. Weinfeld, *Social Justice*, 54, 84.

19. Idolatry, as we will see in chapter 5, refers primarily to placing trust and property into the oppressive hands of the governors of a highly centralized government and economy.

20. Weinfeld, *Social Justice*, 49.

21. Ibid, 159.

22. Weinfeld, *Social Justice*, 173.

of tectonic changes among nations) are times when the blessings and curses of the covenant, which we will review below, come into obvious play. Judgment thus refers both to positive attendance upon righteous government (i.e., the granting and enforcing of rights and responsibilities) and a meting out of negative consequences against unrighteous government involved in the suppression of rights and of land-holding. In the days of Moses/Aaron, Samuel/David, Josiah/Jeremiah, and Ezra/Nehemiah, positive judgment was meted out and great benefit obtained, for at least a period of time. In the days of Ahab, Ahaz, Zedekiah, Antioches Epiphanes, and Herod, negative judgment was poured out of heaven by the hand of God and of earth by the hands of men.

In Moses' Israel, the first law—the first commandment—is a call to perpetual re-enactment of Decalogue political values as against a culture backsliding toward monarchy, idolatry, political dependency, or heavy religious denominational uniformity. In Israel, each individual, from "captains of your tribes, (and) your elders" to "your little ones, your wives" make a compact with God to enforce the laws of human rights. (Deut 29:10–13; see also Exod 19:8) In fact, this citizenship pledge requires citizens to take civil action to reclaim their own rights and the rights of others when abrogated. Many scholars argue that the political covenantal re-enactments associated with Noah, Abraham and David excuse the citizen from individual responsibility for political action and place it on the shoulders of either God and his providential will or on the shoulders of the prophet. They argue that the blessings of the covenant are "unconditional," rather than conditional on the behavior of the people. It is not our purpose to argue here the tenability of such a distinction.[23] But virtually all scholars believe the Mosaic covenant required citizen energy and popular choice as the key variable in deliverance from harm. This inevitably leads to rivalry and potentially to conflict over religious and political values. But such competition is good if the speech and the actions of the parties are reasonable and ethical.

Indeed the principle historian of early Israel, the so-called Deuteronomistic writer, included a clear indication of the original intent of the first commandments[24] in several astonishing verses which we relate

23. For the traditional view, see Anderson, "Covenant," 139.

24. We use the plural here to tip our hat in the direction of the Jewish sense that the Protestant first and second commandments do seem to go together and perhaps form

here in full: "And when thy son asketh thee in time to come, saying, What mean the testimonies, and the statutes, and the judgments, which the Lord our god hath commanded you? Then thou shalt say unto thy son, We were Pharaoh's bondmen in Egypt; and the Lord brought us out of Egypt with a mighty hand . . . And the Lord commanded us to do all these statutes . . . that he might preserve us alive, as it is at this day." (Deut 6:21–24) The Hebrew word translated here as "testimonies" means pact, or covenant.[25] A law is indeed a testimonial of a past experience. The law of free exercise in Israel is a testimony of the lack of political and religious freedom in Egypt, just as our own Bill of Rights is a testimony to the demeaned status of political and religious enfranchisement of the colonists under the regime of King George III at the time of the American Revolution. The intent and meaning of the covenant charter of laws is simply to enact the kind of political, economic and religious freedom that the descendants of Jacob did not have in Egypt, that is, to enact the rule of humane law rather than the capricious rule of an autocrat. We will see that the word "alive" refers not so much to actual living, breathing physical life, as satisfaction and happiness. It is this "blessing," as opposed to "cursing," that the Israelites expected their foundational law to render to the citizenry, as we will see below.

In any event, the free exercise commandment, together with the anti-autocracy commandment, trigger the first and most fundamental step in organization of the government. It divides the government into two seats of power, the public and the private, the state and the church. Moses takes on secular government functions for himself and delivers the religious functions to Aaron. (Exod 28–29) Each cultural sector is henceforth expected to respect the independence of the other at all levels of government. Political freedom requires checks and balances between the powers in society. Israel is subsequently careful to disarm the ability of the secular power to overthrow the cult denominations, and the ability of the cult denominations to take the government captive. For example, Saul incurs Samuel's wrath, and violates the constitution, when he usurps priestly duties at a critical time in the campaign to rebuff the Philistines. (1 Sam 13) On the other hand, priestly houses in the days of Greek colonialism usurp the secular power and earn the

---

one commandment; see the *Ten Commandments*, Segal and Levi, eds., 6.

25. Walzer, *Exodus and Revolution*, 85.

Biblical Captivity

disrespect and revolutionary opposition of major sectors of Jewish society. (for more on this see chapter 6)

RELIGIOUS LIBERTY IN THE ANCIENT WORLD

In this brief section we will review the problem of religious liberty in the ancient world in general. In this connection, it is appropriate to revisit a comment made in my first essay on this subject: "Bible students have made much of the notion of the Exodus as liberation from physical slavery. But they have not been so careful to discuss the most fundamental kind of slavery, that of religious slavery. Liberation from physical slavery is surely what is necessary to establish occupational rights, physical health and other social benefits. But even a more significant form of liberation is that from the shackles of conscience. Without the exercise of free thought and belief, even economic freedom cannot mean much."[26]

We see evidence in ancient Near East extra-biblical sources of other struggles to achieve just this kind of intellectual freedom to worship and to participate in government. Egypt herself had learned the lesson of the importance of religious freedom in earlier times. Proclamations from the 4th Dynasty (about 2500 BCE) onward freed farmers in the vicinity of the temple from slavery in the service of the government and its sectarian god.[27] In the period of the Sixth Dynasty (2345–2181 BCE), King Pepi II freed the worshipers of the god Min in Koptos from slavery so that their labor and offerings could be disposed in service of their preferred god alone. The law freeing them was posted on stelae at the gate of the temple.[28] Seti I issued a proclamation in 1300 BCE, close to the time of Moses, that protected temple estate employees of the god Osiris, making them "immune" from slavery to other causes.[29] The Hittites at the time of Moses (in the 13th century BCE) also granted liberty to holy estates from participation in national labor projects. Thus, in proclamations of freedom given to slaves in many kingdoms of the Fertile Crescent by reformist leaders, workers are freed from state obligations so they can devote their discretionary resources to the private

26. Shinkoskey, *Do My Prophets No Harm*, 111.
27. Weinfeld, *Social Justice*, 101.
28. Ibid, 80, 101–102.
29. Ibid, 136.

interests of their God, rather than to the personal interests of single-minded rulers. Captives of the prior state regime effectively had to pay obeisance to the policies of the king rather than the policies of a more liberal and humane source of power. In this sense, Moses is merely asking Pharaoh for the favor that many humanistic kings of Egypt in the past have been willing to grant.

The epigraphy of the Middle East shows with increasing confidence that the ancients were cognizant of "modern" worries like personal privacy, protection afforded the lives, labor and private property of persons,[30] and notions of free political and religious expression. They were much more frequently overrun by marauders than many modern cultures are (see chapter 2), and thus were likely to be a good deal more sensitive to the problem of abrogation of human rights, and versed in proper solutions and preventatives. We saw this in the sensitivities and acrobatic avoidance mechanisms demonstrated by Abraham with respect to rulers in Canaan and Egypt. Proclamations of economic and religious freedom were issued by kings and won by reformers[31] throughout the Mediterranean and Near East a thousand years before Moses and a thousand years after him. Written laws are evidence of reform movements and political pressure as much as political control efforts, and indicate a time-honored tool to curb despotism.

In the north of Mesopotamia about 2420 BCE, Enmetena of Lagash "established liberation" for the people there. Urukagina did so as well, about 50 years later, in 2370 BCE. The Sumerian reformer Urnammu, living 2111-2094, 400 years before Hammurabi, made reforms in favor of the poor and oppressed. Ishme-Dagan did likewise in 1953-1935 BCE as did the Sumerian Lipit-Ishtar around 1900 BCE.[32] The laws of the Akkadian city Eshnunna are dated from the 1800s BCE. During the time of early Assyrian ascendency (1900-1700 BCE), the inhabitants of the Assyrian colony of Cappodocia were extended rights of freedom.[33]

Proclamations of political rights and law are also found near to the time of the Abrahamic migration, variously located from 2100 BCE and

---

30. Westbrook, *Tigris*, 1:33, 51.

31. For the ability of citizens to petition government for redress of grievances, see Hittite inscriptions detailed in Westbrook, *Tigris*, 1:157.

32. Ehrlich, "Israelite Law," 421.

33. Weinfeld, *Social Justice*, 92.

Biblical Captivity

1600 BCE.[34] Reformist kings used the opportunity provided them at their coronations to enact justice and establish new yardsticks for good conduct in their realms, often extending worship rights to a variety of denominations. A string of liberal Mesopotamian rulers sprung up in the eighteenth century, after Abraham was likely gone. Samsuiluna pursued reforms in the period 1749-1712; Hammurabi, as much a strong-arm ruler as a reformer, promulgated his laws around the turn of the 17th century[35] (1728-1686 BCE); then Ammi-Saduqa exempted certain citizens from military service during his reign, which spanned the period 1646-1626.[36] He also distinguished between agricultural loans, which could be released, and consumer or business loans, which could not.[37] Six hundred years after Moses, Esarhaddon proclaimed a form of religious and economic freedom in Assyria around the time of Hezekiah's son Manasseh.[38] (680–670 BCE)

It is hard to imagine kings making political and religious reforms for constituencies who are indifferent to them. It seems obvious that while an annalistic history was typically written by parties close to the monarch, and glorified his personal efforts above the efforts of others, pressure applied by the people had to have been responsible for much of the impetus to reform.[39] Even colonized nations could protest. In fact, Ugarit protested the economic pressure placed on the free citizenry by the Hittite emperor, and won a reform.[40]

Urukagina and his people, like Moses and his people much later, likely achieved great political traction among neighboring cultures for instigating liberation and a body of rights. A reasonable amount of in-migration to their polities likely resulted from them, especially if similar liberties were granted to resident aliens. This attraction appears to have swelled the party of the Israelites with a variety of hangers-on upon their exit from Egypt during their 40-year tenure in the wilderness even

---

34. Millard, "Abraham," 37–40.
35. Anderson, *Old Testament*, 602.
36. Weinfeld, *Social Justice*, 89.
37. Westbrook, *Tigris*, 153.
38. Ibid, 61, 66, 99, 102, 109, 141.
39. See Horsley, *Jesus and Empire*, 61–63, for a discussion of the separate traditions of the elite versus that of the village communities.
40. Westbrook, *Tigris*, 158.

The Constitutional Tradition of Ancient Israel

before they entered Canaan, and also after they entered. For example, Kenites joined with them and enjoyed an allocation of land.[41]

THE COVENANT AND ITS CURSES

Israel's performance as individual citizens and as a nation is measured in terms of adherence to her foundational political system, the covenant law commonly known as "the commandments," or Decalogue, and also to the broader legal system that springs from the Decalogue, frequently referred to as the "statutes." (Deut 27:10) The blessing that is expected from keeping the covenant foundational law—its positive outcome—is the independence of the people at all levels of society. The cursing associated with the covenant, as we suggested above, is the consequence of neglecting the governing charter. That consequence is one or another form of political captivity.

At the time of his retirement from the political judgeship of Israel, Moses delivers a farewell address which outlines these blessings and cursings. (Deut 27–28) Joshua mentions them again later, when the government is re-established in Canaan. (Josh 23–24) The Decalogue charter of rights and responsibilities, first given at Sinai some "40 years" earlier is to stand as a bulwark against the common fate of communities in the ancient Near East—internal political instability, foreign oppression and aggression, forced migration, and ultimately economic and intellectual enslavement. On the positive side, the ten great statements are devoted to promoting community stability, local autonomy, and political longevity based on a socio-economic system of perpetual maintenance of "inherited" land within the clan or local government grouping exercising stewardship of the land.

The commandments and the statutes not only regulate the polity and sanction misbehavior, but also to teach the citizenry the way they are expected to lead their lives. The original laws and the later packaging of them in a historical wrapping are to serve as instruction, or "torah." In particular, Torah is a testimony of Israel's prior experience in both the Canaan of their ancestors (a good outcome), and the Egypt of their ancestors (a bad outcome).

---

41. Halpern, "Kenites," 4:17–22.

Biblical Captivity

Moses recalls in the first three chapters of Deuteronomy—the beginning of his speech—their experience in the wilderness after leaving "Horeb." In the fourth chapter he reminds the children that they must "hearken . . . unto" and "do" the laws. (Deut 4:1) "Hearken" invites the people to listen to what the laws are saying, the intent and purpose of the laws and not just their bland proscriptions and their high-sounding encouragement. They must contemplate the testimony and the story that the laws convey. If the people "hearken," they will know what the laws are designed to accomplish and what the laws are designed to prevent. They will then not hesitate to "do" them, that is to enforce them, respect and cherish them, and renew them when necessary. Moses adds that the people must not change the laws, "add" or "diminish" them. (Deut 4:2) Jesus of Nazareth, for his part, commends the same understanding of the foundational law in his day: "One jot and one tittle shall in no wise pass from the law." (Matt 5:18) He agrees that hearkening to, or studying, the laws, however, is only the beginning of righteousness. (Matt 5:20) What remains is to do them on a daily basis. (Matt 5:21–48)

If the people hearken and do—sentiently enact and enforce—they will be blessed with security in their lands, ways and possessions: "The Lord shall cause thine enemies that rise up against thee to be smitten before thy face . . . (they shall) flee before thee seven ways." (Deut 28:7) But if they do not hearken and do, "the Lord shall cause thee to be smitten before thine enemies . . ." (Deut 28:25) The result of this smiting is captivity: "And (thou) shalt be removed into all the kingdoms of the earth." (Deut 28:25) Elsewhere, in a text of the Torah perhaps re-touched at a much later time, this curse of captivity is re-iterated: "I will scatter you among the heathen . . . (and you will) pine away in your enemies lands." (Lev 26:33, 39)

The captivity that they will experience is religio-political captivity at root: "Thou shalt (there) serve other gods of wood and stone." (Deut 28:36) In fact, both of the two great oppressions that the Exodus and the Sinai constitution were designed to overturn, religious and economic oppression, will recur: "(Ye will) serve other gods . . . neither shall the sole of thy foot have rest . . . (ye shall be) sold unto your enemies as bondmen." (Deut 28:64–65, 68) In essence, they will be like Joseph sold into Egypt, and the children of Israel sold into wholesale slavery several hundred years later by the hand of Pharaoh.

The Constitutional Tradition of Ancient Israel

What is so difficult about captivity, internal or external, is that it is extremely hard to get out from under. For example, once the northern kingdom goes into captivity in Assyria, those tribes seem never to have been heard from as an independent political entity again. The southern tribes come back to Judea after several generations of captivity in Babylon, but then, for the next 600–700 years, are governed as political puppets of much greater nations. Once Joseph was sold into Egypt, the great Palestinian community promised to Abraham was blockaded, interrupted, delayed, forestalled, for 400 years. It was this earlier experience that the historian Moses drew upon to warn his people. If they neglected the laws like the sons of Jacob did when they imprisoned Joseph, "Thou shalt be only oppressed and spoiled evermore, and no man shall save thee." (Deut 28:29) No successful prophet-deliverer came to Israel in Egypt during the intermediate stages of those 400 years, at least not one strong enough to return her to Canaan, or to alleviate the long term of oppression of individual intellectual and economic power under the House of Seti. Not until Moses. None came to Israel either during the half millennium of political vassalage after release from the Babylonian captivity. Not even the Maccabees, the Herodians, John the Baptist, Jesus of Nazareth, Paul of Tarsus, or the great rabbis of the Tannaitic period, were politically strong enough to return Israel to permanent independence in her ancestral homeland. The curse of captivity is monstrous and effectively permanent. It must be avoided, even at great cost.

Moses spells out the details of the history of captivity of nations when he lists the negative consequences of reverting from the kingship of a God of humane law back to the arbitrary and injurious law of autocratic kings. All the strength, beauty and pleasure of family and community independence will be lost, and a once proud and prosperous people will go mad with mourning and misunderstanding. Marriage, homes, beloved animals, children, possessions, and familiar landmarks all will be lost. "Thou shalt betroth a wife, and another man shall lie with her . . ." (Deut 28:30); "Thou shalt build a house, and . . . not dwell therein" (30); "Thy sheep shall be given unto thine enemies" (31); "Thy sons and thy daughters shall be given unto another people, and thine eyes shall look, and fail with longing for them all the day long . . ." (32); "The fruit of thy land and all thy labors, shall (another) nation . . . eat up . . . " (33); "Thou shalt be mad for the sight of thine eyes which thou shalt see." (34) All this happens because the people will be exiled to a place "which neither thou nor thy fathers have known . . ." (36) The place of exile will not even be an ancestral homeland of any kind. The loss will be even greater than the level of loss for other peoples taken captivity in the ancient Near East. That is because Israel has something that others do not—genuine democratic freedom. When a people so fortunate as Israel "observe and . . . do all his commandments," they are "set on high above all nations of the earth." (Deut 28:1) They are like ancient Tyre, (Ezek 28:13–15), Ethiopia, (Amos 9:7) Syria, (Amos 9:7)—a people to whom all eyes are drawn. But if they do not observe the commandments, they are like a "hissing" (1 Kgs 9:8) and a "byword." (Job 17:6; Deut 28:37) They are booed like a corrupt referee at a basketball game.

Nonetheless there is hope at least for a partial or eventual salvaging of their civilization, because God does not stop working through prophets to try to get the job of independence done again. Isaiah suggests, "The Lord shall set his hand again the second time to recover the remnant of his people, which shall be left, from Assyria, and from Egypt, and from Pathros, and from Cush, and from Elam, and from Shinar, and from Hamath, and from the islands of the sea . . ." (Isa 11:11) But this second time does not come for another 2,000 years after the second temple is destroyed. Prevention is better than the cure.

Ezekiel gives assurance that the problem of captivity is not a threat to Israel alone, but to other peoples who find artificial satisfaction in their own lives and who perhaps provide a dab of human rights every now and again for their neighbors. Such a nation is Egypt, when she is in the hands of a benevolent ruler. Still: "I will scatter the Egyptians among the nations, and will disperse them through the countries." But then Egypt, too, like Israel, can potentially be brought home; "I will gather the Egyptians from the people whether they were scattered . . . I will cause them to return . . ." (Ezek 29:13–14) Natives exiled from Egypt, of course, are not new on the scene in Ezekiel's day. The story of the return of the exile Sinuhe to his Egyptian homeland is one well known in the ancient world, since it dates from the twentieth century BCE (see chapter 3). Interestingly, a decent living can sometimes be had after dislocation since the goal of a conqueror is often to assimilate the elite of the conquered society into the conquering society and invest

The Constitutional Tradition of Ancient Israel

them in the political way of life there.[42] But the level of happiness that comes from self-government is difficult to attain under such circumstances, as Psalm 137 suggests. There is danger in assuming too much satisfaction with life under forced exile.[43]

The prophets Jeremiah (Jer 33) and Ezekiel (Ezek 34) devote extensive narratives recalling the same kinds of blessings and curses elaborated by Moses. For Jeremiah, the "houses" and "cities" of his day spill out their men to ward against the "Chaldeans," but because they neglect the commandments those houses and cities will only be filled once again "with the dead bodies of men." (Jer 33:4–5) Some 250 years later, the writer of Chronicles sees Jeremiah's prophecy of desolation in Judea fulfilled, because the princes of Judah did not redeem the people from economic and intellectual oppression as they should have. (2 Chr 36:21) Jeremiah, like Moses, holds out a distant hope for "return." Just as surely as the people choose cursing over blessing, God chooses and works to "bring . . . health and cure." (33:6) He will do this by means of revelation through prophets: "(I) will reveal unto them the abundance of peace and truth. I will cause the captivity of Judah and the captivity of Israel to return." (33:7)

For Ezekiel, the "shepherds," or leaders, of Israel "feed themselves" (they become fat) rather than their flocks. "Because my flock became a prey" (34:8) [are held captive by their leaders] God will have compassion on them: "I will deliver my flock from their mouth." (34:10) "They shall dwell safely and none shall make them afraid." (34:28) Ezekiel's optimism apparently resulted from the growing remnant of priestly activists who gathered around him in Babylon and hoped to return to Israel and build a new temple there. The optimism which infected the exiles was eventually scaled back quite a bit when it became clear that Israel would not be free to re-constitute an independent nation in Judea and to build a fantastic new temple, but rather would eke out an existence as a nation in vassalage to Persia and would construct only a shadow of the old temple in Jerusalem. (Ezra 3:12)

---

42. Lewis, *Ancient Tyranny*, 97–104.
43. Smith-Christopher, *Theology of Exile*.

Biblical Captivity

CONSITUTIONAL PROVISIONS TO PREVENT OR CURB THE RAVAGES OF CAPTIVITY

In the introductory paragraphs of chapter 1, and in section 1 of this chapter we noted that Israel's Decalogue is a response to two main oppressions known by the children of Israel in Egypt—the repression of labor power and the suppression of political/religious conscience. The Decalogue was designed to prevent similar oppression from ever arising in Israel.[44] The fact that the northern region of Israel did exist as an independent nation for some 500 years after Moses, and the southern region for some 600 years after Moses, attests to the sturdiness of the democratic constitutional system. We noted that the civilization underwent several self-correcting revolutions which brought about either schism (1 Kings 12), or renovations of rights (2 Kgs 23), and that such political activity was from time to time witnessed in Egypt and Mesopotamia as well as at the hands of reforming kings there.

Ancient proclamations of liberty typically provided a manumission of both the body and the mind, so we should not be surprised to see that Israel's law does as well. The manumission formula for freeing a slave included the opportunity to devote himself to a particular god.[45] In Mesopotamia, there was a widely held belief that enslavement of the devotees of a god angers all the gods, and subjects the land to desolation and punishments.[46] In Israel, such enslavement brings an indictment from Yahweh: "I will make your cities waste . . . I will bring your land into desolation." (Lev 26:31–35; see also 2 Chr 36:21) Of King Manistusu in twenty-second century Akkad it was said "he freed thirty-eight cities from corvee and from levy, that they might serve on behalf of the temple of the god Shamash alone."[47]

From time to time the major gods in heaven freed the minor gods from service by an act of the grand council of gods. As a result, mankind, according to one Mesopotamian creation theory, were then asked to shoulder the responsibility of devotion to the major gods in place

---

44. The Decalogue's first commandment addressed religious liberty, and its fourth commandment enacted a mandatory day of rest to prevent both chattel slavery of citizens and rigorous, punitive labor.

45. Weinfeld, *Social Justice*, 81.

46. Ibid.

47. Ibid, 16.

The Constitutional Tradition of Ancient Israel

of the minor gods.[48] In this view, the captivity of the minor gods in heaven was taken as a platform for discrimination against the minor gods on earth. A better interpretation might be that such a heavenly circumstance should encourage a council of the authorities on earth to carry out a similar proclamation of freedom for the people devoted to the minor gods, so that those gods might have access to their own clientele of devotees. From such machinations of thought, a theory of religious liberty might well have been given theological support in ancient Mesopotamia. As a practical matter, it is easy to envision that the widely dispersed, small scale settlements of early Mesopotamia provided the kind of religious pluralism which conditioned tolerance of a variety of sectarian worship traditions within developing regional city-state systems of government.[49]

It is the position of this essay that Israel's first commandment enacts political and religious liberty, and that its fourth commandment enacts economic liberty as against enslavement of the citizen's labor power and land and other economic holdings. The people were to work hard and long, but only six days out of seven. They were then to have a day of rest by law. The law of Deuteronomy also specified that after seven years indentured servants were to be freed, and after 49 years lands sold out of the hands of their original owners were to be returned. (Deut 15; Lev 25) Jesus' Sermon on the Mount can be seen as a promotion of economic and intellectual freedom of the kind suggested by Moses and other Near East reformers. Jesus said that it was not possible for man to "serve two masters . . . Ye cannot serve God and mammon." (Matt 6:24) It is clear from the sermon that the oppressive economic and political practices of the political authorities constitute the "mammon" that Jesus speaks of. For example he suggests that the failure to enact economic reform/mercy on the most private and local of levels, the "forgiveness of debts" among contracting parties, is the hallmark of "evil." (Matt 6:12–13) Lack of such forgiveness on a larger scale is surely, then, an even greater locus of evil. Political leaders contract with the people, but they have not forgiven. What God suggests is the best policy is that the intellectually "poor in spirit" (this condition is referred to as "the oppression of the poor" in Ps 12:5 and "sigh(ing) by reason of the bondage" in Exod 2:23) must be lifted out of such abasement, and

---

48. Ibid, 17.
49. Bauer, *History*, 18, 32–34, 36–38.

the economically "meek" must "inherit the earth," that is, have their property and lands returned to them. (Matt 5:3, 5) The Sermon on the Mount provides a formula for political and economic freedom and re-enfranchisement just as much as the Lord's Prayer for forgiveness of debts is a suggestion that such freedom is favored by God in heaven.

The first and fourth commandments are key constitutional enactments to prevent and cure captivity, and thus are positioned early in the Decalogue in its first table of five. The sixth commandment, however, is also an essential protection against the kind of oppression and captivity that results from the state's political killing of its own dissident citizens, and, alternately, its mustering of them into expansionist military enterprises without sanction of the constitution or consent of the people. The eighth commandment, the prohibition of theft, curbs the government's authority to expropriate the property of citizens and international neighbors as well, and thus is an anti-captivity provision too.

The tenth commandment—prohibiting coveting of the neighbor's wife and possessions—is positioned at the end of the Decalogue and sums up the fundamental dual concerns of the book of Exodus, with its concern for the individual and for the neighbor. As we mentioned above, Decalogue provisions apply to government and employers and the property of neighbors as well. The best translation of "neighbor" in the Hebrew Bible is "citizen." Jeremiah's interpretation of the problem that the tenth commandment addresses is instructive here. He complains that King Jehoiakim "useth his neighbor's service without wages." He is referring to forced labor on the king's building projects. The king expropriates the wealth of the citizen neighbors of his realm for his own glory and majesty.[50] (Jer 22:13) This is contrasted with the young king's father Josiah, who previously was light-handed with respect to mandatory public labor. The Decalogue's tenth commandment thus provides a broad encouragement for the Sabbath year labor release law of Deuteronomy 15 (release of debts every seven years) and the Jubilee year land release law of Leviticus 25 (through which ownership reverts to the original owner's family). These periodic, mandatory remissions of economic burdens imposed on the poorer classes by the aristocracy apparently result from usurious lending practices and overbearing central government taxation of labor and property holdings.

---

50. Weinfeld, *Social Justice*, 54.

Such failure to rollback economic burdens leads to days of judgment whereby the curses/consequences of the covenant law are fulfilled. For example, Jeremiah sees the aristocracy's sun-setting of Zedekiah's labor release law as a defining factor in the resumption of the siege of Jerusalem and eventual fall of the southern Kingdom.[51] (Jer 34:17) Extending the period of indenture past the seven year period essentially defrauds the neighbor of his property and offends the tenth commandment: "Thou shalt not covet thy neighbor's house, his field . . . or anything that is thy neighbor's." (Deut 5:21) For this reason Jeremiah rails, "Ye have not hearkened unto me in proclaiming liberty, everyone to his brother, and every man to his neighbor . . ." (Jer 34:17)

The tenth commandment thus re-iterates and expands the general principles of the first and fourth commandments by noting that the broad national policies of the First Table are to be enacted into specific local commercial and behavioral ordinances, along the lines generally outlined in the Decalogue. Thus Israel's Tenth Commandment is much like America's own Tenth Amendment, which makes clear that local law-making bodies are free to fill in the gaps where federal lawmaking does not enumerate specific policies. The problem is that localities in Israel took too much liberty in re-defining the creditor/debtor accountability relationships and thus offended the spirit of the Tenth Commandment. The nation was now poised to learn the actual consequence of such greed.

PERSONAL AND CORPORATE CURSING: AN EARLY HISTORICAL SCIENCE IN THE BROAD ANCIENT NEAR EAST MILLIEU

One who curses exercises condemnatory speech and action against another. The idea of cursing carries with it both primitive and progressive notions for ancient Israelites. A curse can be prediction, wish, vow, conspiracy or overt action. It is a warning of consequence. In the ancient Near East, a curse is pronounced by God or the gods, kings, scribes, priests, military officers, court prophets, individuals, treaties and statutes. Bible stories and characters use these condemnatory vehicles for affecting or predicting the outcome of current and future events, and

---

51. Ibid, 88.

Biblical Captivity

develop several of them in a way that suggests a science devoted to the subject. Israel's prophets deliver extended curses called oracles of doom, or "woe" oracles, against their own or other nations. These predictions are essentially calls for the nation to stay out of treaty alliances which commit the people to wars in defense of other nations,[52] calls to shun despotism, and calls for the people to redress the oppression of the poor and uneducated at home.

The curse of a prophet is essentially a prediction about the future that is well informed by a study of the past.[53] In Deuteronomy 27–28, Jeremiah 33, and Ezekiel 34, the curse describes everything debilitating that Israel can possibly suffer if and when it neglects its own sacred foundational constitution, the Decalogue, with all its progressive safeguards, rights, and responsibilities. When the nation begins to embrace religious and political values long associated with nature worship and despotic kingship, it activates the curse of God, prophet, and constitutional commandment law, opening a Pandora's box of natural, social, legal, economic and military consequence. The nation subjects itself to internal and external conquest and captivity.

The removal of mankind from the Garden of Eden, wherein there was political innocence and ready access to God's presence, constituted the original curse of mankind by God. This initial "fall" was followed in time by the curse/consequence of the flood, the confusion of tongues and scattering of nations about the earth, and the development of nature religion, strongman tyranny, and hereditary kingship. Throughout all time it has been the effort of God, prophets, and law-abiding citizenries to reverse the consequence of inhumanity and lawlessness triggered by events like the fall and other departures from humane law in the communities of mankind. Those consequences are summarized by one author in six words starting with the letter "d": defeat, disease, desolation, deprivation, deportation, and death.[54] While eastern Sem-

---

52. Gottwald, *Kingdoms*, 32.

53. Jotham predicted woe for those citizens of Shechem who supported Abimelech's violent usurpation of power, and in time, they experienced misgivings about the kind of political process so characteristic of the autocracy Israel had been subject to in Egypt, and the consequences, or curses of their decision-making as well. (Judg 9:7–15, 57) It has been suggested that Jotham's curse was also an encouragement to oppose Abimelech, a calling of the citizenry to action; see Schipper, *Parables and Conflict in the Hebrew Bible*.

54. Stuart, "Curse," 1218.

The Constitutional Tradition of Ancient Israel

ites normally attributed the issuing and fulfillment of curses to the authority and action of a particular god, western Semites, the Bible peoples among them, normally understood that curses could emanate just as easily from the mouths of men and women, since socio-political consequences are rightfully based on observable patterns of human behavior.[55]

Curses can be progressive and appropriate, primitive and inappropriate/ illegal in nature. Appropriate curses are those which are arguably true, reasonable, ethical, consensual, even scientific. They are those meted out by God, predicted in scripture, and accurately foretold by sentient scribes, priests and prophets. They are executive orders given out by kings/leaders and military orders carried out in the field by generals, including confiscation or destruction of booty. (Josh 6:26, 7:1, 12; 1 Sam 15:23) They are the stipulations of penalty generally or specifically agreed upon in treaties, contracts, and the laws of the land. (Judg 21:18; Neh 10:29; Matt 26:74; Acts 23:12) Curses are also accusations or prosecutions in court. (Prov 30:10) A curse may also be a sense of shame or guilt felt by an individual or pronounced by another. They are natural as well as human-aided consequences for ignorant behavior.

Inappropriate curses (behaviors which curse) are those which are false, unreasonable, in-humane, unethical, unilateral, and/or patently illegal. They include sorcery (Isa 47:9), sedition (2 Sam 16), mindless retribution/blood revenge, cursing parents (Exod 21:17; Lev 20:19), cursing the disabled (Lev 19:14), cursing God (Lev 24:11–24), and enacting aggressive imperialism. The New Testament yearns for a time of universal education and salvation for ethical mankind which will bring about the cessation of the curse of iniquity: "And there shall be no more curse." (Rev 22:3) This reprises Jeremiah's sense of the ultimate blessing possible for a people when the law of common sense is written in the hearts of each human being. (Jer 31:31–33) Jesus taught that this goal could be reached when individuals combated ill-wishes and harm with love rather than with vengeance: "Bless those who curse you." (Luke 6:28) This is a matter of fighting fire with water, hate with love. Jesus' "new" commandment of loving one another is as old as the hills, but its power had been forgotten. (John 13:34) However, if the people to whom Jesus sends his apostles do not accept the path of blessing, he authorizes a sort of mock curse against them, the shaking off of the

55. Brichto, *Problem of Curse*, 12.

Biblical Captivity

dust of their shoes "for a testimony against them," as the emissaries left town. (Mark 6:11)

There is a type of Old Testament curse which is viewed by its modern readers in juridical hindsight as marginal at best, or of dubious value, and at worst indicative of a contradictory, hypocritical, violent element in the nature of the Hebrew God himself. The God of the Hebrews, and the gods of other ancient Near East nations, made a practice of judicial determination of guilt by using a technique of physical "ordeal" when there was no witness or substantial evidence of crime.[56] The book of Numbers recalls such a criminal procedure used to establish marital infidelity in the absence of hard evidence of an alleged extramarital affair.

In this case, the priest invites the suspect to drink "bitter water," which may or may not cause a "curse." If the woman drinks the water and it has the effect of swelling the belly or causing sufficient infection ("rotting of the thigh") so as to cause infertility, she is deemed to be guilty and has already suffered part of her punishment, the rest of which is endured as she lives out her life in the community. (Num 5:27) If she is not taken with illness or sterility, she is found to be innocent and is free to conceive children with her husband.

This seems a travesty of justice to the practiced modern mind, since immunological or biochemical reaction to a particular substance would seem to have little or no correlation with the existence of a behavioral transgression. It is certainly conceivable, on the other hand, for example, that the medical science of the Hebrews had the sophistication to establish some kind of link between physiological stress factors resulting from guilty pleasure and the production of neuro-chemicals which in turn interact negatively with the test substance.

But perhaps there is a psycho-forensic factor operating here that makes the "bitter water" test into a reasonably sophisticated truth serum in the hands of the court. Individuals accused falsely of heinous crimes, then and now, are willing to go to the mat to establish their innocence, since good reputation is a highly esteemed prize for those who work hard to build it. If the accused woman agrees to subject herself to the test and retains fertility, she absolves most of the fears of her husband about her infidelity. The key here is her willingness to undergo this primitive lie detector test. There is an indication in the text that she

---

56. Conrad, "Curse," 145; see 1 Kgs 8:31, 2 Chr 6:22.

has a choice, as she is encouraged to say "Amen, amen" to the procedure. (Num 5:22)

If she then undergoes the test and gets sick and/or loses fertility, her willingness to participate might be understood by the court as a mitigating factor. She herself believes she is innocent, or else she believes she can suffer the illness and heal. In the eyes of some, she is guilty because of her body's reaction to the test, and she certainly suffers acutely and possibly chronically because of that reaction. But her courage to undertake the ordeal encourages her husband and the court that she is willing to risk such suffering to have a chance at restoring even just part of her reputation. Perhaps in accepting the ordeal she is spared the second punishment indicated by the law—"be(ing) a curse among her people." (Num 5:28) Declining to participate may equally well have been taken as evidence against her, although this is not explicitly stated. In such a case it seems there would be no judicial determination possible for the husband. Possibly the woman is then liable to live under the cloud of uncertain commitment to the marriage at home, or even to divorce. In sum, this particular legal text in Numbers describes a principle which may or may not have been accurate, even if at times effective in establishing guilt. (Num 5:18–27)

The western world which inherited the Judeo-Christian tradition from Palestine still used the practice of physical ordeal nearly two millennia later. The citizens of Salem in New World Massachusetts, for example, dipped suspected witches into the river to see which of them might survive and thus be exonerated from guilt. Perhaps then and there too, willingness to participate was a factor in the beneficial outcome of the case, assuming, of course, the accused witch survived.

In general, however, those who curse or take captive without reasonable cause, or without reasonable outcome, become subject to the same curse they enact upon others, in a sort of "what goes around comes around" captivity karma. Thus when the Sumerian city of Umma unrighteously wreaks havoc against the Sumerian city of Lagash, a scribe of Lagash writes in 2350 BCE that the same fate awaits Umma. This prediction, or curse, was fulfilled when Sargon I crushed Umma twenty years later.[57] In the Bible, the many references to "taking captivity captive" (Ps 68:18; Isa 14:2; Rev 13:10) indicate that there is recognition

---

57. Bauer, *History*, 94, 98.

in Israel, as well as among the communities of nations, that aggressive kings earn the enmity of others, that not all neighboring kings will return love for spite, and that the oppressed will eventually be freed.

Indeed, God places Abraham in an environment of "bless(ing) those who bless, and curs(ing) those who curse." (Gen 12:3) This is an ethical imperative related to political and religious freedom. Abraham must receive and assist those who bless or accept his progressive, prophet-based culture, and he must legislate against those who do not uphold it—enforce measured, legal consequences against them. But it is also a fact of life that there will be indiscriminate, retributive violence against those who violently curse or abuse others in the environment Abraham is settling in. There will be those who return cursing (violence) with more cursing (violence). God takes responsibility for the retribution ultimately meted out against imperial powers by those who desire blood revenge. While he does not condone it, he acknowledges that it does happen, and it happens in the world he created.

Meanwhile, Israel is to reverse circumstances of oppression forced upon them only when they have the power to do so successfully, and with minimal violence. Hence, Jehu effectuates an overthrow of the House of Omri with a palace coup rather than a national bloodbath. Jeroboam effectuates the secession of the north from the united kingdom with little or no violence. Daniel operates with a mind to serve at the pleasure of the court in Babylon, while at the same time using honest words rather than swords to engage Nebuchadnezzar with the notion that his administration will ultimately fail, presumably because of his personal political behavior.[58] Jesus's admonition to Peter to return his sword to its scabbard in the Garden of Gethsemane is a reflection of the same propensity of the freedom God of Israel to avoid violence. (Matt 26:52)

---

58. Smith–Christopher, *Theology of Exile*, 186.

5

Captivity Through the Old Testament Eras

Soon after the people accept the Decalogue at Sinai, Israel experiments with new-found freedoms. People in close proximity to Moses criticize his decisions, propose to share power with him, temporarily depose him, and encourage the people to experiment with radical forms of democracy. These incidents include Aaron (the golden calf incident, which occurs virtually at the same time as the Decalogue revelation and is the people's solution, and possibly Aaron's, to a vacuum of power in the community while Moses is away); Miriam (jealousy over Moses' Cushite wife and possibly the influence that culture has on him); Korah (objection to the Aaronic priesthood); and Dathan and Abiram (objection to the concept of singular prophetic political leadership of the nation).[1] These matters are settled either by exhortations, clarifications, negotiations, or civil strife. Ultimately, all of these incidents help to define the government and the private institutions only recently acclaimed at Sinai. In particular these events set a precedent for solutions to problems of religious and political tension after settlement, and establish that peace and success is a result of staying the course of prophet-mediated nation-building.

When the Israelites camped at Sinai, they were in a legal "state of nature."[2] They did not yet have law to govern them. While Moses was

1. See Numbers 12–16.
2. Spinoza, *Theological-Political Treatise*, 189.

Biblical Captivity

away on the mountain for a period of days, the people asked Aaron for a molten idol, a symbol of monarchic political organization around which they might resort to symbolize the progress they had made in achieving independence for themselves. (Exod 32:1) Their purpose is made clearer by the mention of plans for making "sacrifices of well-being," or peace offerings, (Exod 32:6)—that is, thanksgiving offerings—celebratory sacrifices often made upon the organization of an ancient Near East polity, just as temple building suggests such organization and independence.[3] One wonders whether it is Aaron they had in mind to be king or high priestly leader of the state. Their solemn celebration of monarchic nationhood then turned to "playing" ("revel" NRSV)—flirtatious or sexual partying. In the eyes of Moses, the making of the idol suggested a return to the notion of luxurious kingship like that of Egypt. After all, Aaron had asked the people to turn over their precious metal jewelry to him, so he could make the idol, thus deftly completing a massive transfer of wealth from the citizenry to the new central government, and likely also providing an estate for the new leader, whoever it might be. (Exod 32:2–4)

This was a partisan political movement which threatened to undo the solidarity of the fleeing community, as well as the constitutional deliberations/contemplations Moses had been conducting on the mountain. And it also served later as a justification perhaps for occasional shifts in course for the new society, from strict construction and democratic republicanism to monarchy and political control of the church in Israel.[4]

Moses' expectation all along was that the people should become a democratic society in which each citizen would be part of a "priestly kingdom," that is, part of a well educated and progressive citizenry. Virtually every family would have a priest of God in its midst. (Exod 34:19) The entire people and nation must become "holy," or politically enfranchised as full, trustworthy citizens under God. Indeed, "keeping" the covenant of freedom is the very definition of holiness. (Exod 19:5–6)

At this critical tipping point between democratic and autocratic government, Moses asks the people to reiterate the pledge of allegiance offered to the plan for liberty while still in Egypt. (Exod 4:29–31) He

3. Meyers, *Exodus*, 221.
4. Ibid, 260.

asks, "Who is on the Lord's side?" (Exod 32:26–28) He finds that the intellectual elite of his group, the Levites, who presumably best understood the possibilities of representative government, were willing to root out the "three thousand" rebels who wanted to undermine the democratic experiment before it could even get its constitutional start. (Exod 32:28)

SELF-GOVERNMENT IN THE WILDERNESS (CHALLENGES WITHIN)

After eleven months at Sinai, the people travel north eleven days and settle for an extended period at Kadesh. (Num 13:26; 20:1, 16; Deut 1:46) The stay at Kadesh is basically found in Numbers 11–20, but scholars believe some of the material in Exodus 15–18 reflects the stay here as well.[5] Here, too, they come in contact with other Hebrews, whom scholars believe either had settled there before, or had come out in a second Exodus.[6]

Israel "wandered" in the wilderness south of the Beer-sheba entrance to Canaan for a generation, long enough for adults of the Exodus to pass away and a new generation to come along.[7] (Num 13:26–35; 26:63–65) This lengthy sojourn served an important political purpose. It allowed for a period of instruction and experience in self-government, which in turn helped the Israelites overcome both the fear of independence and addiction to the luxuries of Egypt, the "fleshpots" which they longed for in the wilderness.[8] (Exod 16:2–3) It also allowed the Israelites to wait-out the era of Ramses II, and move forward with the conquest/settlement of Canaan during the time of Merneptah (1224-1211), who was much less interested than his father in menacing the people of Palestine.[9]

The new charter of commandments was rigorously tested during this lengthy stay at Kadesh-barnea in the Negeb south of Palestine. Many years later, when Moses, with the help of the editor of Deuteronomy, looked back on those years, he was able to state, "God led you these

---

5. Anderson, *Old Testament*, 102.
6. Ibid.
7. Ibid, 101.
8. Walzer, *Exodus and Revolution*, 35.
9. Anderson, *Old Testament*, 118.

Biblical Captivity

forty years . . . that he might humble you, testing . . . whether you would keep his commandments or not . . ." (Deut 8:2–3) The springs of Marah, Massah and Meriba (Exod 15:23–27, 17:7), so symbolic of internal Israelite turmoil in the wilderness, are likely located at Kadesh.[10] If in this general area much of their early experience with self-government was obtained, the exercise was clearly quite bumpy, including as it did a variety of rebellions against both the political and religious authority of Moses.

The most clearly secular side of the "murmuring" of the camp can be seen in their complaints of having to eat mana. (Num 11:4-6) Moses' own siblings, Miriam and Aaron, also complain about his marriage to an Ethiopian woman. Perhaps his tolerance of other cultures and their outsider religious traditions goes too far in their minds. (Num 12:1) They wonder, too, if he is taking too much power to himself. They say, "Hath the Lord indeed spoken only by Moses? Hath he not spoken also by us?" (Num 12:2) Once this internal family power struggle comes to a conclusion (Num 12:10–16), a wider disturbance breaks out.

On the surface, the events inspired by Korah, Dathan and Abiram lend themselves to interpretation as a rebellion against Moses' singular leadership of the political and religious movement of Israel. However, one must remember that Moses has already separated cult activity and leadership from government activity and leadership at Sinai. (Exod 18, 29) In spite of this, it is clear that Korah's main objection is to Moses' claim of oracular communication with God and overall political leadership of the nation, which includes a cozy relationship with the main religious denomination lead by his brother Aaron. Dathan and Abiram's main objection is to his secular leadership.[11] It is understandable how Moses' response to it (a purge of the dissidents) can be interpreted as intolerance of pluralism in politics and religion.[12] (Num 16) However, this overall reading is not supported by the context of the events.

Upon initial reflection, it seems the three are merely taking seriously Moses' teaching about democratic access to God. (Num 11:26–29) They complain, "Ye take too much upon you." (16:3) Is this not what

10. Ibid, 102; see Num 20:2–13.

11. Some students of the Bible see this memory as a reflection of later struggles in priestly family leadership during the monarchy and in particular at the time of Josiah. See "Korah", *ABD*, 101.

12. See Shinkoskey, *Do My Prophets No Harm*, 115.

Jethro said to Moses as well? (Exod 18:13–27) Perhaps Moses should decentralize the priestly investiture function he exercised in licensing Aaron and others in the priesthood as he did the secular adjudicative function. (Exod 18:13–27) In this reading, which makes some sense, the mistake seems the innocent one of assuming that Moses' teaching of equal access *to* God also means equal authority *with* God. In this, they mistake the nature of either oracular prophethood or popular political leadership, or both. As an oracular prophet, he has a calling to lead this people and give inspiration to both their secular and religious aspirations. (Exod 32:34) He has something other potential political leaders do not have: the ear of God, and the direct, plenary words of God's mouth to assist him in making his judgments. (Exod 33:11) This, they have to deal with. They also seem to forget that as well as this unique God-connection, the camp have elected him as their first constitutional political leader. (Deut 5:27; Exod 19:8, 20:19) They did so, presumably because of the sturdiness of his understanding of history, politics and science, all of which accrued during his upbringing at the Egyptian court and during the time he spent in the democratic-oriented culture of the Kenites/Midianites.[13] Also, as the political leader he has responsibility, like any other political governor, to regulate institutions such as commercial enterprises, farming, the military, and religious institutions. Perhaps they are just immature and impetuous, but largely innocent of evil-doing.

Upon closer examination, it is clear that Korah, Dathan and Abiram are not merely proposing an incremental reform in priestly operation, but are attempting to commandeer the entire political operation. The New Testament Book of Jude reflects this same way upon the incident. Jude calls Korah a "gainsayer" (Jude 11), suggesting not that he gently rebukes or merely criticizes Moses' leadership, but that he opposes and denies his constitutional leadership and wants to make political gain at Moses' expense. The passage in Jude mentions Korah in the same breath as Cain, which suggests conspiratorial steps to effectuate the violent overthrow of an adversary. Cain and Korah both "speak evil," (Jude 10) that is, promote crime with malicious intent. In fact, Korah, Dathan and Abiram "rose up before Moses with . . . two hundred and fifty princes of the assembly . . . and they gathered themselves against Moses and against Aaron . . ." (Num 16:1–3) The rising is what it

---

13. Halpern, "Kenites," 17–22.

says it is, full-fledged rebellion against the political system only recently enacted at Sinai. Moses and Aaron represent the two major sources of power under the constitution: the public political power of the national government, and the private ethical power of the favored church. These two seats of power constitute the warp and the weft of civic life in the nation.

The rebels assert a platform of anarchic radicalism that, taken to its logical conclusion, would effectively undermine the very structure of this or any other civil government. They believe that all the people of the congregation have equal authority with God and political power equal to that of Moses: "All the congregation are holy, every one of them . . ." (Num 16:3) Finally, they announce that the Lord has left Moses and has situated himself with the rebelling party: "The Lord is among them." (Num 16:3)

If Korah's intent were merely to assert religious diversity, clearly his right under the charter, he might have simply siphoned off a group of followers and led his congregation in peaceful worship amongst other worship groups. His intent, however, goes much beyond this. It is to oppose the entire premise upon which the Exodus is based—the authority of an elected and ethically-minded political leader to lead a people in freedom. He wishes to undermine the constitution, the Decalogue that Moses and the people accomplished by the consent of the people. (Exod 19:8: "All these words . . . we will do.") He wishes to subvert the first frail steps the nation has taken in governing themselves under a temporary legal structure until such time as they settle in a new land and elaborate a more thorough code of laws respecting that same schedule of rights. His position is seductive, because it makes use of the notion that there is a universal system of human rights that people of all cultures at one time or another struggle to achieve. Moses has no quarrel with him on this point.

For their part, Dathan and Abiram, from the tribe of the firstborn Reuben, throw down the revolutionary gauntlet, asserting political judgment on Moses and implying a different form of government is warranted. They say Moses has failed in his political promise, as if the warp and weft of political life is instant economic gain. All men can see this: "Wilt thou put out the eyes of these men?" When Moses summons them to a meeting, they reply with finality, "We will not come up"

(Num 16:14), a response tantamount to a declaration that the journey to Canaan by a unified constitutional camp is over.

Korah's rebellion against the church is as thorough-going as his rebellion against the secular law and its leader. Moses asks, "What is Aaron, that ye murmur against him?" (16:11) The tribe of Levi from which Korah hails has responsibility for teaching the law and serving in the lower echelons of church organization. God has given them the freedom to "approach" him (Num 16:10) and officiate in the congregation, but they do not have authority to speak for God in their own local groups and make policy for the church separate and apart from the headquarters of the denomination. That authority belongs to Aaron, the high priest. Moses challenges them on this point: "Seek ye the priesthood also?" (16:10) But they, like Cain, also are persecuting the newly organized church (essentially its method of sacrifice) and the chosen system of worship of most of the sojourners as well. Their intent is to destroy Aaron's priesthood as much as to promote their own.

But this is not their only transgression of civic good sense. The 250 princes who are using censers to officiate in their own separate rites are political figures from the large and powerful tribe of Reuben.[14] (Num 16:2) Moses sees that these leaders have taken over the priestly function and added it to the political. As "princes," they ought not to be usurping the priestly function of any local cult by burning incense in censers symbolic of priestly authority. In fact, it is not good to involve incense in civic ritual at all. (Isa 1:13) Such activity offends the sensibilities of an anti-autocratic church as well as an anti-monarchic state, which variety of culture the children of Israel are laboring to construct. These politicians are temporizing with the separation of church and state, and with the de-luxuriation of civic and religious ritual which the sojourners have labored so hard to institute. They are going back to the idolatry model of government just as surely as they did in the incident of the golden calf, and are diminishing the free estate of religion required at all levels by Israel's constitution. The crimes of the rebels, in sum, are three-fold: political sedition (speech) and treason (action) against the state; internal rebellion against and even persecution of a legitimate church organized under law, and thus promoting public disorder; and

---

14. In fact, the existence of 250 clan leaders in one tribal faction alone suggests a tremendous commitment to political and religious localism in the migrating community of Israel.

Biblical Captivity

despotism, the depositing of both major sources of local human political power into the hands of individual politicians.

Moses, for his part, believes he has been betrayed and that any argument about his ethical record is out of line. "I have not taken one ass from them, neither have I hurt one of them." (Num 16:15) Here he indirectly suggests the intent of the rebels is to do just that, to commandeer the wealth of the people still loyal to Moses, and, if civil war breaks out, take many lives. From all outward appearances, they intend to set up a feudal system of government with an oligarchic triumvirate of Korah, Dathan, and Abiram serving as rulers in cahoots with local baronies lording it over the clans, under the pretense of instituting radical democratic individualism. In some respects this is an early form of a twentieth century "people's republic," a thinly veiled system of dictator-directed regional commands. They smear Moses with the very crime they themselves commit: "Wherefore then lift ye up yourselves above the congregation of the Lord?" (Num 16:3) They accuse him of monarchy: "Thou make thyself altogether a prince over us." (Num 16:13)

Moses understands this is full-fledged rebellion, and understands quickly it is the Lord's will to take severe action: "And the Lord spake unto Moses and unto Aaron, saying, Separate yourselves from among this congregation, that I may consume them in a moment." (Num 16:20–21) Moses pleads for mercy, and states his view that the rebellion has been stirred up by one man: "Shall one man sin, and wilt thou be wroth with all the congregation?" (Num 16:22) God agrees to a more moderate course, to have the loyalists separate themselves from among the camps of the three rebel leaders, and to keep their hands off the rebels' personal belongings: "Touch nothing of theirs, lest ye be consumed in all their sins." (Num 16:26) Moses then announces that the rebels will suffer some kind of natural consequence, an act of God that comes "not … of mine own mind," (16:28) for he has opposed any such general punishment of the duped rebels.

What then ensues is either an actual earthquake, or something of similar destructive magnitude—perhaps the term "the earth opened its mouth" is a euphemism for a political purge—that befalls the immediate households of Korah, Dathan, and Abiram.[15] (Num 16:30–33)

---

15. One specialist notes that the physical conditions of the Arabah rift valley explains their swallowing up by the ground. The sojourners had camped on a mud bog covered by a hard layer of clay that was softened by storm rains. The ensuing breakup

In addition, the lighting of 250 coal-hot incense burners in an unprotected outdoor environment sets off a conflagration—perhaps assisted by lightning—that takes the lives of the princes-turned-priests: "And there came out a fire from the Lord, and consumed the two hundred and fifty men that offered incense." (35) Ironically, then, the political fire of rebellion against constitution and people occasions a physical fire that immolates the tents and lives of the usurpers as well. This is the story of Korah.

EXTERNAL THREATS AGAINST THE CAMP OF ISRAEL

Threats against the camp loom from outside sources too. A migrating or nomadic people in general are insecure in the ancient Near East, but Israel is even more so due to its size and its political pretensions, as we will see below. In the encampment in the northern Sinai, and later in the march toward Canaan, threats to the religio-culturo-legal autonomy of the people continually bedevil the Israelites. The earliest episode is at their settlement at Kadesh, where the Amalekites apparently feel threatened and launch an unprovoked attack. (Exod 17:8–13; Deut 25:17–18) God expresses concern that Israel take a deferential view of the continuing presence of the Amalekites, and pursue a circuitous route into Canaan rather than stir up the Amalekites again by traveling through their territory. (Num 13:29) As they move along this long and indirect route, God also implores Israel to avoid "distressing" Edom, Moab and Ammon. (Deut 2:5, 9, 19) They are to practice what they preach. However, when the Israelites respectfully ask for permission to tread lightly through Edom they are rebuffed. (Num 20:14–17) After they add that they are willing to pay for any water they use, normally offered freely to strangers, they are rebuffed again. (Num 20:18–21) They are not treated as they wish to treat others.

The Israelites are also attacked by the King of Arad in southern Canaan. (Num 21:1–3) Then, King Sihon of the Amorites denies their request to pass peacefully through his territory (Num 21:21–32) and comes out instead to confront them in battle. (Num 21:23) Next, Og of Bashaan aggressively engages them. Finally, Balak of Moab is inspired by political jealousy and insecurity to such an extent that he hires a

---

of the crust led to their engulfment in the labile mud. See Kitchen, "Exodus," 706.

prominent and respectable prophet of Mesopotamia to curse the culture of the Israelites. Balak apparently wants no contamination from the democratic propensities of the tribes.

Before we cross Jordan with the tribes, we pause here to review briefly the story of Balaam. (Num 22–24) Balak asks the non-Israelite prophet Balaam to "curse me this people; for they are too mighty for me: peradventure I shall prevail." (Num 22:6) This politician, in typical kingly fashion, wishes to bend God's will to his own, and thus provide justification for attacking, and a prediction that if he does, he will win. (Num 24:11) Balaam fears the powerful tug of political intrusion into religious affairs, and asks the king if he may go off by himself to consult with God on his own terms. (Num 22:18; 23:3, 15)

Apparently, Israel already has managed to share a good deal of information about her political structure with various groups of people throughout the region. Balaam recognizes that a particular form of secular government not unknown to him exists among the Israelites and is reluctant to condemn it, as the political leader of Moab wishes him to. He summarizes, "Lo, a people dwelling alone, and not reckoning itself among the nations." (Num 23:9) Here "alone" suggests the idea of an experiment in political organization not fitting the usual pattern of governance. We learn throughout the subsequent narrative that this means one not interested in making treaties of friendship and mutual protection with neighbors (Exod 23:32), and without monarchic government. Both policies single them out among the close-knit fraternity of Near East nations. It is clear to Balaam that Israel's democratic government and religious plurality is unencumbered by the machinations of state priestcraft.

THREATS TO CONSTITUTIONAL GOVERNMENT DURING JUDGES AND KINGS

Joshua's initial plan to occupy Canaan, apparently, was to build a military bridgehead from the Jordan, through Jericho, and fanning out from there via various fords to the central mountain ridge. From there he could then widen the area of occupation.[16] (Josh 6–8) It is true that the Bible details some aggressive engagement with officious kings in

---

16. Herzog and Gichon, *Battles of the Bible,* 44.

Canaan after the Israelites crossed Jordan, both sides apparently understanding their systems of government are mutually exclusive. Joshua defeats associations of southern/Amorite and northern/Canaanite kings.[17] (Josh 10–11) Once the tribes disperse to their assigned homelands in the interstices between Canaanite lowland city-states, they function as separate and nearly autonomous political units, subject to loose control under the confederation principles of the Decalogue.

The large coastal communities extant in the land before Israel crossed Jordan were supplemented, so archaeologist have found, by a noticeable increase of small villages in the central highlands where much of Israel settled. Thus, the material findings reflect the broad dispersion of political power in the land after the conquest suggested by the famous phrase, "In those days there was no king in Israel; all the people did what was right in their own eyes." (Judg 17:6) During the period of Judges there emerged only one rather central and extensive regional government, that of the Ephraim/Manasseh/Benjamin/Gilead bloc.[18] Most of the stories of the Book of Judges have to do with this grouping, and Pharaoh Merneptah refers to them on a stele found in Thebes from 1200 BCE.[19] The Galilean tribes were separate from this group, and the Judean tribes as well, off doing their own thing.

During that 200-year time frame, various confederation-elected Judges supervise tribal military conscription levies and deal with various external threats. Othniel, Ehud, Shamgar, Deborah, Gideon, Jepthath, and Sampson are notable in this regard. They repulse threats from the north, south, east and west: Mesopotamians, Amalekites, Midianites, Moabites, Edomites, and Philistines. Israel's confederation of tribes is thus threatened not only by political aggression from the lowlands of the Syro-Palestinian land mass, but from semi-highland tribal groups arrayed in a tight circle round about and in between her positions. One author understands that this was a period of complex political interactions during which some Canaanites were convert citizens, some were neutrals, and some were allies with Israel.[20] Antipathy to the kingship arrangements of most of these societies during this period is seen in

---

17. Ibid, 54–55.
18. Miller, "History of Israel," 330.
19. Ibid.
20. Gottwald, *Tribes of Yahweh*, 555–83.

the scorn heaped upon enemy monarchies, who are satirized.[21] Those who allied with Israel are Rahab, Gibeon, the "man from Bethel," and the Adullamites.[22] Some of these reflect kinship relations going back in time, perhaps even to patriarchal days.

Israel is threatened within its own multi-tribal structure as well by individual subversives and cross-tribal aggression. First there is the incident of Achan in the time of Joshua. Achan transgresses the constitutional statute prohibiting self-aggrandisement during war, deriving, it seems, from the eighth commandment against theft. (Josh 7:24–25) Then there is an internecine conflict between the Gileadites lead by Jephthah and the Epraimites, a dispute apparently over presige and honor in warfare (Judg 12:6), but likely also an ongoing expression of alienation felt between the tribes who settled east of Jordan as against those settling to the west. (Josh 22; see chapter 1) Next is the matter of the retribution against the Benjaminites resulting from the Levite concubine incident. This involves a deep socio-political rift welling up and exacerbating the usual cross-tribal envies, after the kidnap/murder of an Ephraimite citizen goes un-extradited and unpunished. (Judg 20)

The debacle of the reign of Gideon's son Abimelech is especially important with regard to our theme of captivity. The generally well-thought-of Gideon himself, after an exemplary effort to rescue the constitution from the culture of Baal nature worship that captivated so many Israelites, earns the enmity of the historian by taking on priestly duties at the same time as his civic secular duties and apparently, thereby, inspires his son's excesses. Abimelech multiplies the sin of his father many-fold by acting like a typical Mediterranean tyrant. He first organizes a clan power base (Judg 9:1), corrupts that power base using the seductive lure of monarchy (Judg 9:2), raids the temple treasury, thus diminishing the status and estate of the church (Judg 9:4), and finally commits political murder in order to consolidate his power. (Judg 9:5) His three-year tyranny as strong-arm ruler of the city-state of Shechem is ended by the people, but it is not long after that all of Israel is drawn into kingship, albeit a better brand of kingship organized reluctantly by Samuel—elective, limited kingship based on constitutional law, and featuring separation of cult and crown. (1 Sam 8)

21. Gottwald, *Politics*, 43.
22. Ibid, 56.

Captivity Through the Old Testament Eras

Israel continued to experience the threat of conquest throughout its period of transition to monarchy. Those events punctuate the stories of Samuel, Saul, and David. Saul resists the imperial incursions into Israelite territory made by the Ammonites (1 Sam 9:1–10, 16, 11) and the Philistines. (1 Sam 13; 1 Sam 28–29, 31) A particular problem was that the Philistines had established garrisons in the Israelite hill country territory in order to collect tribute.[23] Early in his own career, David assisted with the effort to waylay Philistine imperial incursions into Judah (1 Sam 17) and invasion of the Amalekites from the south. (1 Sam 30) Once ensconced in a seat of unified command over the north and the south (2 Sam 2, 5), he repulsed the Philistines again. (2 Sam 5:17–25) He then undertook a number of imperial adventures of his own, perhaps under the guise of pre-empting aggression which might arise out of the Transjordanian kingdoms to the east and the Syrian kingdoms to the north. Thus he makes war against Moab, Edom, and Ammon, and Damascus, Hamath, and Zobah (2 Sam 8:2–24, 10:1–11.1, 12:26–31) and subjects these polities to tribute in the style of ancient Near East imperial monarchies. (2 Sam 8:10–11)

Internal jealousy and oppression reached a critical mass at moments throughout the period of Saul and David as well. Before David obtained assent to his leadership from the north, there was a "long war" between the house of Saul and the house of David. (2 Sam 3:1) Saul was evidently jealous of the charisma of the young David, which from the beginning he had attributed to his relationship with Yahweh, the God of the ancestors. That God exhibited a radical doctrine of heavenly favor extended to a nation living under a constitutional law which limits central power, protects the churches from control by the government, and elevates the rights of the poor and oppressed. (1 Sam 17:37, 45–47) This civic religion was clearly a threat to Saul's habit of commandeering the prerogatives of the mainstream churches. Saul directly threatened the new constitutional monarchy brokered by Samuel, based as it was on religious liberty, when he killed the priests of Nob (1 Sam 22) and usurped priestly functions for himself. (1 Sam 13:5–15)

As might be expected in a society given over to political and religious pluralism, David's leadership is threatened by several individuals, notably his own son Absalom, (2 Sam 15–19) and by Sheba, who was supported by the northern tribes. Both of these certainly

---

23. Gottwald, *Politics*, 47.

had constitutional standing to organize and stand for election. (2 Sam 20:1–22) David himself tests the boundaries of constitutionalism when he undertakes a census, widely understood among the anti-centralist landowners as the first step in setting up a system of central taxation and military conscription. (2 Sam 24:1–17, 1 Chron 21:21–27) This directly offended the sixth commandment. In addition, society suffers from a variety of internecine intrigues playing out within the house of David, including the enmity between Amnon and Absalom. (2 Sam 13–14)

For his part, Absalom ultimately usurps the throne from David using a tyrant's ploy of democratic reform. (2 Sam 15:1–7) He retains mercenaries (2 Sam 15:18) and entertains a plan for regicide. (2 Sam 17:2) He also carries on promiscuously in the manner of ancient Near East autocrats (2 Sam 16:20–23), thus acting in all ways like Samuel predicted bad kings are wont to act. Another son of David, Adonijah, also usurps the throne, that is, has himself crowned king outside the orderly process of succession. (1 Kgs 1:34) In fact, it was David's prerogative to appoint a successor who would then stand for election, and he had apparently signaled his intention to appoint Solomon. (1 Kgs 1:13) Adonijah got as far as to obtain the support of one of the high priests and a general of the army before his plot was foiled.

Solomon, for his part, is able to successfully build the central bureaucracy (1 Kgs 4) and create the standing army that his father was unable or unwilling to do. (1 Kgs 4:26–28) He built fortresses (1 Kgs 5:13–18; 9:15–24; 10:26), and taxed the people in the form of mandatory national service and also in the form of gold. (1 Kgs 4:22, 5:13–18; 9:15–22; 10:14–25) Solomon eliminated political rivals Adonijah and Abiathar (1 Kgs 2:26–27), but to his credit, not through murder. Solomon's centralization measures were challenged by means of rebellion of the territories held in captivity by David. Edom, aided by Egypt, rebelled against him. (1 Kgs 11:14–22) Damascus rebelled and broke away from the united monarchy.[24] (1 Kgs 11:23–24) Solomon, having overstepped the national budget, was forced to cede land to Tyre to pay off the national debt. (1 Kgs 9:10–14) Solomon's policies engendered political rivals in Hadad (1 Kgs 11:14–22), Rezon (1 Kgs 11:23–24), and Jeroboam, who deserted to Egypt after a constitutional scholar/prophet named Ahijah encouraged a breakup of the unified kingdom. Jeroboam

---

24. Gottwald, *Politics*, 51.

lay wait there in order to lead a revolution after Solomon's death. (1 Kgs 11:26–40)

When Solomon's son Rehoboam declared his intention to further consolidate central power, as against the traditional political and economic perquisites of local civic units and landholders, Jeroboam seized the opportunity to rebel, and successfully lead a movement of the northern tribes to secede from the union. (1 Kgs 12) That there is often an ideological/religious basis for political power-flows in the ancient world is demonstrated by Jeroboam's construction of two national shrines in the north, at Bethel and Dan, so that both his people's political and religious allegiances could be satisfied on one soil, and through him. (1 Kgs 12:25–33) During the subsequent two-state period, lasting roughly from 900 to 600 BCE, each of the two kingdoms—Israel and Judah—are subjected to, and subject other states to imperial captivity in the form of tribute-taking, conquest, cession of land and enslavement of peoples. A good part of the politico-religious enmity and skirmishing during this period takes place between the two brother nations themselves.

The variety of kingship that began with Saul changed rapidly in only four generations of political leadership. It started with the severely limited military kingship of Saul, balanced by Samuel's presence essentially as a Prime Minister. Samuel, for example, continued to direct domestic and judicial affairs. The kingship was then diverted in the direction of ethical, unitary, divine hereditary kingship in the person of David. It next morphed to the secular wisdom-oriented kingship of Solomon, and finally dead-ended in the heavy handed despotic monarchy of Rehoboam. It was during Rehoboam's reign in the south that Shishak of Egypt invaded Judah and nearly destroyed the southern kingdom. (2 Chron 12:4) The narratives and historical reports about Rehoboam thus substantiate the Biblical political notion, which says that a nation and its leaders who take people into captivity (in this case its own people) will be subject to captivity themselves. (Ps 68:18, Isa 14:2) Rehoboam suffered the loss of half of the kingdom initially, and nearly lost the rest of it due to his personal ambition, which was deeply at odds with traditional constitutional local government in Israel.

The initial political and religious enmity which occasioned the breakup of the united monarchy of Israel portends what becomes an interminable series of political, military, economic and religio-cultural clashes between the two nations.²⁵ For example, before the end of Jeroboam's tenure in the north, Israel loses some border cities in Benjamin to Judah's Abijah. (2 Chron 13) One king in the south, Jehoshaphat, and one in the north, ironically the usually suspect Ahab, pursue reconciliation between the two states, but rapprochement does not last past their lifetimes. Ahab's method for the reconciliation is by means of marriage diplomacy. He gives his sister Athaliah to be King Joram's wife. But that gesture is challenged by the revolutionary fervor that plays out in the north at the time of Elijah and Jehu. These two reformers see the intermarriage as a move by Ahab to establish Baalist influence in or control over Judah. Athaliah soon enough constructs a sanctuary to Baal in Jerusalem. (2 Kgs 11:18) In addition, she exhibits a good deal of naked ambition of her own, none of which is good for Yahweh, the prophets, or the people.

Prior to the Jehu revolution, the third revolt against aggressive kingship chronicled by the Bible since the return to Canaan, King Asa in the south and King Baasha in the north duel with each other over control of the travel and trade routes. Baasha begins his rule with a political purge of the house of Jeroboam and then, in an aggressive move, fortifies Ramah, only a few miles away from Jerusalem. Asa repels the invasion of Zerah the Ethiopian (2 Chr 14:6–14), and then bribes Benhadad of Syria to break his treaty with Israel and align with Judah, a policy which Asa apparently undertook without measuring the will of his people. When a dissident seer protests this Syria policy, Asa takes a harder line with his people by suppressing the prophet and dissident factions within the populace. (2 Chr 16:7–10) The traditional way of thinking, expressed succinctly by Isaiah (Isa 8:12), is that Judah should focus on her own internal constitutional challenges and mind her own business among the nations rather than participate in the shifting external alliances which sap her resources and invite retaliatory maneuvers from offended kings and nations. In the meanwhile, Benhadad shows good faith with his new partner Judah by attacking Israel and subjecting eastern upper Galilee to his control. Ultimately, however, Asa earns a positive mention from the Deuteronomistic historian for his conservative constitutional reform, related to removing idols and cracking down on homosexuality. (1 Kgs 15:9–15)

---

25. Much of the flow and detail, though not necessarily the analysis, of the following discussion is indebted to Gottwald, *Politics*, especially chapter 3.

Captivity Through the Old Testament Eras

The north turns more sharply than the south, it seems, from constitutional kingship, as we begin to track an extraordinary pattern of royal murders, political assassinations, and coups there. Baasha's successor Elah is murdered and deposed by Zimri, who soon enough commits suicide, leaving the throne to Tibni. At this point the north splits into two camps, one loyal to Tibni and those loyal to Omri. Omri ultimately muscles out Timni and celebrates by conquering Moab and enriching his throne with tribute money. This imposition of captivity on a neighboring nation is requited soon enough by Moab, as well shall see below. The economic oppressions of Omri against his own citizenry are remembered and blasted by Micah some 150 years later, apparently because they set a precedent for economic exploitation, which subsequent kings in Israel enjoyed to the fullest. (Micah 6:16) Omri initiates in the north one of the things that his predecessor Jeroboam rebelled against in the united monarchy—hereditary kingship. Four generations of Omrids rule until Jehu incites rebellion against the corrupt dynasty. Jehu, exasperatingly, establishes his own hereditary monarchy, presumably on the firmer footing of devotion to separation of church and state and the socio-sexual ethics required by the civil religion of Yahwism, rather than the political and social ethics of Baalism.

During the time of Omri's son Ahab, establishment of religion is taken to be a perquisite of the king's family, and rivalry between the Baalist established church of Ahab and the ever diminishing cadre of Yahwists reaches a fever pitch. We see the reciprocal killing of the priests of the north's two principal religions told in the Elijah cycle of stories. (1 Kgs 17–18) Ahab makes war against Damascus (1 Kgs 20:1–25), and for his international intrigues earns a siege of his capitol city Samaria and a close brush with captivity. He shows his disregard for traditional constitutional protection of clan property in the debacle depicted in the Naboth story. (1 Kgs 21) Ahab and Jeshoshaphat together invade Ramoth-Gilead (1 Kgs 22:1–37), but Ahab dies during the process, a death predicted by three prophets in consequence of his imperialistic activities and his domestic oppression of the people.[26] (1 Kgs 20:42; 21:20–24; 22:13–28)

Asa's son Jehoshaphat, as we have seen, allies with Ahab in order to try to win back southern territory held by Syria in Ramoth-Gilead. He blesses the political marriage of his son to Ahab's sister, and campaigns

---

26. Gottwald, *Politics*, 62.

Biblical Captivity

in Moab to put down a rebellion for independence from the captivity imposed there by Omni. (2 Kgs 3:6–27) Jehoshaphat also repulses an attack by the Ammonites. (2 Chr 20:1–30) He acts the part of the imperial monarch by taking tribute from Edom, and gifts from Philistia and Arabian tribes. (2 Chr 17:11) However, he does make a conservative reform of sexual ethics, for which he is remembered positively by the historian. (1 Kgs 22:46) During the reign of Jeshoshaphat's son Joram, some of the mischief done in David's day is undone, as Edom successfully revolts and renews her independence, and Libnah secedes from the Judahite kingdom. The Philistines and Arabs oppressed by Joram's father Jehoshaphat enact yet another episode of Biblical captivity karma by attacking Judah and killing most of Joram's sons. (2 Chron 21:16–22:1)

Jehu is credited with overthrowing the corrupt dynasty of Omri and instituting an isolationist policy like that remembered from the day of Judges. This neutralist policy was not without some political consequence, as Jehu soon lost his kingdom's territory east of Jordan to Hazael of Damascus.[27] But Jehu's foreign policy is vindicated before long when Assyria's Adad-nirari III pressures and weakens Syria. Elisha encourages Israel to defend itself against Syria during the time of Jehu's son Jehoahaz, a simple defensive activity bereft of most of the consequences of treaty-triggered military activity. (2 Kgs 6:8–23; 13:14–19) Jehoash, son of Jehoahaz, recovers some cities taken by Damascus, and plunders Jerusalem's temple during a border skirmish with Judah's Amaziah. Jehoash's son Jeroboam II recovers more of the lost territories, but his rule is associated with the increasing economic disparities between Israel's economic classes so lamented by Amos. (Amos 1:1; 7:10–17)

During her five year reign in the south, Athaliah suppresses many of the southern royal family members and also marginalizes Yahwist leaders by accommodating Baalism as the state religion in Jerusalem. After her overthrow, the Davidic prince Joash makes constitutional reforms and renovates the temple of Yahweh in Jerusalem. Joash bribes Syria, repeating the protectionist strategy used by Asa, and raids the Temple treasury to do so. (2 Kgs 12:17–18) A curse is incurred by Joash when he denies religious liberty to the prophet Zechariah. He soon after violently loses his life. (2 Chr 25:14–24) The curse of captivity is also experienced by Joash's son Amaziah, who lashes out at Edom and also

27. Gottwald, *Politics*, 64.

at Israel. Amaziah embraces Edom's gods, thus eschewing the constitutional tradition of political Yahwism, and is then defeated by Israel. (2 Chr 25:14-24) Amaziah's son Uzziah (Azariah) wages an expansionist war against the Philistines and plants Judahite colonies on Philistine soil. (2 Chr 26:6) He also takes tribute from Ammon. (2 Chr 26:8) This is the general political state of affairs at the time of the domestic and international political commentary of the four great literary prophets of the eighth century Bible—Amos, Hosea, Micah, and first Isaiah.

After the rule of Jeroboam II in the north, Israel is ruled by six kings in the space of one generation (753-723), four of whom are assassinated by their successors. This is a heady Bible commentary on the insecurity and violence that is associated with constitutionally unchecked hereditary kingship. During this period of time a new great power, Assyria, takes the Near East stage and violently expands its domain. Assyria subjects Israel first to financial/economic captivity in the form of tribute, and ultimately to political/military conquest.

When the Assyrian Tiglath-pileser began to campaign in Syro-Palestine, Menahem of Israel enacted a tax of silver and paid tribute to him. After him, Pekah used another time-honored, but ultimately futile tool to forestall captivity: he entered into an alliance with Syria and reached out to Judah, asking them to join the coalition. Ahaz of Judah aligned instead with Assyria, placing Syria-Israel in a pincer position. Tiglath-Pilaser then moved against Israel and conquered Galilee and Gilead, taking captive half of Israel's population, leaving only Ephraim and Manasseh free. Assyria soon overthrew Syria as well. Israel's King Hoshea paid tribute to the new Assyrian king Shalmaneser V. After a space of time, Hoshea, in desperation, shunned tribute payments and turned to Egypt for help. Shalmaneser then captured Samaria after a seige and terminated the northern kingdom altogether, deporting much of the remaining half of the population. (2 Kgs 17:5-41; 18:9-12)

After Uzziah, Jotham of Judah warred with Ammon and imposed tribute on it. (2 Chr 27:5) The next king, Ahaz, made his bid to ally with Assyria under duress, since Israel/Syria had put Jerusalem under siege. Edom and Philistia seized the moment to attack Judah also. (2 Chr 28:16-18) It is in the context of Sennacherib's siege of Jerusalem that we find Isaiah's prediction to Ahaz's son Hezekiah that Assyria would not prevail. (Isa 36-37) Hezekiah had paid tribute to Assyria, but had prepared against an invasion by constructing a siege-busting

Biblical Captivity

water system for Jerusalem. After Sennacherib abandoned the siege, Hezekiah continued to pay tribute.

Hezekiah's son Manasseh is said to have oppressed his people violently during the course of his sixty year rule. Manasseh presumably continued the flirtation with Babylon that Hezekiah had initiated in his attempt to find answers to the Assyrian threat. (2 Kgs 20:12-19; Isa 39) When Manasseh's son Amon was assassinated, Amon's son Josiah enacted a sweeping ethical and democratic constitutional reform in conjunction with the will of the landholders and based on the newly discovered ancient book of Deuteronomy. Josiah intercepted Egyptian troops on their way north to war in Syria, and died engaging them in battle. (2 Kgs 23:29; 2 Chr 35:20-22)

The Bible's note that Pharaoh Neco appointed Judah's next two rulers, sons of Josiah, and took tribute from them, is meant to remind its readers that alliance with great powers inevitably plays out on a bad way, as "friendship" turns to dominance of the lesser by the greater. Soon, another of Judah's "friends," Babylon, muscled Egypt out of the area and the second son paid tribute to Babylon for three years before deciding to rebel. Babylon then laid siege on Jerusalem and deported high level officials and skilled workers, in a first deportation in 597 BCE. Babylon now had the power to appoint Israel's kings and did so. Jeremiah counseled Judah against turning to frail Egypt for friendship in order to get help against Babylon (Jer 29:3), but King Zedekiah rebelled against Babylon anyway. Babylon besieged the city a second time and Jerusalem fell and was destroyed in 587 BCE. (2 Kgs 25:1-70) Babylon deported large numbers of the population at this time, and ordered a third captivity deportation a few years later. (Jer 40:7; 52:30)

The elite population of Judah were in Babylonian exile for about 50 years and were not able to return until Persia overran Babylon in 538 BCE. Cyrus, followed by a series of other Persian kings, facilitated the return of the exiles to Judea under Persian-appointed governors, including Jerubbabel, Nehemiah, and Ezra. After some 200 years of Persian overlordship, Palestine was overrun by Alexander in the late fourth century. For about 150 years not much is known about the politics of Judea until the Seleucid Syrians conquered the area, and the Maccabeans revolted against the heavy-handed rule of one of their kings in 168 BCE. After a brief period of Jewish independence under the Hasmoneans, the Roman Pompey entered Jerusalem in 63 BCE

Captivity Through the Old Testament Eras

and Palestine came under Roman control for the next several hundred years. The long highland Hebrew tradition of rebellion against imperial power ultimately lead to a final round of oppression, captivity and extermination, as the Jews learned in the Jewish Wars of the first and second centuries after Christ.

BIBLICAL REPORTS OF IMPERIAL CAPTIVITY IN PALESTINE IN THE SECOND TEMPLE PERIOD

The Second temple period (539 BCE to 70 CE) is characterized by long silences in the Biblical record. However, coming as it does after 600 years of relatively independent national living, this period of time has no less importance for the theme we develop in this book. Basically it constitutes a 600 year period of captivity, with only a brief period of independence between Greek overlordship and Roman overlordship during the second century BCE. It is a period of time during which all the curses of socio-political turpitude predicted by the prophets of the Bible come home to roost. The Second Temple era is not a period of time, I suppose, that prophets and psalmists are want to wax on about. And this half millennium was only just the beginning of national evaporation for the people of Moses, for at the end of it there would be another 2,000 years of alienation from the land for the Jews before they returned once again to control the land of Palestine in 1947 CE.

The dark spots or holes in the Biblical record during the intertestamental period fall roughly into six spans of time: from 582 to 538 (from the fall of Jerusalem to the advent of Cyrus), 538 to 520 (from the proclamation of Cyrus to the rebuilding of the temple); 516 to 458 or 445 (from new temple to the time of Ezra/Nehemiah); from 458 or 398 to 175 (from the last time of Ezra/Nehemia to the events precipitating the Maccabean revolt); from 164 to 142 (from the conclusion of the Maccabean revolt through the early part of the Hasmonean dynasty); and from 68 to the New Testament, (from Pompey's entry into Jerusalem to the birth and life of Jesus).[28]

Gottwald posits four specific explanations for the political information gap during the colonial era. First, the final authors/compilers of the Hebrew Bible regarded pre-exilic times as the golden age and

---

28. Gottwald, *Politics*, 69.

Biblical Captivity

were "de-politicized" (de-moralized? privatized? embarrassed?) by the destruction of the northern and southern kingdoms. Second, they deemed it advisable to avoid writing about the colonial experience in critical terms in order to not displease their Persian, Greek, and Roman rulers. Third, information about certain periods of colonial dominance was unavailable to them. Fourth, "advocates of conflicting programs for restoring Judah were so preoccupied with legitimating their agendas by documenting and appealing to the more distant Israelite past that they had little time or interest to records the events unfolding in their lifetime."[29]

Biblical information regarding the hegemony that Babylon exercised over Judahite survivors of the failed rebellions is limited. The Jewish people in Egypt are wholly lost to Biblical view after Jeremiah's explanation of their presence there. (Jer 41:16—43:13) Those in Babylon appear briefly in Jeremiah and Ezekiel. They also appear in Second Isaiah, during the period roughly between 550 and 538. (Isa 40-55)

As to those remaining in Palestine, there is mention of a Persian appointee, Gedaliah, who engaged in a civil war with the king of Ammon. This king may have had some Israelite blood in him and may have wanted to revive Israel independent of Persia, and of course, Ammon. (2 Kgs 25:22) The third and final deportation to Babylon in 582 may have been in reprisal for the assassination of Gedaliah. These three deportations of landed people, together likely, with educated priests, politicians, and scribes and skilled artisans, gave rise to the sense of "the empty land" extolled in Lamentations. Among those left on the land, many appear to have been put into forced labor. (Lam 5:13) Those in exile in Babylon also appear to have been put to slave labor, possibly to work on abandoned Babylonian sites that Nebuchadnezzar wished to rebuild.[30] (Ezek 3:15; Ezra 2:59, 8:17) Ezekiel and Jeremiah, in large measure due to their political and historical sentience, warned of a prolonged absence from their homes. (Ezek 14:1-3; 20:1-3; 33:30-33; Jer 29:20-23) Many of the less educated folk likely did not want to accept this admonition. A messiah movement apparently developed around the idea of the triumphant return of Josiah's son Jehoiachin to Judea (2 Kgs 25:27-30), and another around the idea of the raising up of Jerubbabel to rule Israel. (Hag 2:19-23)

29. Ibid, 96–97.
30. Gottwald, *Politics*, 99.

Many of the aristocracy, on the other hand, seemed to have assimilated politically, if not always culturo-religiously, into Babylonian society, as the Daniel and Esther stories seem to indicate. There Daniel and Esther play willing and prominent roles in court life while maintaining a private attachment to the civic worldview and religion of their ancestors. In the next section we will review the significance of the Decalogue admonition about molten idols in the context of these stories, and compare the Israelite experience of political idolatry with the experience of idolatry in Greece. The extreme derision of molten idolatry found in Second Isaiah (Isa 41:29; 44:9–20; 45:20—46:7) is apparently an attempt to divert exiled Israelites from inordinate attachment to the Babylonian culture of dependency upon great kings and imperial adventurism.

The Persian period begins with Cyrus' appearance in Babylon, and his liberation of Jews who wish to return to Palestine. The early portion of the 200 year period of Persian ascendancy in the Middle East (539–332) is treated by Biblical authors as mostly benign, although there is some evidence of a revolt against Persian rule around the time of the rebuilding of the temple. For example, there are no prophetic oracles against Persia in Haggai and Zechariah like those found in the writings of earlier literary prophets against other nations, although in them there is some expression of mild resistance to Persian rule. Persian kings seem to act out of personal desire or ignorance of facts[31] (Dan 6; Esther) rather than active malevolence. Judaic heroes such as Sheshbazzar, Joshua, Zerubbabel, Ezra, and Nehemiah seem to be encouraged by the Persian authorities rather than discouraged. One explanation of the Bible's apparent disinterest in the aggressive imperial activities of Cambyses from 530–522, and Persian depredations in Asia Minor, Greece and Egypt in the fourth century, is that those events did not define Judaic civilization as much as other events.[32]

Judah is a subdivision of a regional Persian governmental satrapy consisting of all of Syro-Palestine and known as "Beyond the River." Judah is a mere skeleton province under Sheshbazzar, somewhat strengthened under Zerubbabel during the time the Jerusalem temple

---

31. Gottwald, *Politics*, 101.

32. For a summary of the Persian/Greek conflict in this period, see Ruzicka's essay, in Lewis, *Ancient Tyranny*, 224–237.

Biblical Captivity

is rebuilt, and in decline after Zerubbabel until Ezra and Nehemiah.[33] Ezra the priest is commissioned to promulgate the laws of the ancestors (the "laws of your God") among the returnees to Palestine, and Nehemiah the prince is commissioned to rebuild the city. (Ezra 7:25–26; Neh 2:5) The splitting apart of the power of political reconstruction into the secular and the religious by the Persians roughly mimics the balance of power organized by Moses at the time of the early Israelite state at Sinai, and reflects the division of power between prince and priest in evidence throughout the period of nationhood in Israel.[34] During the Greek period, on the other hand, instances of disregard of this fundamental separation of private and public power come to be more frequent and more glaring.

During the Greek period, for example, certain Ptolemaic and Seleucid rulers seem to take over aspects of the administration of the religious sector of their empires and also allow local puppets to administer both sectors as well. While the Maccabees seethed under the injustices inspired by such an arrangement, the Maccabean/Hasmonean leaders who ruled during the period of independence fell into the same trap. This disrespect of Decalogue-prescribed separation of powers during colonial times led to the formation of major new split-off sub-cultures of Judaism, in particular the Pharisees and Essenes, both of which parties longed for separation again. The Sadducee priestly families, on the other hand, inherited unitary political-religious rulership from the Hasmoneans and enshrined it as the standard for governance during the Roman period. It was their corruption of Decalogue political ethics, as much as Pharisee theology heralding the end of prophecy, that Jesus roiled so much against.

The Bible, while disinterested in Persian imperial activities swirling around outside Palestine before Alexander's conquests in the late fourth century, is vitally, although obliquely, interested in direct Hellenistic colonial rule in Palestine after Alexander's death in 323 BCE. Alexander's political offspring became rulers of a northern kingdom with headquarters in Syria (Seleucids), and of a southern kingdom with headquarters in Egypt (Ptolemies), and these two kingdoms competed for hegemony over Palestine over the next 150 years.

33. Gottwald, *Politics*, 103.

34. Separation of cult and state will be explored more thoroughly in an upcoming essay.

Captivity Through the Old Testament Eras

The book of Ecclesiastes was probably written in Ptolemaic Greek times[35] in the third century, during the 200–300 year period of silence of Biblical historical narrative from Ezra/Nehemiah to Maccabees. The book is a philosophical-political treatise—not a history—so it does little to shed light on specific events. But it does provide its readers with a negative assessment of hereditary monarchic government (as opposed to consensual governmental leadership), formed with the Ptolemies immediately in mind. In one bitter sentence, the author summaries and introduces our upcoming discussion about political idolatry, which we define as political support given to a system of celebrity families, who think much more of themselves than they are actually worth to the people. The (political) Preacher writes: "Better is a poor and wise child, than an old and foolish king, who will no more be admonished. For out of prison he comes to reign whereas also he that is born in his kingdom becometh poor."[36] (Eccles 4:13) A wise young commoner is a better governor for a people than a blooded monarch who does not listen to advisers and comes out of prison to reign when his party overthrows the current monarch's reign. An abler restatement of Samuel's lament about kingship can possibly not be found.

In the Book of Daniel, the Macedonian kingdom of Alexander is the fourth beast to prance about the Mediterranean world. Assyria, Babylon, and Persia are the first three. We must wait 200 years to learn about the next great beast, Rome, lamented in the Book of Revelation. In Daniel, the first ruler spoken of is Alexander, and Antiochus Epiphanes IV is the latest in a series of Greek rulers alluded to in the work. This last is the one who desecrates the second temple in Jerusalem in 167 BCE, producing the Abomination of Desolation. (Dan 7:7–8, 19–27; 8:5–12, 20–25)

In Daniel, the kings of the north (Seleucid Greeks) and kings of the south (Ptolemaic Greeks) struggle against one another over a century of time in the third century BCE. This sad story concludes with the greatest tragedy of all, the extinction of local Palestinian human rights by a northern king. (Dan 11:2–39) No greater example of the near total oppression of a peaceable and democratic people on a tiny strip of land located between squabbling empires could possibly be found, lest it be

---

35. Coogan, *Old Testament*, 490.

36. The JPS version reads: "For the former can emerge from a dungeon to become king; while the latter, even if born to kingship, can become a pauper."

the treatment of Israel captive to Pharaoh in Egypt a thousand years before.

We learn from Greek historiography, and from Judahite writings excluded from the rabbinic canon (but included in some versions of the Christian Old Testament), about the political events of the Maccabee revolutionaries from 175–161 and some of the independent kings down to 134 BCE. The Hasmoneans ruled in total for about 80 years before being swept away by Roman imperial power. Ben Sira, writing in Jerusalem abut 175 BCE, is the only securely datable Judahite document dealing with the constitutional matters (torah) of such great interest to the earlier literary prophets. He believes he writes in a continuous tradition of prophetic-stature constitutional writers, and is not aware of a closed canon of scripture as of his own day.

MOLTEN IDOLATRY IN THE BIBLE AND ANCIENT NEAR EAST

Idolatry is the political system that provides so much grief for peaceable peoples in the ancient Near East. Wood and precious metal, in fact, are merely long-standing symbols of the human political tendency toward domination, deprivation, and war. They do not, of themselves, a dictator make. A hint as to the considerable antipathy that the political constitutional theorists of ancient Israel have with wooden image-making and with molten idolatry is given in a statement by Second Isaiah: "The smith . . . (and) the carpenter . . . maketh it after the figure of a man, according to the beauty of a man . . ." (Isa 44:12–13) Israel is committed to the rule of law, not to rule of man. When humankind makes its rulers into celebrities, the strength of humane law inevitably declines. The only real celebrity is the law, and the Spirit of peace and honor which inspires it. While the nations about Israel brought molten images of their anthropomorphic gods or of their powerful great king rulers into battle, Israel brought a simple box, an ark containing the covenant—the constitutional law of the nation. It was the opinion of the political prophets from Moses to Samuel, Elijah and Amos to Jeremiah, and anonymous prophets working underground during the colonial era from Second Isaiah to the author of Daniel, that participation in the local administration of humane law is more profitable for people than vain veneration of autocratic rulers badly corrupted by wealth and power: "Behold, they are all vanity; their works are nothing: their molten images are wind and confusion." (Isa 41: 29)

Second Isaiah's long paragraphs blasting idolatry, in the context of the repression of exiles under which he labored, begs for the definition we present for it in this section. Idolatry is at heart a matter of politics and constitutional law. It is a matter of the "civic religion," the ethics and the science of self-government that hangs in the balance between family and local government and central regulation of all aspects of social, economic, and political life. In this particular worldview, Second Isaiah joins hands across the Mediterranean with Greek and Roman philosophic exponents of representative government like Plato, Aristotle, and Seneca.

The Deuteronomistic and Chronicalist historians of Israelite culture join hands with classical historians like Herodotus and Thucidides in Greece and Cicero in Rome. The pages that were absent from the history of free and representative government in Israel, because the nation was in captivity there, were boldly present in the pages written by the free and independent nations of the northern Mediterranean.

While the Israelite historians warned about the danger of molten idols made by Aaron, Jeroboam, and Micah (the householder, not the prophet), Greek historians were equally effusive about the danger of the molten "bull" cast by the Greek tyrant Phalaris of Acragas. Historians of his reign associate it with the same vectors of political domination and senseless monarchic celebrity luxury that Amos associates with the northern kingdom, where Jeroboam's molten bulls were installed in the national cathedrals of Bethel and Dan.[37] (1 Kgs 12:28–29) In Israel, the molten idol is associated with the hiring of "priests of low level," that is beholden to the king rather than to the people or God. (1 Kgs 12:31)

Power-hungry kings and tyrants need great amounts of wealth to purchase the services of mercenary soldiers to keep them in power. Like Abimelech did in time of Judges, and later Israelite rulers during the time of certain of the effeminate kings of Israel and Judah, they raid the treasuries of the temples and diminish the estate of the private/religious sector to bolster the power of the central government sector. (Judg 9:4–6)

---

37. Lewis, *Ancient Tyranny*, 156.

Alexander of Pherae, one of the most notorious tyrants in Greece, demonstrated all the sexual promiscuity, domestic oppression, and imperial adventurism that Samuel warned was characteristic of systems of autocratic rule. (1 Sam 8) He expropriated the production of the precious metal mines for himself, minted coins to pay his mercenaries, gave gifts to foreign dignitaries, and paid bribes to stay in power.[38]

The minting of coins bearing one's name, or personal emblems, or one's facial profile is another type of molten idolatry associated with autocratic political rule. When the autocrat mints coins on a national level rather than a regional or local level, this suggests that local interests, and local wealth, have been sacrificed to the interests of the despot. The leader may also place a symbol of his own religious preferences, or a figure of his god, on the coin. In traditions like Israel and Greece, this suggests a fusion of church and state, which directly contradicts Israel's Decalogue commandments.

The tyrant may take the additional step of placing an inscription on the coin elevating himself to a position as the solely bidden leader of the god, or the son of the god. The dictator Hieron equated himself with Zeus on his coins.[39] The Greek despot Antiochus Epiphanes IV (of Daniel's "Abomination of Desolation" fame) put a profile of his own head on the front of his coin, and a depiction of Zeus on the back of it. He also placed an inscription on the coin that read: "King Antiochus, god manifest, bearing victory."[40]

In Rome, the emperor Caligula was extolled, not on a coin, but on a monument, as "Gaius Julius . . . High Priest and Absolute Ruler . . . the God Visible who is born of Ares and Aphrodite, the shared Savior of human life."[41] This typifies the ultimate curse of dictatorial government—in which the worship of an ethical god is replaced with the worship of a capricious, insecure and cruel human being. In the Rome of an earlier time, the people were on guard against this tendency. Cassius was prosecuted by the Senate for attempted tyrannical idolatry. He commissioned a statue of himself to be placed in a temple where it would overshadow or replace worship of the ethical Roman

---

38. Ibid, 68, 70, 143.
39. Lewis, *Ancient Tyranny*, 110.
40. Coogan, *Old Testament*, 506.
41. Ehrman, *New Testament,* 25.

Captivity Through the Old Testament Eras

god worshipped there.[42] At about the same time, the idolatrous Hasmonean rulers of Judea were gaining a reputation for luxury and violence against religious and political opponents, thus mimicking the earlier tyrannical administrations of Saul and Ahab. Antipathy to molten gods, and profiles of or inscriptions about kings on molten coins, extends to molten anything in general. Thus the Jews objected to Herod placing a golden eagle on his renovated Jerusalem temple, and also to Pilate trying to position precious metal military shields in Jerusalem.[43]

KINGSHIP AND TYRANNY IN THE MEDITERRANEAN WORLD

In the section on captivity in the period of Judges, we introduced the subject of the usurper of power, a scenario of political captivity which can take place in a representative government almost as easily as in a monarchy. Abimelech was an early and obvious model for the failure of constitutional representative government in the time of Judges. (Judg 9) A tyrant, by definition, sidesteps the legal process for election or succession and arrogates additional power throughout his rule by clandestine or forceful means.[44] Saul, who was elected to serve the purposes of constitutional government as a limited monarch, was the first of many kings in Israel who abused power by marginalizing political rivals, such as David, and negating constitutional precepts. Absalom and Adonijah both usurped power from David and ruled for brief periods of time, although it may be that their political efforts were justified by David's declining popularity and increasing concentration of power. Rehoboam, Ahab, Athaliah, and Manasseh each ignored or overthrew constitutional mandates and took the government where they personally wanted it to go. Athaliah committed political murder (2 Kgs 11), Rehoboam made monstrous increases in taxes (2 Chron 10), and Mannasseh severely oppressed the population and "shed very much innocent blood." (2 Kgs 21:16)

Greece and Israel maintained trade links with one another, from the time of Judges down to the time the Greek empire overran Palestine

---

42. Lewis, *Ancient Tyranny*, 50–51.
43. Goldenberg, *Nations*, 44.
44. Lewis, *Ancient Tyranny*, 2–3.

Biblical Captivity

in the intertestamental period.[45] But Greece and Israel shared more than a commitment to commerce. Greece, like Israel, had her own period of "judges," notably in the sixth and fifth centuries when Israel's own constitutional government had been destroyed and she was in exile in Babylon. Like democratic Israel, democratic Greece experienced periods of tyrannical rule from the seventh century down to the first century BCE.[46] Greece was completely free of obvious tyranny only for a brief period of time, about 466–405. But, even so, this 60-year period spans the years when Pericles took Athens into a dangerous and unnecessary war and exhibited the secrecy of political activity and manipulations of the population which characterize the later stages of constitutional government of nations headed for despotism.

The incipient tyrannies of Periclean-type policies were in evidence in Greece and other areas of the Northern Mediterranean in the "archaic" seventh and sixth centuries, and were evidenced in the person of Pisistratus in particular (560-527 BCE). In Rome, Tarquinius Superbus in the sixth century ruled autocratically and inspired Rome's revolution in representative government.[47] Outrageous tyrannies were in evidence in the Peloponesian section of Greece, in Thessaly, Sicily (especially at Syracuse), in Heraclea in southern Italy, and in Ionia and Caria of Asia Minor. In the first century BCE, Rome implemented the Greek model of elective autocracy for a period, before moving on to the bald dictatorships of the Empire.[48] The Roman dictatorial system of government was eventually overthrown by Germanic tribes fleeing from Attilla the Hun.

Greece, like Israel during the Bible period, was a politically independent highland buffer zone between great empires. Israel faced threats from the North in Syria, the East in Assyria and Babylon, the south in Egypt, and the west in Philistia. Greece faced imperial domination emanating in the north from Macedon, in the south from Carthage, in the west from the Etruscans, and in the east from Persia. In fact, the very state power that liberated Israel and allowed her to return to Judea—Persia—soon enough turned dreadfully imperialistic and overran Asia Minor, portions of the Greek homeland, and Egypt.

45. Smith, *Palestinian Parties*, 57–81.
46. Lewis, *Ancient Tyranny*, 3.
47. Lewis, *Ancient Tyranny*, 17.
48. Ibid, 6.

Often it was a threat to national security that gave the excuse for political figures to stretch the boundaries of constitutional propriety. In such cases, the central government typically usurps local militias and musters them into a standing army. They also implement new forms of national taxation on top of local levies, in contradiction of statute or custom. David attempted to take a census for the purpose of building a standing army, but was rebuked by Nathan.[49] Roman and Sicilian tyrants got away more easily with tinkering with citizenship registers, in their considerable efforts to better collect taxes and raise armies.[50] Saul and David, as well as usurpers throughout the Mediterranean, used mercenary troops to carry out many of their political objectives.[51] (2 Sam 20:7, 23) Such mercenaries are not typically loyal to the interests of the native people they are fighting against, and their presence can come to be deeply resented. In Greece, foreign mercenary troops served typically as a palace guard.[52] In Israel, David's mercenaries are simply referred to as "David's men," or as Cherethites and Pelethites, and were likely ensconced near him as well.

Tyrants and kings might also contract political marriages with ruling families of foreign powers, who might help to keep them in power during difficult times. David, for example, married Saul's daughter for this purpose,[53] and Solomon married a daughter of Pharaoh. (1 Kgs 3:1) Egyptian pharaohs accepted Mitannian and Kassite princesses from Mesopotamia as wives for their sons, in order to cement oligarchic cross-national relations. They also frequently depended upon gifts from foreign leaders, as David did from Hiram of Tyre. (1 Chron 14)

Ambitious elected or hereditary leaders might also build cities for political patrons and give land grants to soldiers in the process of establishing a dynasty. Thus did King Asa (1 Kgs 15:23), and King Ahab when he built a new capitol city at Samaria. In Greece, tyrants used the "new capital" strategy to attempt to destroy the political identify and heritage of a previous city and tradition.[54] Tyrants and despotic kings often made treaties of friendship without consulting the wishes of the

49. Coogan, *Old Testament*, 260.
50. Lewis, *Ancient Tyranny*, 109.
51. Coogan, *Old Testament*, 243.
52. Ibid, 259.
53. Coogan, *Old Testament*, 238.
54. Lewis, *Ancient Tyranny*, 104.

Biblical Captivity

people of the land, or after ignoring the counsel of prophet advisers, as Asa did with Ben-hadad (2 Chron 16), and Ahaz with Assyria.

Kings in Israel, particularly in the north, acted like Near East despot dynasts by committing an endless series of regicide usurpations, as we showed above in Section 3.[55] Kings might also expropriate the lands of their subjects, as Ahab did in the case of Naboth; tyrants in Greece and Rome did the same as well. Tyrants also frequently closed the gap between church and state, as Saul and Uzziah did (2 Chron 26:18), and as did the Denomide tyrants in Greece.[56]

Tyrants and despotic kings also used population relocations: baldfaced deportations of populations whose lands they wished to take, or whose traditions they wished to disrupt. Israel's own experience of captivity at the hands of Assyria and Babylon is a fine example of this.[57] The Sicilian tyrants constantly relocated the local populations of the island to suit their need.[58]

At the same time, in order to curry favor with the people, tyrants may frequently champion the rights of the poor, liberating (and even arming) slaves, as Euphron did in the 360s at Sicyon, north of Sparta in the Peloponnese and as Zedekiah did at the time of the Babylonian siege of Jerusalem. They also at times promoted reforms, such as the distributing of land and food to the people.[59] They might also liberate formerly captive cities, as David did in Israel, and Ducetius in Sicily. Both David and Ducetius also bolstered a cultic center in a native area, carrying out their work at the urging of an oracle from God.[60]

Tyrants might also seize money from temples to pay their mercenary troops as Dionysius did in the late fifth and early fourth century Asia Minor,[61] or to pay tribute to neighboring powers and thus keep themselves in power: se, for instance, as Ahaz (2 Kgs 16), Athaliah (2 Chron 24:7), Hezekiah (2 Kgs 18), and Menahem. (2 Kgs 15) Nebuchadnezzar (2 Kgs 25:13–17) carried off the Jerusalem temple treasury

---

55. Coogan, *Old Testament*, 294.

56. Lewis, *Ancient Tyranny*, 130.

57. Christopher-Smith, *A Biblical Theology of Exile*, 27–74 (Violence and Exegesis: The History of Exile)

58. Lewis, *Ancient Tyranny*, 95–118.

59. Ibid, 50–51.

60. Ibid, 38.

61. Lewis, *Ancient Tyranny*, 68.

to support his own royal tyranny in Babylon, and Epiphanes carried off the replenished wealth of the Jerusalem temple to support his tyranny in 167 BCE as well.

Benevolent tyrants and despotic kings alike might also extend the boundaries of their kingdom in search of land, resources, laborers, and fame, as David did after unifying Israel under his rule. Good behavior after battle is to dedicate war spoils to the public or priestly treasuries of the land (2 Chron 18:11) and bad behavior or tyranny is to raid those treasuries or keep the war booty for oneself, or to pay mercenaries to keep oneself in power.

Much is known about Rome's cultural-economic problems once she embraced tyranny. Tyrants in Rome enacted policies which crippled the local agricultural economy and pushed ex-farmers into the cities. Slave laborers from conquered countries replaced production by local artisans. Population declined due to war and disease. The plebians, or poorer class, became addicted to entertainment, holidays, and sporting events. Heavy taxation was imposed in order to support foreign adventurism. Government bureaucracies became corrupted, and hiring was increasingly based on political patronage rather than ability. There was a decline in learning associated with devotion to luxury in the upper classes. A culture of celebrity and dependence replaced a culture of knowledge and self-reliance.[62]

---

62. Ellis and Esler, *World History*, 151.

6

Captivity in the New Testament

OUR THEME THROUGHOUT THIS essay suggests that the legal writers, literary prophets, historian-annalists (authors of Kings, Chronicles, etc.), biographers (Daniel, Esther, Jonah), psalmists, philosophers, and editors/compilers of the Hebrew Bible/Old Testament are supremely concerned about preventing the political curses which rake over the land and the people when they shirk the original constitutional law of ancient Israel. Respecting those "ten words" sustains economic prosperity, independence from other nations, and local clan and family rule—in brief, blessings. Neglect of the Ten Commandments by means of aggregation of wealth into the hands of a super-wealthy and powerful oligarchy, immersing the nation in international politics, and concentrating power in an ordinary Near Eastern central kingship or a tyrannical presiding officer, leads to a myriad of curses.

We have seen that Palestine was enveloped for 600 years in the web of consequences resulting from these kinds of overall failings with respect to the Decalogue. The last chapter of that captivity comes into prominent relief in the New Testament. The teachings and activities of Jesus, as well as his predecessor John the Baptist, and his successors Paul and the other apostles of the reconstituted constitutional faith, are best seen as particularistic answers to the political situation of domination and oppression in Palestine. These answers are situated in a broad milieu of other, similar efforts and answers discernible just before and just after the time of Jesus. These other political writers and movement mentors, like Jesus, are concerned about blessing and cursing too.

Ancient Near East political oppression comes in three flavors: domination by foreign powers or by domestic political puppets of those powers; domination by indigenous government leaders within a context of relative national independence; and domination by priestly denominations of religion that either nuzzle-up to the foreign powers for protection, get cozy with indigenous political parties, or rule their cults in a caustic or corrupt way.

The principal architects of the crooked political structure of late second century Judea, the Hasmonean dynasts, acceded to power with the Maccabean revolt about 165 BCE, and did not relinquish their firm hold on Judean society until 63 BCE. They were indigenous oppressors. Mattathias first led the revolt, after which leadership passed successively to his sons Judas Maccabee, Jonathan, and Simon. The government had the character of a familial military monarchy from the beginning. The technical onset of the Hasmonean dynasty begins with Simon's accession to rule in 142, as Simon makes a formal declaration of independence from the Seleucids of Syria at that time.[1] This independence is recognized by Demetrius II, who concedes peace, immunity from tribute, and remission of tax arrears. Judea is captive to this foreign power no longer.

Simon's achievement is celebrated, moreover, in grandiloquent style, as though he were a great king dynast. There is considerable festival and ceremony upon the occasion of his expelling of the Hellenistic garrison from Jerusalem. Simon also seizes the moment to have himself acclaimed not only presiding officer (ethnarch) of the new nation, but also commander of the armed forces, and high priest of the Jerusalem temple, thus seizing all important sectors of socio-political power for himself.[2] The grant of high priesthood power was offered to Simon and his offspring "forever," so Simon took care to claim power vertically for his progeny, as well as horizontally for himself in his own day. In fact, though he shunned the title of king, he wore the purple robe and exercised the power of a dictator or emperor. No assembly of clan elders could be convened without his consent.

---

1. Rajak, "Hasmonean Dynasty," 69.
2. Ibid.

Simon's son John Hyrcanus took the additional step of minting a coinage, which to his credit was aniconic, that is, without display of a human figure. Nonetheless the coin glorified Hyrcanus as an equal, or perhaps more-than-equal, party in tandem with the people. It boasted the words "Johanan the high priest and the community of the Jews." John's son and successor Alexander Jannaeus (103-76) took the additional Hellenistic step of calling himself king, as well as high priest, in complete disregard of Israelite and Judaic tradition and law. He acted like the sort of adulterous king Samuel warned against, when, as high priest, he feasted in public with his concubines. It was at this time that the predecessor group of the Pharisees broke finally from the politicized religion of the Jerusalem temple.[3]

During the generations of the Hasmonean dynasty, aggressive campaigns were carried out against "idolators," that is, religio-cultural minorities living in the Jewish territory whose ethics did not comport well with Torah, Jewish instruction and law. Jonathan, for example, attacked coastal regions in Philistia, Samarian territory, and also campaigned in Galilee and Lebanon. Alexander Jannaeus acted like a great king expansionist as well, by conquering territories belonging to Syria, Idumea, and Phoenicia.[4] In a number of cities, Jannaeus took local populations as slaves.[5]

The military efforts of the Hasmoneans seem to have been assisted by a political agreement with the increasingly imperial Roman Senate, which had an eye to assist a traditional ally. But Rome perhaps also contemplated feasting on Judea as a colony at some point in the future.[6] Jewish friendship treaties with Rome were re-newed until the end of the rule of John Hyrcanus in 104 BCE.

When Pompey overtook Jerusalem in 63 BCE, he honored the Sadducee political faction by empowering Hyrcanus II, son of Jannaeus and Salome, to continue as a political high priest, and thus marginalized the Pharisee wing of Judaic religion, which was opposed to unifying the political and religious functions in one person.[7] The Essene sect had

---

3. Rajak, "Hasmonean Dynasty, 70.
4. Josephus, *Ant* 13:395.
5. Rajak, "Hasmonean Dynasty," 73.
6. Rajak, "Hasmonean Dynasty," 72.
7. Ibid, 70, 76.

many decades before taken to the Judean desert and other parts north, to practice their civic life and religion outside of the larger public eye.

Herod the Great, hailing from an Idumean family that had converted to Judaism, had married into the Hasmonean family and had assisted Rome with its military campaigns in the region, defending against the Parthian invasion. Herod pledged unwavering support, and provided considerable gifts and bribes to whatever Roman official was ascendant in the region. Ultimately, he was thus rewarded by Octavian with a great deal of personal power as a Roman client king. (JW 1.394-95; Ant 15.187-201; III-162) Because he paid respect to the surface requirements of Jewish political religion—shunning the overt idolatry of using representations of human beings or animals in artifacts associated with his regime, and promoting circumcision—there was no great religious reason for discontent during his reign, from the point of view of the mainstream priestly faith. He did introduce pagan Hellenism, with its entertainment and sports venues, to Jerusalem, but that did not seem to bother Sadducee leadership overmuch. But, in contrast to these cultural issues, the political and economic concerns about his leadership were so compelling that upon his death, Judea sent a delegation to Rome requesting that the region of Palestine be annexed to Syria rather than continue under the hardships imposed upon them by the house of Herod.[8]

Herod fancied himself a Near East great king. His absolute authority was made clear on his coinage. Though he avoided a representation of his profile, he asserted himself as "Herod the King." He gave no ancillary recognition to any other local political authority such as the Hasmoneans did. In fact, he convened only mock legislative councils (called the Sanhedrin) and only for the purpose of rubber-stamping his decisions, disseminating new executive orders, or making a case for his latest appointments or executions. He banned meetings of citizens, as well as any kind of larger mass assembly. He used spies in Jerusalem and in the countryside to detect opposition to his rule. He executed and confiscated the property of entire families when any one member showed an inclination to oppose him.[9] He appointed and manipulated the high priesthood, using his own relatives in its offices.

---

8. Levine, "Herod the Great," 168.
9. Josephus, Ant 15:365–68.

Herod required a loyalty oath from the citizens of his realm.[10] Some 6,000 Pharisees refused to provide the oath to him. He also declared the date of his accession to the throne as a national holiday.[11] He conducted vicious purges of his political opposition throughout his reign. Forty-five leaders of the major political faction that had opposed him were executed.[12] He tortured relatives and friends of such opponents.[13] Later, he beheaded another opponent, and placed potential rivals under house arrest. He executed his brother in law for dissent against the regime, and for fomenting revolt. He executed many of the remaining vestiges of the Hasmonean family. He even executed his own wife Mariamme, and her two children, out of insecurity over the instability they could cause his regime.

Herod's political oppression was necessarily undergirded by economic oppression. In order to protect his rule from rivals and uprisings against it, he raised huge sums of money to finance garrison cities throughout his realm, which under Roman patronage had expanded even beyond that which had been achieved by the Hasmoneans. The expenses needed for maintaining a lavish court and his huge army, which included foreign mercenary bodyguards from Europe (Greeks, Germans, and Gauls), he raised from agricultural taxes and sales taxes. He also expropriated the wealthy of his political opponents, including their lands, which he turned into personal estates. He imposed customs duties along the trade routes he controlled, especially Nabatean trade from the Arabian peninsula, and ocean trade through his ports. He owned and exploited copper mines on Cyprus. He did not hesitate to raid tombs as well. He opened the tomb of David and took 3,000 talents from it.

This was the kind of legacy that, had a Deuteronomist or Chronicalist historian written his epitaph, would have earned him a summary mention such as: "He did evil continually," or "No one in Israel did worse than him." In fact, he likely rivaled Solomon and Ahab as far as expropriating the resources of the people for his state building program. He likely outdid Rehoboam in the level of taxation he imposed upon the people. It is possible he killed as many or more of his own people

---

10. Horsley, *Jesus and Empire*, 32.

11. Josephus, *Ant* 15:423.

12. Ibid, 15:5

13. Horsley, *Jesus and Empire*, 41.

than Manasseh did. It is possible he hired more mercenaries than David and pursued foreign alliance and entanglement as thoroughly as Ahaz. It would have been the kind of record that would have inspired Old Testament prophetic activity in its wake, as indeed it did.[14] The entire Christian movement can be laid at the feet of Herod and his partners, the emperors of Rome, who gave their own personal interests much higher priority than those of their subject peoples.

In summary, Herod can be said to have been notoriously agile in his romance with the Roman overseers, while at the same time committing bigamy with the surface elements of Judaic constitutional culture. Although he died, according to Matthew, just after the time of Jesus's birth, his sons Archelaus, Herod Antipas, and Phillip the Tetrarch, and their cousins Bernice, Agrippa I and Agrippa II, form the contemporary backdrop of Jesus's life and ministry in Galilee and Judea. Another cousin, Herodias, whose second marriage was disapproved by John the Baptist, had the Baptist killed in an act of repression of political speech not unfamiliar to the region. Josephus indicates that this murder took place because John was a political threat to Herod Phillip,[15] a threat perhaps not so much to replace him, but to sully his finely glossed political sheen.

Herod's son Archelaus' accession to rulership in Judea was the occasion of widespread revolt.[16] He essentially presented "modern" Israel with its own Rehoboam moment, during which he appeared before a public assembly and heard the assembly's urgent plea for easing of taxes and release of political prisoners. Like Rehoboam 900 years earlier, he told the citizenry to go to hell. He then killed thousands during the course of his recriminations.[17]

In light of this background history, the story in Matthew about the events surrounding the visit of the Magi to Judea near the end of Herod's thirty year reign does not seem particularly surprising. Jesus' concerns about life in Galilee and Palestine were largely conditioned by the political high-handedness of Herod in the decades of his parents' upbringing in Judea. But Herod's response to the Magis' visit rings a particularly ominous note for the conditioning of the political life of the

14. John the Baptist, Jesus and others, discussed in section 1 below.
15. Witherington, "Herodias," 175.
16. Horsley, *Jesus and Empire*, 41.
17. Ibid, 46.

young teacher/healer. Three eastern wise men told Herod that they had come to pay homage to a future King of the Jews. Herod asked them to return with news of his whereabouts, but after visiting Bethlehem, discerning his murderous intent, the wise men decided not to do so. Joseph and Mary subsequently took the child to Egypt, thus avoiding the slaying of infants in Bethlehem and surrounding areas. (Matt 2) Upon Herod's death, Jesus' parents avoided the Herod-like regime of Herod's son Archelaus in Judea, and went to live instead in Galilee. (Matt 2:22–23) One supposes that the stories of the political and migratory events surrounding his birth was not left unmentioned to the young political critic by his parents and relatives.

THE CONTEXT OF ROMAN RULE IN THE JESUS STORY

A student of the New Testament period must understand that the political and religious movement of Jesus takes place not only against the backdrop of the repressive monarchy of the Herodians, but against the backdrop of the larger emerging monarchy/emperorship of the Romans. It is important to understand that Jesus was conscious of, and much of his thinking and action was dictated by, the repressive power of Rome in Judea.

Rome had been a virtuous republic roughly from the time of its beginning in 510 BCE down to the time of the three great Punic Wars, from 264 to 146 BCE. By then, Rome had traded domestic tranquility for the international strength that often tempts a republican nation. Partly in response to foreign aggression, and partly because she could do so, Rome expanded her territory from the Italian peninsula to include Sicily, Corsica, and Sardinia. By the time of the last Punic War she decimated the state of Carthage in North Africa, and then launched wars further afield, through which she overthrew Macedonia, Greece, and parts of Asia Minor, all of which became Roman colonial provinces.[18] Rome inflicted a defeat on the Seleucid regime of Antiochus Epiphanes at the time he was attempting to wipe out Judean culture in Palestine in the mid-first century BCE. Where Rome did not conquer directly, she forged alliances or client-like friendships. By 133 BCE

---

18. Ellis and Esler, *World History*, 133.

the Roman Empire extended from Spain to Egypt, ringing the entire Mediterranean.

Conquest and control brought great riches to Rome: war booty, taxes and tribute, and commerce. A new aristocracy emerged, which used slaves from conquests on huge local Italian estates, called latifundia. Local small farmers and artisans fell into poverty, unable to compete with the slave estates, and thus had to sell off their lands. Many of these now landless persons moved to cities like Rome where they became a restless class of unemployed, reliant on free bread and soothed by state-sponsored entertainments. The political establishment became steeped in corruption. When political reform was instituted by the Gracchus brothers in 133 CE and 123 CE, the Senate, representing the wealthy class, turned against its own people, engineering political murders and street violence. This led to civil war, creating a classic opportunity for tyrants.

The Senate pitted itself against populist political leaders who employed common people in their armies. Julius Caesar, who gained popularity with his conquests in Gaul—modern day France—warred against the Senate's general Pompey. Pompey had previously curtailed pirate raids of Mediterranean vessels and befriended Herod in Palestine. For his part, Pompey had deeply disappointed the Judeans when, after having been invited into the city to rescue one Jewish faction from another in 64–63 BCE, he proceeded to carry out a massacre on the temple grounds, and apparently profaned the temple by entering into its holiest precinct.[19] After defeating Pompey, Caesar put down revolts around the Mediterranean, and then returned to Rome, where he forced the Senate to make him dictator with absolute powers. In time, Caesar was killed by defenders of representative government, and another civil war resulted. Caesar's grandnephew Octavian (also known as Augustus Caesar) overcame Anthony and became the first emperor, or life-long dictator of Rome. Herod, initially supporting Anthony, switched his allegiance to Octavian.

At first Rome's new form of government was not yet a hereditary kingship, but rather much like a very powerful, life-long presidency or "principate," with the Senate playing a residual role. The governing emperors of Rome, some of them extraordinarily despotic, played a defining role in important moments in the development of Christianity:

19. Goldenberg, *Nations*, 42.

Biblical Captivity

Augustus Caesar (27 BCE–14 CE; Luke, Acts mention him); Tiberius (14–37; period of Jesus' activity); Caligula (37-41); Claudius (41-54; dating of Paul's earliest letters); Nero (54-68; dating of Gospel of Mark); Titus (79-81); Domitian (81-96; dating of Matthew, Luke, Acts, John, Revelation).[20] After Domitian there came a series of somewhat less oppressive emperors like Trajan and Hadrian (117–138), and later Marcus Aurelius, who died in 180 CE. The next hundred years after Marcus Aurelius saw political and economic turmoil, the decline of learning, and the continuing rise of vice and entertainment. The unwieldly empire was ultimately divided into two parts by Diocletian in 284 CE, with a system of co-emperors. These co-emperors were not always keen to share power. In one 50 year period, some 26 emperors reigned, many overthrown by "army democracy," usurpers trying to institute reforms of some kind. In 312 the Emperor Constantine gained the throne, defeating his co-emperors, then built a new capital at Constantinople. He also granted toleration to Christians, and proclaimed the Nicean Creed as the orthodox doctrine of Christianity.[21] Rome was defeated by foreign invaders in 378 CE, and Rome itself was sacked in 410 CE. Then Atilla the Hun, starting in 434, ransacked Christian Europe. Like Nebuchadnezzar 1,000 years before, he was thought to be sent by God to punish backsliding nations, and so was called the "Scourge of God."[22]

Ironies attend Rome's relationship with Judea in New Testament times. Rome knew about Judea's history as an independent nation, and its rebelliousness during the period of Greek rule, and thus understood its present desire to be governed by indigenous rulers. Thus, latitude was given to Herod. But Rome also knew about Judea's 600 year long history of colonial occupation and its slavish dependence upon foreign rule during that period, and thus also deemed Jews to be in a poor position to understand Rome's fresher representative tradition. Jews, they felt, were superstitiously devoted to complex interpretations of ancestral laws, which occasioned in them an exclusivity and awkwardness that made a client relationship difficult. For their part, Jews in Palestine understood that Rome had eliminated rivals in the Mediterannean and disliked that Rome now insisted on total loyalty or "fides" from its client states. Rome had transformed itself from a representative government

---

20. For this chronology, see Ehrman, *New Testament*, 27.
21. Ellis and Eller, *World History*, 148; Bauer, *History*, 6, 11.
22. Ellis and Eller, *World History*, 149.

into an autocratic one, while still fancying itself democratic. Many elements in the Jewish tradition understood that Rome now exercised the same kind of hegemony over others that it once hated in the world about it.

Roman citizens at home and abroad now worshiped their own central government leaders as divine benefactors of the world, as can be seen from an inscription from the province of western Asia Minor ("Asia"): "Providence . . . has brought our life to the climax of perfection in giving to us Augustus, whom it filled with strength for the welfare of men, and who being sent to us and our descendants as Savior, has put an end to war and has set all things in order . . ."[23] Furthermore, Rome's generals and emperors made dramatic boasts of their manly political prowess in subjugating smaller nations and peoples, and placed these boasts in inscriptions on the temples of homeland religious denominations, and on coins and public monuments and in literature, in much the same fashion as the despotic Pharaohs and Assyrian dictators of previous millenia.[24] They also conducted glory parades in the capital city, and piled up the spoils of victory in heaps before the admiring home crowds.[25]

Rome had the power to escalate its level of control and instigate military terror if its clients did not submit and defer on a consistent basis. This included the use of crucifixion against rebel leaders and their associates, and even of genocidal slaughter or enslavement of inhabitants of towns where there were consistent or severe violations of treaty or order. The political factions in Judea were a constant irritant to Rome, given that some of them were insistent upon devotion to a kingship of God (that is, of ethical law), a markedly different form of kingship than what Rome offered its subject states. In fact, Judea, and most particularly Galilee, were regions where Roman retaliation for political organizing and action was particularly evident and consistent over a 200 year period, beginning with Pompey in 64 BCE and lasting until the conclusion of the Second Jewish War in 135 CE.

The political roiling in Palestine during this 200 year period consisted of four large revolts and the Roman responses to them: Herod's War in 40 BCE; the revolts of 4 BCE—inspired by both Judas and

23. Horsley, *Jesus and Empire*, 27.
24. Ibid, 22, 26.
25. Ibid, 27.

Biblical Captivity

Athronges; the First Jewish War of 66–74 CE; and the Second Jewish War of 132–135 CE (under Bar Kokhba). Within this broad envelope there were also a number of additional, particularly urban revolts, as well as a number of specifically rural insurrections. Some of these subsidiary events were aimed at humanizing the policies of Roman kingship, and some had the goal of the restoration of Israelite messianic kingship—constitutional monarchy featuring a God-appointed local indigenous ruler. The urban events included the protest of political and economic policies inherited by Archelaus in Jerusalem at the time of Herod's death in 4 BCE, and the riot at a mid-first century CE Passover gathering in Jerusalem. The rural events included a messianic movement in the area of Nazareth after Herod's death: the massive, peaceful demonstrations across the countryside when Pilate sent soldiers into Jerusalem bearing military standards with images of Roman gods on them; and the incident involving Caligula's ordering of his own image to be installed in the temple, which precipitated a widespread agricultural strike.

There were, as well, a number of prophet-led political movements aimed at restoring Davidic messianic leadership. These included the mid-first century CE movements led by Theudas the Prophet, the Egyptian (Jewish) prophet, and Jesus ben Hananiah.[26] Finally, there were a number of "scribal" movements, both literary and activist, which featured educated priestly, legal or academic leaders or enclaves agitating for traditional ancestral freedoms. These included scribal backing for some of the revolts above, and the penning of politico-religious literature like the Testament of Moses and the Psalms of Solomon, as well as writings uncovered at the Qumran community of the Essenes.[27]

Nestled yet further inside these broader envelopes of political educating, organizing, and uprising are the activities of John the Baptist, Jesus, Paul, and other Jewish-Christian dissidents whose stories grace the pages of the New Testament, and the Christian apochrypha and pseudopigrapha. We will review some of the largely extra-biblical events summarized above in the context of the Jesus story which follows below.

The political movements of John the Baptist and Jesus, as well as those movements and uprisings during the earlier time of Herod the

26. Horsley, *Jesus and Empire*, 51.
27. Ibid, 82, 84.

Great and the Hasmoneans, together with the movements and uprisings of Jewish people after the time of Jesus (such as the First Jewish War in 66 CE, the Diaspora uprisings in 115–117 CE, and the Bar Kokhba revolt of 132–145 CE), are all the natural result of generations of local repression by empires and their puppets. They reflect, as well, the same kinds of political and cultural concerns expressed by reformers like Moses, Gideon, Deborah, Samuel, Elijah, Jehu, Hezekiah, and Josiah on the same land long before the Greek and Roman subjugations. Indeed, they reflect the same kinds of concerns raised two thousand years after Jesus on the same land in the revolts against the manipulations of dynasts and puppet tyrants in the largely Islamic world of the eastern and southern Mediterranean today.

The biblical Jesus movement was sandwiched in between several repressive events, forming its political context. One of the seminal incidents for Jesus, certainly, was the political murder of John the Baptist. Some of John's followers eventually joined the Jesus movement, but many of them continued in their devotion to John for generations after. Another of these was the large rebellion which took place in Galilee in 6 CE, when Jesus would have been a very young child. Judas of Galilee led a rebellion so significant that Josephus believes it sowed the seeds of rebellion that led to the first Jewish war of independence in 66 CE and the destruction the temple in 70 CE. In 6 CE Quirinius, the Roman governor of Syria, held a census of the population and an inventory of the property of the new territory of Galilee that had been placed under his supervision. Judas, in response, argued that the people of the land ought to submit themselves to God alone, who supports human rights, as against the authority of a despotic colonialist king who musters farmers into his war machine, and forces the sale of sacred ancestral lands due to the burden of tribute taxation imposed upon them.[28] Judas' sons, like the sons of Maccabee 175 years before, followed his example, and helped lead the rebellion in Jerusalem shortly before the First Jewish War. Two other of his sons were crucified by the Romans. Eleazar,

---

28. Jesus, for his part, slightly softened this philosophy by teaching that it was reasonable to pay tribute if it was not too onerous to do so (Matt 17:24–27), although it was clear to his listeners that the government the emperor represented was less than fully ethical.

Biblical Captivity

probably Judas' grandson, led the defense of Masada after the fall of Jerusalem.[29]

The name of Jesus' companion Mary Magdalene suggests another of Jesus' intimate connections to the political weariness and repression of the day. Her hometown was probably Magdala, also known as Migdal.[30] It was at Magdala where a generation or two before hers the Roman warlord Crassus (in 52 BCE) slaughtered many of the city's residents, and enslaved 30,000 others in the area, leaving abject devastation as a heritage for the surviving locals to feed upon.[31] Then, Herod conquered the area at the behest of the Romans in 40-37 BCE, establishing a rigorous administration over the area that left its residents smoldering with dissent. Mary of Magdala had every reason to look for the political acuity and social solace that her mentor had to offer her.

Only shortly before Jesus's parents removed him from Judea to Egypt, after the death of Herod in 4 BCE, the Roman general Varus burned towns in Judea and Galilee and crucified 2,000 rebels for their political activity. Galileans, in particular, were chaffing under Rome's installation of Antipater as the local ruler there.[32] He taxed them heavily to support construction of two new capital cities, Tiberias and Sepphoris, which dominated the nearby villages of Lower Galilee.[33]

Shortly after Jesus' death, at the hands of the Roman powers, and at the hands of the puppet political administrators in Jerusalem, there were revolutionary activities in Samaria, north of Jerusalem and just south of Galilee. The Roman governor Pilate put to death Samaritans under the influence of a "nameless man" who organized a group to meet at the base of Mt. Gerizim. They assembled at the village of Tirathana. Their leader told them he would reconnect them with Moses at the summit of the mountain, and presumably undertake political activities after that. Pilate (whose rule extended from 26–36 CE) attacked the group with cavalry and infantry. It was said that he "took many into captivity."[34] Of the Samaritan experience, one author notes, "No less than the Jews, the

---

29. Cockerill, "Judas," 1090–1091.
30. Strange, "Magdala," 463–464; Pritchard, *Concise Atlas*, 105.
31. Horsley, *Jesus and Empire*, 60.
32. Horsley, *Jesus and Empire*, 28.
33. Ibid, 60.
34. Josephus, *Ant* 18:85–87.

Samaritans resented foreign rule and oppression."[35] Pilate also during this time attempted to install military standards in Jerusalem, and also tried to install gilded dedicatory shields in the temple area, provoking near-riots.[36] Indeed, Caligula, also, attempted to have his statue placed in the Jerusalem temple, which provoked a farmer's strike, and national outrage.[37]

Indeed, just before the Roman governor Fadus' rule, and only a few years after Jesus' death, while nominally respecting Jewish religion, Agrippa I, like his grandfather Herod, placed a heavy burden of taxation on Galileans and Judeans alike for his building projects, and made lavish gifts to gentile cities. (Ant 19.299–311, 327, 331–52) In addition, he used a gentile pagan festival to suggest that he shared in the divinity of Caesar.[38]

Around 45 CE, during the governorship of Fadus in Judea, and about the time Paul was traveling on behalf of the new Jesus movement, Theudas led a large group to the Jordan river to reenact something like Joshua's crossing and political conquest of the land, promising a (symbolic?) parting of the waters there. Fadus sent a cavalry unit which took many alive and killed about a third of the group.[39] Acts 5:36 refers to this incident in a statement made by Gamaliel. Fadus also repressed the Jews of Perea, killing or exiling Jewish leaders[40], and suppressed a sort of Jewish Robin Hood-type character named Tholomaus.[41]

About a decade after Fadus, in 56 CE, a Jewish prophet arrived from Egypt during the time of Felix. This revolutionary announced that he wanted to make the walls of Jerusalem fall down. Felix killed 400 of his followers and took 200 of them alive. The prophet escaped, reorganized, and arrived at the Mount of Olives with many thousands in tow.[42] The Book of Acts mentions that Paul was initially mistaken as the Egyptian prophet who provoked this rebellion, indicating that

---

35. Horsley, *Jesus and Empire*, 163.
36. Goldenberg, *Nations*, 43.
37. Horsley, *Bandits*, 165.
38. Ibid.
39. Josephus, *Ant* 20:97–98.
40. Ibid, 2–4.
41. Horsley, *Bandits*, 166.
42. Ibid, 168.

Paul's activities were considered to have decidedly political overtones. (Acts 21:38)

Josephus says that all of these kinds of messianic activities centered around a common theme. "Under the guise of divine inspiration," various charismatic figures would lead people "out into the wilderness so that there God would show them signs of imminent liberation."[43] Jesus himself seems to have believed he could command such a group of ready revolutionaries from out of the local population (Matt 26:52–53), but seems to have wanted instead to lead his people in more passive resistance to despotism, although he knew that even that would cost him his life. (Matt 16:21; 17:22–23)

Just before the First Jewish War of 66–74 CE, the Roman Gessius Florus plundered the Jerusalem temple, taking a huge amount of gold to suit his greedy rule.[44] It had been fully a hundred years since the time of Pompey that a Roman had subjugated the Jewish people so profoundly and directly. The uprising itself took place also against the backdrop of Nero's political pogroms back at home in 66 CE. Thus this uprising, while having some basis in religious concerns, is firmly ensconced in a setting of increasingly oppressive imperial brutality. In 67 CE the Zealot group tracked down the high priestly group, complicit in the Roman shenanigans, and took them captive as traitors. Simon bar Giora organized a force south of Jerusalem and proclaimed an emancipation of slaves. The Roman emperor Titus, a few years later, engaged in mass slaughter of the people of Jerusalem, destroyed the temple, and refused to accept peace terms offered by factions in the city. He set the city ablaze, and ultimately, Josephus says 1.1 million people perished in the siege, although Tacitus gauges only about half that many. Simon was ultimately taken to Rome, and executed in public to underscore the glory of the regime.[45] Many subsequently perished at Masada, apparently taking their lives to avoid becoming slaves.

For their part, the Essenes, who had gathered in the Judean desert near Qumran, seem to have looked for some kind of support to overcome the oppression of the empire and its puppet government. Their

---

43. Josephus, *Jewish Wars*, 2:259
44. Goldenberg, *Nations*, 42.
45. Horsley, *Jesus and Empire*, 50.

War Scroll expresses confidence that the armies of heaven would overcome the enemies of the elect.[46]

The Bar Kokhba revolt, in 132–135, is the last gasp of militant Jewish nationalism, and is styled as the Second Jewish Revolt. Serious unrest in Judea after the destruction of the temple in 70 CE had led to the strengthening of garrisons in the region.[47] Along with this, Hadrian had prohibited circumcision throughout the Roman Empire, and this offended Jewish sensibilities in Judea.[48] Rome then announced its intention to convert Jerusalem into a pagan city sacred to Jupiter, and to rename it Aelia Capitolina. Simon bar Kokhba and his revolutionaries created a short-lived independent state. He reversed the large-scale land appropriations by the Romans[49] and issued coinage in the name of a free and independent Jerusalem. However, once the revolt against these plans was suppressed, Rome enforced the renaming of Jerusalem, and the name stuck for the next 200 years.

JESUS ON HIS OWN: THE TEMPTATION AND THE SERMON

The Christian church, by and large, has done a poor job of interpreting its own scripture. Jesus is most often presented as a Sabbath day spiritualist, beckoning followers to an eternal after-life, whose achievement is best worked out by means of church attendance, observance of the sacraments, and support of the priest or pastor. Thus, Christ is seen as a religious leader, and the New Testament as a book of religion. However, the cultural-legal tradition that Jesus defended so forcefully ("one jot or one tittle shall in no wise pass from the law, til all be fulfilled"; Matt 5:18), is better seen as a socio-political tradition, one built around nationhood rather than priesthood. It is a tradition steeped in the idea of national political independence for a people who choose to govern themselves under a humane constitutional law.

In other words, Jesus was concerned about exactly what Moses was concerned about 1,200 years before. He was concerned about the

---

46. Horsley, *Bandits*, 183.
47. Isaac and Oppenheimer, "Bar Kokhba," 599.
48. Goldenberg, *Nations*, 45.
49. Isaac and Oppenheimer, "Bar Kokhba," 600.

Biblical Captivity

political oppression of minority groups, whose enfranchisement in fact might actually lead to better results for government than if elite economic and political interests remained in charge. His most fundamental and constant theme was about political governance—that is, the organization and operation of "the kingdom." (Luke 10:19; Matt 7:21; John 3:3; Mark 11:10) This was to be an earthly civic kingdom, not a spiritual kingdom of the eternal afterlife where only the elect would participate. In this earthly kingdom all would play a part and receive civic blessings. (Matt 19:29) He let his followers know that governance of the land ought to be in the hands of each and every citizen. (Luke 17:21) Jesus Christ did as Moses did in Egypt. He confronted the political authorities non-violently, setting an example for how disciples and future generations should act in any community where their rights might be taken away from them.

This new kingdom was not to be organized on the basis of a shining new priestly capital city, with the ordered lands and monuments of an aristocracy or an oligarchy leading the way. It was rather to be an entity "not made with hands" (Mark 14:58), an interim movement of self-empowered and self-governing people, living, working, and meeting by the wayside, not needing or overly respecting central power. It would organize in and around—in the cracks of—the illegitimate kingdom, so that it would be in the world but not of it. It would organize right in the midst of the kingdom of despots. This was to be a mostly quiet, decidedly non-violent political movement, which would promote egalitarian social interaction between the sexes (Luke 10:38–39), the healing of old psycho-somatic wounds (Matt 4:23; 1 Cor 12:9), educational meetings in the public halls of local government called synagogues (John 18:20), and forgiveness by the middle class of the debt owed to them by the poor. (Matt 5:40; Luke 6:29) The wealthy, well, they were beyond repair. (Mark 10:25)

Jesus' teachings and activities were civic and philosophic in nature, not ecclestiastic. In our terms today, we might call call his work social scientific. He was concerned about all aspects of the person, in all the contexts of an individual life, not just the Sabbath day context, and not just its religious thinking and beliefs. He was concerned about social, economic, political, cultural, and scientific views, venues, and objectives. When he recruited supporters, he wooed them with exactly this nation of wholistic salvation—renovation and improvement that would touch all aspects of social society as well as individual living. He wanted to extract people from their current captivity in the entire fabric of contemporary life that was tightly wrapped around them. Hence he told a couple followers, "I will make you fishers of men." (Matt 4:19) His intent was to remake the whole person and thereby the whole society. Men were to be plucked out of their environment like fish were pulled from their watery world. And the men, like the fish, were not to be returned to their former habitats once reformed by their deliverers.

In fact, religious worship seemed to be only of somewhat marginal interest to Jesus, compared to his broader civic interests. In one passage, after he provides a healing service to a patient, he urges his client to go see his priest in order to take care of his religious duty, suggesting that the healing was not a faith healing, but a medical one. (Matt 8:1–4) After Jesus appears in the synagogue in Nazareth at the start of his civic activity, we do not find him in a "church" building again, unless it is when he returns to his former home in Galilee. (Matt 4:23, 13:54) His biographers do not report on teachings in the synagogue, except for the announcement in Luke 4.18 that his mission will be a civic one. They seem to focus on his activities in the public sphere and the sayings he is remembered for there. Even so, the synagogue is a multi-purpose, part public/part private building that is used as often as a non-denominational civic center as it is a religious venue, and it is likely Jesus resorted to the synagogue from time to time for its secular environment as much as its religious environment (John 18:20), in the same way he used the temple in Jerusalem. His overtly spiritual experiences are not in church, but in nature—by the waters of a river (Matt 3:13–17), on a mountain (Matt 17), or in a grove or garden. (Matt 26:36)

On the other hand, his "ministry," as presented in the four gospels, seems to resemble almost a political stump tour. He meets with, organizes, and provide services to people in every conceivable kind of social setting. He engages people in the open countryside, at people's homes, along the roadside, on board boats or ships, in cities (Matt 11:20), by a lakeside, at weddings, next to sick beds, in the desert, along the coast, and in rented or borrowed rooms. A huge concern is "Jerusalem," the national capital, the seat of government (as we would refer to "Washington" today), and he mourns openly for how things are done there. (Matt 23:37) His visits to Jerusalem and to its temple there were for the purpose of civic teaching and protest, rather than for presentation

Biblical Captivity

of sacrifice or worship. In fact, while his parents presented him at the temple in a rite of apparently religious dedication soon after his birth (Luke 2:22), once he was old enough almost to exert his own free will, his interest in Jerusalem and its temple was to debate with the "doctors" (scholars) who congregated there about "business" matters of the political kingdom. (Luke 2:41–52) When he returned there as a mature adult, he situated himself in the sections of the temple that were open to the public, the courtyards where all manner of instructional, legal, economic (Matt 21:12), and political activities were normally carried out. These courtyards were essentially the national counterpart of the local governmental "gates" of the cities and towns.

Jesus steeped himself in the traditions of the founders and early reformers, interpreters, and compilers of the history of the nation, those documents first known as "the law and the prophets." (Matt 22:40) Their grand concern, and his, was the "covenant," the foundational Israelite law known as the ten commandments, or ten "words." The law, the commentaries on civic life, and later the stories, rituals, wisdom and customs of the nation were put together in a book having three divisions: the "torah," the "prophets," and the "writings." These were documents that expounded the scintillating doctrines of civic independence, representative rule, and human rights and responsibilities that had animated the Israelite/Judaic culture for over a thousand years. This sacred history chronicled not the ecclesiastic doctrines of a church, but the political science and constitutional law of a land and nation characterized by a wide variety of churches and political parties.[50]

Jesus' overall view of government is expressed in the experience of the second (according to Luke) "temptation" in the wilderness. At this moment, which was likely the culmination of a lifetime of study, thinking, and experience, Jesus is shown the autocratic monarchies of the earth and the "power" and "glory of them," but quickly and decisively shuns that form of government as a political paradigm in favor of a God-mediated covenant of human political rights and responsibilities. (Luke 4:5–8) This rights program is quickly thereafter announced in his hometown of Nazareth (Luke 4:14–20), and turns out to be exactly that reform program first enunciated by Isaiah several hundred years before. (Isa 61:1–2) Both Isaiah and Jesus are committed to a program of relief of the poor, release of the victims of oppression, education of

---

50. See Smith, *Palestinian Parties*.

the ignorant, and empowerment of the marginalized of society. They are both community activists, prophets who study history and predict the future based on their evaluation of the foibles of humankind and the propensities of power. They are culture critics and advocates of the original intent of the constitutional law.

Jesus is not unaware of the legal traditions of the broader Middle East. The first indication of the path he chooses, as we have said above, is given in his movement announcement in Nazareth, where he reiterates the political doctrine of Second Isaiah, who lived 600 years before and half-way around the known world in Babylon. When he announces his program in Galilee he positions his objective squarely in the realm of the kind of First Commandment reform that political reformers have made their bailiwick from time immemorial. His task is to teach, promote, exemplify, and ultimately die for the right to live in a culture of Decalogue political ethics. He reads from the Isaiah scroll at Nazareth and declares his goal to fulfill the prophecy he has just read: "to preach deliverance to the captives." (Luke 4:18; Isa 61:1)

He will follow the life objectives outlined by Isaiah. He will demonstrate the iniquity of political and religious conflict and captivity. He will educate and enfranchise people to take peaceful control of their own lives and assert their God-given human right to self-government and self-expression. In particular, he will expound a right to a life free of political, religious, and other spiteful killing.

It is not without significance for our theme that Jesus announces an extraordinarily civic focus at the outset of his ministry when he repeats several of the highly charged concerns mentioned in Isaiah 61:1-2. Jesus' politics-infused experience with the Spirit (Luke 4:1, 18) encourages him to "preach the gospel to the poor" ("preach good tidings unto the meek"; Isa 61), the content of which curriculum is then defined in a series of promotions of civic rights and responsibilities encompassing much of the citizenship mentality found in the Decalogue:

- "heal the broken-hearted" ("bind up the broken-hearted," Isa 61; in essence, instill hope in the midst of repression)
- "preach deliverance to the captives ("proclaim liberty to the captives," Isa. 61; in essence, announce the need for civic liberation of the oppressed)
- "recovering of sight to the blind" (a reference to understanding

Biblical Captivity

- responsibility for self-liberation and educating others in the way Jesus is educating them; cf. Matt 23:16; Isa 56:10)
- "set at liberty those that are bruised" ("open the prison to them that are bound"; Isa 61; another reference to agitating for human rights reform)
- "to preach the acceptable year of the Lord" ("the day of vengeance of our God"; Isa 61; a reference to a day of blistering consequence for the civic malfunctionings of the past)

When Jesus refers to preaching "the acceptable year of the Lord," (4:19) it is as much to say his mission is to lobby for religious liberty and for restoration of all the great commandments, since the Day of the Lord, or the Year of the Lord in the ancient Near East, is a time when God, through his anointed reformers, whether princes or prophets, proclaim a release of debts, or of slavery, or of oppression of religious minorities, or of a church taken captivity as a result of war.[51] (Joel 3:17; Ezra 1, 6,7; Isa 42, 52) Such a year is akin to the Sabbath year of rest in Lev 25:4, the year of "the Lord's release" in Deuteronomy 15:2, and King Zedekiah's year of release of servants in Jer 34:8–22.

Together, the brief verses of Luke 4:18–19, and their precursors in Isaiah, constitute a middle Eastern type proclamation of freedom for an oppressed people, a proclamation issued by one who has authority and power to do so—that is, either a sitting ruler or a bidden prophet.

Jesus sees a renaissance in understanding of the foundational law as the primary vehicle for accomplishing these lofty goals. He sees the Decalogue as a political system of blessing for the citizens of the land. (Matt 5:1–11) Those blessings are positioned by Matthew squarely in the context of Jesus' discussion on several of the great governmental principles of the Decalogue charter. (Matt 5:17–48) Neglect of the Decalogue inevitably leads to the curses of political apathy—oppression, sickness, captivity, and death. (Matt 23; Mark 1:34; Luke 1:79, 9:60, 11:37–54, 21:24; John 11:25)

The socio-political blessings expected are those outlined in detail in the Sermon on the Mount. These are re-statements of political blessings generally outlined in Deuteronomy (Deut 28, 30:15, 19), and also in the teaching of the Old Testament prophets, such as Jeremiah. (Jer

---

51. Weinfeld, *Social Justice*, 100, 110–111.

27:12–13) Indeed, the positive blessings which accrue to the good folk in this New Testament treatise echo the raising up of the oppressed in Old Testament times. The sermon terms "poor," "mourn," "meek," "peacemakers," "pure in heart," and "accused falsely" all have a long-standing political meanings.

In the sermon, the poor are rescued from their exploitation and find an honorable place in the kingdom. Similarly, in Psalms, "The expectation of the poor shall not perish . . ." (Ps 9:18), and "Setteth he the poor on high from affliction . . ." (Ps 107:41) In Jesus' world "the tribes of the earth" mourn the loss of land, freedom, good government. (Matt 24:30) Similarly, in Proverbs, "When the wicked . . . rule, the people mourn . . ." (Prov 29:2) In the sermon, the meek finally receive an inheritance by which they obtain socio-political enfranchisement in the community. Similarly, in Psalms, "The meek will he guide in judgment . . ." (Ps 25:9) Also, "The Lord lifteth up the meek . . ." (Ps 147:6)

The problem of (usually imperial) war is a critical one for Jesus and the New Testament peoples as well as Jesus' recent Old Testament tutors as well. In the Ptolemaic period of the 300s BCE, Jerusalem was captured a dozen times.[52] Palestine was ravaged by as many as 200 military campaigns in the 260 years from the death of Alexander to the conquest of Jerusalem by Pompey.[53] During the Roman period, the people saw uprising and reprisal after uprising and reprisal, as we have noted above. Captivity and oppression are thus foundational, definitional issues for Jesus of Nazareth. Jesus looks for more of the same kind of imperial, oppressive civilization in the Near East as long as the institutional powers operate on the basis of the laws of earthly monarchs who eschew the poor and oppressed. For example, he predicts that soon enough war will destroy the temple. (Matt 24:1–2) In the Book of Revelation, which we will examine a bit more below, the imperial beast makes offensive war often. (Rev 11:7; 13:7; 16:14; 17:14; 19:19; 20:8) God makes war twice, but his is only a war of words, "the sword of my mouth." (2:16) His is a war of righteousness.[54] (Rev 19:15) Only when the ambitions of men are limited by the commandments of God can war be limited. (Micah 4:3; Zech 9:10; Hos 2:18–23; Isa 2:4) The war that Paul envisions is a battle not against people but against the

---

52. Smith, *Palestinian Parties*, 63.
53. Ibid, 64.
54. Klassen, "War in the New Testament," 871.

institutional governing structures that lie behind them. (Eph 6:11–14) It is the kingdom that Christ teaches—the rule of ethical law—that his disciples are asked to pray for and bring to all the earth. (Matt 28:19)

Captivity refers to two things in Jesus' day. It means external oppression of the nation of the kind imposed by Rome in Palestine—loss of free use of the land and its produce, loss of national independence, loss of free labor power, and loss of free expression of intellect and religion. It also refers to the enervating practices entered into by the local political structure—priests and princes—over the past several hundred years, and more pressingly, the licentious mentality of the ruling Sadducees and their compatriots—the scribes, tax collectors, and high priests in the present day. It is the peacemakers who work to roll back both kinds of captivity. The peacemakers will be called "the children of God," the best and real citizens of the nation. (Matt 5:9) Methods of humiliation, intimidation, and violence used by tyrants and emperors in the ancient world, such as crucifixion, ultimately serve only as viral examples of the injustices of empires, and thus serve as a great political and ethical teaching tool for Christians. (Gal 3:1) Non-violence, educated pacifism, even martyrdom serve the purpose of atonement—bringing citizen and heavenly king together in harmony.

In the sermon, the peacemakers are called "the children of God," a political designation suggesting empowerment to govern as well-enfranchised "sons," as villagers subject to a mother city (or a father constitutional law; Isa 51:17–18). In the Old Testament, the Decalogue enfranchisement program leads to peace: "Behold, I give unto him my covenant of peace . . ." (Num 6:26) When all have a voice, all feel fulfilled and quieted. (1 Chr 22:9) Citizens are asked to "speak peace to their neighbors" and to "do good; seek peace, and pursue it." (Ps 28:3, 34:14)

In the sermon, the "pure in heart" will "see God," a blessing suggesting honorable, independent civic standing among nations and a status as progressive, democratic, and scientific. This recalls the blessing in Deuteronomy: "All the people of the earth shall see that thou art called by the name of the Lord . . ." (Matt 5:8; Deut 28:10; Num 24:5–9) Those in the sermon who are "accused falsely" find a "reward in heaven," that is, in the new political order inspired by heaven, which enforces honesty and truth. So, those in former times who "smite the neighbor secretly" will ultimately find a comeuppance. (Deut 27:24)

Jesus groups civic blessings under three summary headings: judgment, mercy, and faith. (Matt 23:23) Judgment is a category which encompasses not only judicial equity, but good government at all levels and in all its functions. Mercy is a category of action to be taken by individuals and by government to rescue those who are unfortunate, and elevate them. Faith is a category whose depth is measured by personal experience with natural, spiritual and legal actions and consequences, and by knowledge of history. Deprivation or neglect of any of these categories promotes wider and wider disparities in social, economic, and political equity.

True to his word given at the outset (Luke 4:18), Jesus targeted Jerusalem and its fraudulent civic authorities for the culmination of his ministry and his civic lobbying. Here he confronted religious and political authorities who had persecuted new religious leaders like John the Baptist and the Essenes, and other political and religious dissidents. Those priestly politicians committed political crimes under the Decalogue constitution of freedom and human rights. Jesus was concerned that Jerusalem had become Egypt for the children of Israel once again, oppressing minority groups who saw themselves in a better light than the powerful authorities did. Like Moses, he confronted the authorities with a message about those rights and about the proper responsibilities of government, when he "cleansed" the temple of its spurious trafficking in idolatrous cultural artifacts and money-changing.

Jesus' proclamation of freedom—that is, his encouragement of them to be free-willed and independent agents of government (see Section 3 below)—at the beginning and again at the end of his ministry, and at all points in-between, was directed toward healing them of their political indifference and uncertainty, their defeatism and slavish mentality, and enfranchising them to publish their sense of his message. In the course of the next hundred years or so, dozens of religion-writers took advantage of the liberty they saw in Jesus to express their religious views in written and publically-shared form. Only four of those many "gospels" were eventually included in the New Testament scripture, but many other gospels, and many other "acts" and "apocalypses," have been uncovered in whole or in part, all pertaining to the "liberty" announced by Jesus.

Also, whereas before Jesus John the Baptist made a bold proclamation of civic rights and reform, aa did the Maccabees and others like

Biblical Captivity

the Hasidim, Zealots, and others before John, there came after Jesus those who stood to offer their opinions and their lives for the cause of individual freedom—Paul, Stephen, Peter, and the many bold speakers and martyrs of the first and second centuries. Like, Jesus, Stephen and Paul reminded their hearers of the history of free thinking and action in their nation and offered encouragement that it ought to be that way still. (Acts 7, 13, 17, 20–24, 26)

Jesus Christ, as clearly as any bearer of new light understanding, takes the legislative intent of Yahweh's first commandment to heart. He wishes to record or remember or re-establish the freedom program promoted by the God of the Exodus and summarized in God's name.[55] (Exod 3:13–17, 20:24) The time and circumstance are once again propitious for both God and man. There are many psychological and physical healings and much elevation of thought and independent action among the new body of believers. These result, in part, from the fact that Jesus, like Paul after him, takes care to exercise his right of both political speech and religious liberty by boldly teaching what he believes is the proper interpretation of the Mosaic socio-political culture, and by demonstrating in his activity the political ethics required of citizens in order to renew that culture.

The New Testament provides abundant witness that the two basic forms of captivity we outlined for Old Testament days—external and internal—apply with equal vigor to New Testament times. With respect to external captivity, there are two varieties. First, there is culturo-economic imperialism or vassalage of the sort evidenced by tribute payments, and occasionally heavy-handed Greco-Roman projection of religious and political values onto the citizenry in Palestine. Second, there is the physical captivity of persecution, imprisonment and exile of religious dissidents, and the slaughter and enslavement of political rebels who rise up in active dissent against the occupying regime. There are also two forms of internal captivity. The first is schism and jealousy among once friendly parties, frequently solved by secession or civil disengagement or war, evident in the Samaritan/Judean politico-religious split, and the northern verses southern tribal split long before that. The second is the ongoing, seemingly irredeemable domination of one political party or class or religious party over another, regardless of the status of dependence or independence of the nation. This can be seen in

55. Shinkoskey, *Do My Prophets No Harm*, 87.

Jesus' day in the form of the oppression of minority political parties by the Herodians, and persecution of new light politico-religious groups by both the Pharisees and Sadducees. The kingdom is a society free of this captivity.

The Essenes understood both forms of internal captivity. Their political and religious beliefs have been brought to light by the Dead Sea Scrolls. Politically they believed in local Palestinian self-determination, and thus could not accept Roman appointment of puppet governors or ruling families. They lived in wilderness exile after their split with mainstream Judaic priestly groups at the time of the Maccabean revolt. One of the scrolls uncovered at Qumran, a commentary on the book of Habakkuk, reveals that the future persecution spoken of by that prophet speaks to the persecution of the their own cult, and its leader, the Teacher of Righteousness, by the Hasidic forerunners of the Pharisees in the second century BCE.[56]

Jesus' "kingdom" prophesies are rooted in First Commandment ideology related to freeing political and religious captives. Mark writes, "Now after that John was put in prison, Jesus came into Galilee, preaching the gospel of the kingdom of God, And saying, The time is fulfilled, and the kingdom of God is at hand: repent ye, and believe the gospel." (Mark 1:14–15) The word "repent" surely has as much a civic connotation as a personal ethical or religious one. The gospel or good news of Jesus, is the possibility that the people can form a society which refuses to imprison people like John the Baptist. Those intolerant of the beliefs of others must repent or change their way of thinking, and believe God intends to have a society dedicated to free intellectual expression. In teaching thusly, Jesus fulfills the prediction of Isaiah about God's coming Servant who is to release prisoners.[57] (Isa 42:1) Jesus makes clear this kingdom is a physical and earthly one—one in which "every one that hath forsaken houses, or brethren, or sisters, or father, or mother, or wife, or children, or lands, for my name's sake, shall receive an hundredfold, and shall inherit everlasting life." (Matt 19:29) Also, the people who form this earthly political community will come "from the east . . . west . . . north . . . south and shall sit down in the kingdom . . ." (Luke 13:29–30)

---

56. Coogan, *Old Testament*, 365.
57. Weinfeld, *Social Justice*, 45.

Biblical Captivity

He will teach, in his many parables and stories, and in the personal respect he pays to denominations outside his own, the duty to provide human rights to minorities and the poor, and the release of those who have been imprisoned for conscience' sake. He turns the political and religious culture of celebrity of his day on its head, saying that greatness is not the work of a leader who imposes his charitable will on the few or discriminatory objects of his affection, but rather the work of one who is "your servant," who protects the interests of all others, not just those he chooses to patronize. (Matt 23:11) The service that a truly great one performs is the performance of justice and righteousness—the correction of inequities and injustices, or "judgment," the weightiest matter of the gospel. (Matt 23:23) Here, good government is seen to be the pillar upon which good religion can stand.

Again and again in Matthew and Luke, Jesus returns to the theme of political-religious prisoners. These two gospels self-consciously stress a connection with the Mosaic past as expressed in traditional Jewish concerns. The ones who are most favored of God, he suggests, are ones who "visit" those in prison. (Matt 25:31–46) When he lauds those who in the future can be said to have "visited me" [when in prison] (Mt. 25.36), he promotes the need to attend to those unjustly imprisoned for their beliefs, and a recognition that such imprisonment is wrong. Whoever serves as a vehicle for "loosing" or freeing those who are "bound" on earth, will find their efforts recognized and rewarded. (Matt 16:19)

Jesus' theme of deliverance of the captives is suggested closely by his theme about the raising up of the humble and abased of society. The prisoners will not only be freed, but elevated. Mark relates his teaching, "Whosoever exalteth himself shall be abased; and he that humbleth himself shall be exalted." (Luke 14:11; 18:14) Also, "The first shall be last, and the last first." (Mark 10:30) Jesus' mother is credited with being instrumental in teaching him a concern for the rights of others. She suggests the need to rectify any such deprivation of rights. Of God, she says, "He hath put down the mighty from their seats, and exalted them of low degree." (Luke 1:52)

Those who are "persecuted for righteousness' sake" are lifted up to inherit the "kingdom of heaven." (Matt 5:10–11) They come to understand the importance of free exercise of conscience and thus have the proper mentality to live as sentient citizens in a free society. When Jesus says to his followers that some political or religious persecutors will "cast out your name as evil," (Luke 6:22) he implies legal or criminal judgment against the new movement. When they know what it is like to live without the protection of law for their cherished beliefs, they, like the children of Israel of old, will forevermore be sensitive to strangers like themselves and will be refined through their patience, impassioned for the First Commandment.

The fact that Jesus predicts "coming persecutions" (Matt 10:17) indicates he feels the battle for liberty is still largely a losing one in the ancient world: "They will deliver you up to the councils" of government. Also, both the passages "Ye shall be brought before rulers and kings for my sake . . . " (Mark 13:9) and "when they bring you unto magistrates" indicate political and religious recrimination. (Luke 12:11) What happens all too often are debaucheries of religious right such as the slayings of prophets like Zechariah. (Matt 23:31) Those who are "hated by others, and reviled . . . " nevertheless will find that their "reward shall be great." (Luke 6:20-23) We discussed in an earlier essay the mainstream theological doctrine that brings about

such persecution, the notion that God cannot speak to another prophet after an earlier denominational tradition has codified the writings of an earlier prophet.[58]

Jesus' own life experience reflects the historical picture given in the primordial, patriarchal, Egyptian captivity, and national narratives. The world is constantly embroiled in conflict stemming ultimately from differences in thinking and belief. Those differences lead to death, destruction, oppression. There is but one effective way to make progress against "the world." That is to legally and individually allow for differences in religious beliefs and cultural practices. Jesus sets a personal example in his interaction with lepers, Samaritans, harlots, felons, tax collectors, centurions, Pharisees, high priests, governors, aristocratic Sadducees, scribes, country fishermen, and temple patrons. At the opposite end of the spectrum we find the overweaning political and religious jealousy of King Herod, whose insecurity extends even to jealousy of an infant child born outside of the royal family.

Luke's infancy account sets Jesus' birth in the context of a deeply offensive imperial census, whose purpose is to set a base for tribute tax

---

58. Shinkoskey, *Do My Prophets No Harm*, 60-80.

Biblical Captivity

revenue, and perhaps also to keep track of dissident families.[59] Jesus speaks of the worsening picture of government intervention in the lives of Judeans with the mention of the sacrilege of "desolation" that took place 200 years before in 167 BCE.[60] (Mark 13:14) Indeed, the captivity of mainstream Jewish religious and political interests at that time by the Seleucid king Epiphanes is but a precursor of the captivity of new light Judaism by the Maccabean revolutionaries, who, over time, became establishmentarians and oppressors of the revolutionaries of Jesus' day. Thus the political passion of Jesus is but a variation on the theme of the need to stand up against captivity. That theme is summarized by Jesus' statement that religious persecution is a hate crime, violence without legal justification: "They hated me without a cause." (John 15:25; Ps 35:19; 69:4) He predicts, as we mentioned above, the same for those who take up his name.

Luke's Jesus laments for Jerusalem like the prophets of old. Jesus says "It is impossible for a prophet to be killed outside of Jerusalem." (Luke 13:32–34) This is a wry statement recalling the mainstream church's typical intolerance of new light religion, as the prophets from Amos to Zechariah have lamented. Certainly it is physically possible to kill a prophet outside Jerusalem, but it is not politically possible–not even legal–without the encouragement of the blind guides of Jerusalem and their relegation of the First Commandment to the cultural dustbin. The people love the prophets, but the church leaders and politicians kill them. "Jerusalem . . . the city that kills the prophets." (Luke 13:33)

But current reality is vastly different from what a righteous community looks like. In the short and medium run, the picture is full of intolerance and persecution by jealous citizens, officials, priests, lawyers, and academicians. Even Jesus' best disciples think in terms of glory for themselves rather than for others. Thus he predicts an imminent, painful and ignominious end for himself, and also for his followers, who take up their own cross for free expression. He makes one last effort to exemplify true political citizenship, his calling as prophet and rightful governorship of the people, and indeed the humble kingship of God, in the street theater he plays out in his entry into Jerusalem. He rides in on the kind of colt the people expect their political messiah to be heralded on. This is incredible sarcasm, directed at both himself and at

59. Pilgrim, *Uneasy Neighbors*, 81.
60. Ibid, 73.

the political leaders of Jerusalem, as he knows they view him as an easy target, having brought no army with him. His detractors do their best to mock his pretended kingship during the scourging and suffering on the cross.

THE POLITICAL METHOD OF THE MESSIAH

Jesus' method is critical to understand. It is conditioned, as in fact Bible civic methods are generally, by the political context of the day. Jesus' method is an affirmation of his political theory. Jesus sees the Old Testament prophets as espousing peaceful political methods, the principal method, of course, being law itself: "Great peace have they which love thy law." (Ps 119:165) The goal of the law is peace and empowerment, and the method to obtain that goal is also peace through empowerment. (Mark 9:50; John 16:25–33) The law inspires peace because it allows pluralism. (Mark 9:38–40) Broadly empowered local government brings greatest hope for peace because many voices tied to the humble virtues of family and land are heard, and thus respected, rather than just a few voices whose interests are tied to adventure, riches and domination.[61] (Mark 7:1–13) When government is ruled by men rather than by law, it turns rogue and violent: "The earth also was corrupt ... the earth was filled with violence." (Gen 6:11)

Besides ethical covenant law and the able administration of it, which Jesus calls "judgment" and promotes frequently (Matt 7:2; John 5:22, 9:39), there are a number of other critical methods of civic salvation: education, good citizenship (including redemption—individual acts of rescue and kindness), devolution of power from central to local government (Luke 1:52), and, of course, eschewing violence and war. (Luke 2:14) The methods of civic and prophetic operation are summarized capably in the Decalogue itself. Education is a second commandment imperative: there should be no idolizing, or untoward dependence upon others, but rather self-reliance, which develops out of learning and practicing. Good citizenship is a tenth commandment imperative: citizens must show respect for neighbors. Peaceable living, as opposed to war-making, is a sixth commandment imperative: no

---

61. Horsley, *Jesus and Empire*, 110.

killing. Violence results from ignoring these constitutional principles and lusting for power over others.

The political context of the Roman administration of Judea precludes the methods which often were feasible during earlier periods of time in the nation under the Decalogue constitution: defense of the homeland against foreign aggression (already a lost cause); revolutionary activity to unseat oppressive government (Rome is too large and her priestly puppets in Judea are too strong); or a planting of a new nation in a new world like that undertaken by Moses and Joshua (Jesus promotes civic "missionary" work into all the nations, but cannot do all that much beyond teaching a few sentient disciples before his civic work in Galilee, Samaria and Judea is done; John 16, Matt 28:19).

Therefore, Jesus' method is primarily that which is left to him, that which is ultimately the most fruitful method anyway—instruction and exemplary action, and that which he has, apparently, some training for—healing. Mass education is a legal mandate in olden times, and effectively remains so in Jesus' time. (Deut 6:6–9; Mark 14:49; Acts 13:15) In olden times the educated priests are the teachers. (2 Chron 15:3) A "teaching priest" is one who specializes in political and legal education. (Neh 8:2; Jer 18:18; Ezek 7:26; Mal 2:7) In Jesus' day the priests have the same calling, but they have neglected their duty. (Matt 26:59; Ezek 22:26)

The only really effective way to prevent or ameliorate centralization and thus corruption of government is by a broad and deep program of education of the citizenry. The problem in Jesus' day is that the population have a particularly servile mentality. They have lost both the will and the way to know about their own rights and to assert them. Therefore Jesus goes about the countryside teaching self-government and self-reliance both by didactic method and by means of parables, as we will see in sections 6 and 7 below. He also practices his trade as a healer-physician, which, in tandem with the liberative thinking he plants in people's minds, produces miraculous turn-arounds in overall socio-somatic wellness.

Jesus uses the term "teacher" as a self-identification for himself. (Mark 14:14) Many individuals address Jesus as "teacher," as well. (Mark 4:38, 5:35, 9:17, 38; 10:17, 20, 35, 12:14, 19, 32: 13:1) His disciples come to him constantly for advice about what to think (John 17:6–8) and what to do, and how to select leadership for the movement. (Luke 22:24–30)

Captivity in the New Testament

When his own somewhat servile and dependent disciples cannot figure out how to raise money for the new movement, Jesus instructs them to use the means at their own disposal. The fishermen in his group can go back to fishing to raise money. (Matt 17:27) In order to counteract a lifetime of living dependently upon a central government, as soon as they join with him he lets them know they will need to learn to do this work with "no scrip, no bread, no money." (Mark 6:8) They will need to learn to live off the land and the voluntary largesse of the people before he can hope to send them into all the nations. (Matt 28:19) He teaches them they can use their own native intelligence and experience to provide for themselves. Providing for themselves economically instead of depending upon state largesse is key to the next step, understanding that they can rely upon themselves for important political decision-making as well.

Perhaps the most important curriculum Jesus teaches is that of socio-political self-determination, the local- and family-government mandate of the Decalogue's fifth commandment (honor parents). In fact, he teaches a libertarian idea that individuals have an inherent right, because they have the inherent ability, to govern themselves without much regulation from higher levels of political authority. He teaches that he has learned this about himself: "As the Father hath life in himself, so he has given to the Son to have life in himself." (John 5:26) People have a great deal of creative power within themselves to control and sustain their own lives. If even the fowls of the air and the lilies of the field provide for themselves, certainly a being of higher intelligence can do so as well. (Matt 6:25–34) This is deeply embodied in his teaching: "Behold, the kingdom of god is within you . . ." (Luke 17:21) Jesus, of course, did not mean that mere private or ecclesiastic or cultural authority lies within individuals, but that the actual power of political governance is provided by the Decalogue as a right to individuals, and even more than that, as a responsibility of individuals. This instruction is tantamount to support for a policy of local welfare administration as opposed to administration at the central level of government.

Jesus's promotion of local welfare administration is made explicit in his comment upon the priestly government's "corban" policy. (Mark 7:1–13) Here he criticizes the government's policy for caring for the elderly, which is a corruption of the fifth commandment imperative. A man, under Decalogue law, should respect parental wishes to be cared for by loved ones in old age, as opposed to being "cursed" or pushed aside.[62] (Mark 7:10) But if a child has pushed the parent aside, according to "corban," he can be free of traditional legal consequences by making a gift to the temple state, thus transferring peasant and artisan resources from local use to national use and political distribution. By institution of this policy, temple administrators are selling indulgences—in this case forgiveness of the ongoing responsibility of children to parents—and thus purchasing loyalty to the central government rather than traditional clan or tribal government. This process is inimical to Jesus, and to all the prophets of local self-determination in Israel.

Even in the presence of this corrupting policy, if individuals do not know, or do not have, they need only "Ask . . . seek . . . knock . . ." and it will be provided to them locally by those who do, and particularly by those of Jesus' movement. (Luke 11:9; Mark 6:30–44, 8:1–9) Jesus teaches that he himself, and presumably others also, have power to cast aside a life of servility and take on a new life of empowerment that works for them: "I lay down my life, that I might take it again. No man taketh it from me, but I lay it down of myself. I have power to lay it down, and I have power to take it again." (John 10:18) Furthermore, human beings even have power to forgive sins. This universal power has been co-opted by the priests, who teach they alone can perform this gift to others. (Mark 2:10; Matt 9:6) Jesus teaches his disciples that they have "power to tread on serpents and scorpions [and presumably apply treatment like that given by Moses to his people in the wilderness so they can survive (Num 21:4–9)], and over all the power of the enemy . . ." (Luke 10:19) In fact, he teaches his disciples that each one of them can be like a king who claims to rule by divine right as the "Son of God": "But as many as received him, to them gave he power to become the sons of God . . ." (John 1:12) When they assert such a right, effectively those swelled up with power will be deflated, and those bereft of it power will come into possession of it. (Matt 23:12)

Many have commented on the political philosophy of Jesus' teaching about payment of tribute money to the Romans. Interpreters rightly suspect that this reveals much about Jesus' approach to dealing with imperial government. Peter explains to the tribute collectors that Jesus will be happy to pay tribute. When Peter wonders whether this is proper for their movement to do, Jesus asks him "Of whom do the kings of the

---

62. Westbrook and Wells, *Everyday Law*, 54.

earth take custom or tribute? Of their own children, or of strangers?" (Matt 17:24–27) Peter answered "Of strangers." Jesus explains "Then are the children free." By this he explains, like a political science professor, the difference between a client state governed by a Roman procurator (Judea, Pontius Pilate; see Matt 27:2) and a client state governed by a nominally independent king (Galilee, Herod Antipas until 39 CE).[63] A free people, like those in Galilee, would not ordinarily be expected to submit to a tax to pay a foreign government, like those living under direct Roman government in Jerusalem and its immediate environs. Nevertheless, Jesus suggests they ought to do it anyway, to keep the peace and allow the movement room to operate. (Matt 17:27)

Some in Israel's past gambled with the lives of the people and refused to pay tribute, like Hoshea,[64] Jehoiakim,[65] and Zedekiah.[66] Such a policy was disastrous in each case. Hoshea's policy precipitated the destruction of the northern kingdom, and Jehoiakim's and Zedekiah's policies precipitated the destruction of the southern kingdom. Jesus, like a good political historian, seems to have learned from this and decided not to tempt a superior power.

When the question arises again in a different setting (Matt 22:15–22), Jesus reveals the same thinking, but puts an edge on his answer that his disciples, and astute interpreters of the passage, are able to detect. The Pharisees try to make a rebel of him and induce him to deny the lawfulness of paying tribute by flattering him in front of his disciples. They note that he is a purist in the law of Moses. They say, "Thou ... teachest the way of God in truth ... for thou regardest not the person of men." (Matt 22:16) Jesus understands their purpose and does not worry that some will think him a toady to tyranny if he encourages payment. He explains that the image on the coins they all use makes clear who the sovereign political power is at the moment. It is Caesar, and the people must "render therefore unto Caesar the things which are Caesar's . . ." (Matt 22:21) But when he also mentions that the people must render "unto God the things that are God's," he sharpens his answer considerably. His disciples and many in the crowds about him understand that the things of God ultimately and fully trump the things of Caesar. It is

63. Braund, "Herodian Dynasty," 3:174.
64. Gottwald, *Politics*, 67.
65. Ibid, 84.
66. Ibid, 70.

significant that Jesus does not say "render unto Rome," for he wishes to underscore that as Rome's client states they are being subject not to a reasonable, covenant power but to an autocrat, who provides himself with the wealth that truly belongs to many nations. It is this same autocrat (Augustus Caesar) to whom other client nations like Parthia are required to make religious sacrifices, as if to a God. Jesus' flattery of the dictator is extraordinarily sarcastic. In fact, between the lines he suggests that democracy looms like a giant shadow over dictatorship, and will eventually work its way.

The issue of tribute surfaces yet again at the time of Jesus' appearance before Pilate. Having failed earlier to entrap him, they falsely accuse him now by saying he is "forbidding to give tribute to Caesar . . ." (Luke 23:2) It is a salacious accusation, and Pilate sees it for what it is. They say they know he cannot possibly be supporting tribute, because his movement is a "messiah" movement—of the type common in that time in Palestine. Such movements, like those of Judas, Athronges, and Simon,[67] promote revolutionary overthrow of the existing Roman kingship and the supplanting of it with an indigenous Davidic king. Those movements collect money for their own activities, and not for the king they hope to overthrow. Indeed it has been noised about that Jesus has said "that he himself is Christ a king." But it is Peter who has supposed this, while Jesus never said it. Jesus is the political figure who, by Mosaic law, *should* be civic king, but by no means is it possible that he *can* be. Jesus, knowing Peter's astute perception of Jesus's standing with God could get the movement into trouble, explicitly has asked Peter, "Tell no man that he is Jesus the anointed." (Matt 16:20)

CITIZENSHIP AS SALVATION

Jesus had an undeniably cynical view of the hearts and minds of those autocratic and oligarchic authorities, such as the high priests and the Sadducees, who held political power in the ancient world. When the time was right, their hands were quick to do evil, as corrupt as they were. The socio-political and economic habits of the elite were hard to break. For example, the extraordinarily ethical, but rich young ruler

---

67. Horsley, *Jesus and Empire*, 49.

could sustain almost all the principles and practices of the Decalogue ... except the greatest one. The responsibility to divest his wealth so that the poor might be benefited by it (essentially a second commandment requirement), and then to join a movement to educate and empower the citizenry (a first commandment requisite) was more than he could bear. (Mark 10:17–31)

Jesus understood the politicians of the Jerusalem court and their Roman overseers of the period so well that he felt certain that his teaching ministry would threaten them to the core, and that he would certainly die at their hands. (Matt 16:21–23, 17:22–23) They were mercurial in all their dealings, changing course and judgment according to whim and emotion. He reminded them, "Are ye come out as against a thief with swords and staves for to take me? I sat daily with you teaching in the temple, and ye laid no hold on me." (Matt 26:55) Their actions and their administration of the law were fully corrupt: "They hated me without a cause." (John 15:25) Those of their ilk among the cities and nations of the region could be counted upon to deny basic human rights to those of his movement he would send out to teach as he had been teaching. (Matt 10:23, 23:34; John 15:20) It was said of Jesus, "He knew what was in man." (John 2:25)

Against this great, inertial, corrupt, and corrupting force, Jesus intended to teach the people how to be responsible citizens again, and how to organize into an effective force for good. To those who were interested in his message, he asked simply "Follow me." (Matt 16:24, 8:22; Mark 1:18) But he did not sugar-coat the consequences of such a decision. He challenged his disciples this way: "He that taketh not his cross, and followeth after me, is not worthy of me." (Matt 10:38) One who expected to be a leader in the movement must expect to be martyred. The sacrifice the leadership of a dissenting political movement could expect to make, in the context of a system of political domination, was not a savory one. It was spelled out in a series of statements like the following. "I lay down my life for the sheep." (John 10:15) One must "Give his life a ransom for many." (Matt 20:28) "I will lay down my life for thy sake." (John 13:37) "Greater love hath no man than this, that a man lay down his life for his friends." (John 15:13)

In order to develop this kind of committed leadership, Jesus provided a number of dissertations on the subject of good citizenship. He said that a people who had such a proud heritage of self-government and understood now that they must renew it must not be shy and retiring about the glory of such a system: "Ye are a light of the world. A city that is set on a hill cannot be hid. Neither do men light a candle, and put it under a bushel, but on a candlestick . . . Let your light so shine before men, that they may see your good works . . ." (Matt 5:14–16) When asked about producing a miraculous, religious "sign" to inspire converts and followers, he gave a stinging reply. There would be no such easy accomplishment of progress. It must be done and won by the hard work of social and political activity, by people who criticize authorities, and by authorities who recognize the validity of the criticism: "This is an evil generation: they seek a sign; and there shall no sign be given it, but the sign of Jonah the prophet. For as Jonah was a sign unto the Ninevites, so shall also the Son of man be to this generation" (Luke 11:29–30) This was essentially a call for his hearers to exercise the conviction and courage to stand up against corrupt authority. The proper sign was not religious miracle but civic citizenship and leadership.

The problem with the mentality of the citizens of his day was that for 600 years their ancestors had been subjugated to great powers in the region, and so the people did not know how to be free and independent any longer. They felt that their lives and occupations and voices were a gift of their rulers, rather than a natural right of their very existence. Jesus lamented this fact: "Then saith he unto his disciples, the harvest truly is plenteous, but the laborers are few; pray ye therefore the Lord of the harvest, that he will send forth laborers into his harvest." (Matt 9:37–38) The prophet who summons citizens to civil rights leaves good citizens to watch over the freedoms of the realm as he goes about on his itinerant teaching mission: "For the Son of man is as a man taking a far journey, who left his house, and gave authority to his servants, and to every man his work, and commanded the porter to watch. Watch ye therefore: for ye know not when the master of the house cometh . . . lest coming suddenly he find you sleeping. And what I say unto you I say unto all, Watch." (Mark 13:34–36) Jesus essentially asks for a neighborhood watch program in which neighbors are vigilant to watch for encroachments against lands and liberties. But even parents in Jesus' day teach their children to be dependent upon corrupt authorities. To break the cycle of ignorance and poor parenting, Jesus calls the enlightened among the children to break from the servile mentality of their families and fight against it for a greater cause. (Matt 10:35–37)

The body politic must not wait for God to make judgments about the corrupt powers that be. They must serve as his voice themselves as the prophets did before: "The Father judges no man, but hath committed all judgment unto the Son . . ." (John 5:22) But activism and local government is not an easy job, because the citizenry must "Judge not according to the appearance, but judge righteous judgment." (John 7:24) Those judgments must stand as if they were uttered in heaven by God himself: "Verily I say unto you, Whatsoever ye shall bind on earth shall be bound in heaven; and whatsoever ye shall loose on earth shall be loosed in heaven." (Matt 18:18)

By means of this kind of citizenship education, Jesus built cadres of individuals who valued freedom, independence, and willfulness, and matured the population politically one citizen at a time. These units of freedom were encouraged, by their understanding of the Mosaic law of localism, to coalesce into village-based movements, or "sequestered communities" as one author calls them.[68] These bands of watchful citizens functioned a good bit away from the easy surveillance of Roman and Sadducee rulers after Jesus' death, effectively in wilderness-type rural settings, and even foreign settings. They were to act essentially as Jesus did before his entry into Jerusalem. For three years he engaged in and thus established a pattern of village sojourns, sea crossings, wayside resorting, hilltop sermonizing, garden luxuriating, and wilderness feeding. Paul acted in the same way after his political conversion as well. That the development of autonomous, semi-underground groupings is one clear result of the Jesus movement is visible in the fact that four separate gospels emerged from four separate communities of believers or followers, each emphasizing the themes of his teachings the best way they could. That there were in fact dozens of other Christian communities marginalized and submerged by the mainstream political group that seized Christianity before and during the time of Emperor Constantine seems clear enough from the many other dissident "gospels", "acts," and "apocalypses" uncovered by archaeology and reconstructed through secondary sources over the ensuing 2,000 years.[69]

---

68. Horsley, *Jesus and Empire*, 71.
69. Shinkoskey, *Do My Prophets No Harm*, 176–177.

Biblical Captivity

CAPTIVITY IN THE WORK OF THE APOSTLES

Jesus' predictions about the oppression of individual believers and the captivity of the churches play out in the Book of Acts. Luke, who most believe conceived the book of Acts as a continuation of the story of his gospel, starts the second book where the first account ends, with descriptions of Jesus' appearances to his disciples and his continuing teaching about the political kingdom of God. Specifically, he tells them they will receive the ability to interpret the outlines of the kingdom themselves, through the Holy Spirit. (Acts 1.4) Jesus reminds his followers, as Luke's gospel did, that hope for large heavenly-spiritual events which result in deliverance or destruction should not be their major concern. They should rather be concerned to approach God on their own, with the intercessory help of the Spirit, to deal with the diurnal political realities of life on the planet. "It is not for you to know the times or periods that the Father has set . . ." (1.7) "But you will receive power when the Holy Spirit has come upon you . . ." (1.8) God the Father directs all things before, and all things new. (Acts 5:33–39) In fact, he directs that a new apostle be chosen to replace Judas Iscariot. (1:20)

At the Jewish festival of Pentecost, Peter describes Jerusalem's treatment of Jesus in First Commandment terms. Persecution of him is irresponsible, the work of "Wicked hands." (Acts 2:22–36) The largely Jewish crowd admits waywardness and responsibility, and turns to God for forgiveness and new life. (Acts 2:38–39) Their's is an atonement in the sense of re-commitment to first principles. Their inaction on his behalf is a miscarriage of justice.[70] Baptism is a cleansing of the guilty political conscience.

Once they receive the Spirit, apparently the Spirit of political and ethical knowledge and courage, Jerusalem becomes inhospitable to them. (Acts 3–7) Luke records the appearance of Peter and John before the council for preaching a gospel based on resurrection of Christ from the dead. (Acts 4:10) The council "threaten(s) them, that they speak henceforth no more in his name." (4:17) Peter and John answer by asserting the First Commandment right to free expression. They ask "Whether it be right in the sight of God to hearken unto you more than God . . ." Here "the sight of God" seems to connote legal equity and human right and thus likely refers to a local statute or tradition that the

---

70. Ehrman, *New Testament*, 145.

authorities were trampling on. The authorities had hoped to intimidate the two since they saw they were "unlearned and ignorant men." (Acts 4:13) Once Peter and John couched their argument in constitutional legal terms, the authorities "let them go, finding nothing how they might punish them . . ." This betrays a class-based system of government ethics, under which those who would accept what the authorities tried to impose upon them, were deemed to deserve such discrimination.

When again all the apostles were put in prison without reasonable charge (Acts 5:18), the council of Pharisees and Sadducees this time came up with the legally more feasible accusation of blasphemous libel. They accused the Christians of sidestepping the legal rights of Judeans by persecuting the Sadducee religion. Thus the Sadducees smeared the new movement with the very charge that the movement was essentially leveling against the Sadducees. By teaching Jesus crucified, it seemed the Christians "intend to bring this man's blood upon us," that is, to indict the church leaders for illegal or judicial murder, to tear down God, or worse, overthrow the government-established church. Here is an example of dueling religions, one using the law relating to religion as a club, the other using it as a defense. These were trumped-up charges of a serious nature.

When Peter and John answered that Jesus' mission is to call Israel to repentance, presumably for the shortcomings of the mainstream politicians and churches, "they were cut to the heart, and took counsel to slay them." (Acts 5:33) There was certainly nothing clearly illegal about this, but, nevertheless, they intended to push the sedition charge to its fullest. Gamaliel makes a sixth commandment defense for them. The proof of the pudding is whether the political and religious movement has good and peaceable results, or whether it leads to unnecessary public disorder and violence. He argues that if the Christians know God better than the authorized churchmen—can produce salutary and prescient results for society (Deut 18:20–22), the church must tolerate to them. (Acts 5:39) On the other hand, if they are crackpots, their movement will die out like others of the pretender ilk. This argument saves their lives, but still they are beaten and told not to preach a gospel of calumny directed toward the established church. (Acts 5:40)

The martyrdom of Stephen is cast in free exercise light. It demonstrates that the spirit of oppression is still alive and well among even educated and faithful Pharisees like Saul of Tarsus. Paul's conversion is thus seen as the apprehension of a new understanding of the importance of the tolerant legal love practiced by Jesus. Once he converts to the new faith, Paul learns how it feels on the other side of the leather, and he stands trial for his beliefs in Jerusalem, Asia Minor, and Rome. (Acts 21-28) Paul defends the faith, and the gospel of tolerance, by explaining his own history of intolerance to the court officials. Those officials receive his words more so than the Jews.

Acts records that Paul also found himself on the stand in Achaia in Asia Minor. Here we see another example of Luke's sentiment that Jerusalem persecutes the prophets. The Jews there, as in Palestine, "made insurrection with one accord against Paul and brought him to the [civil] judgment seat." (Acts 18:12) Their charge? "This man persuadeth men to worship contrary to law." (Acts 18:13) Here the Jews refer to the established church "torah" law or ritual of the Jerusalem church, thinking the local government of Achaia will see the wisdom of unitary priestly-secular government and mandatory worship practice like that in corrupt Judea. But Roman Achaia is not Jerusalem. Here there is a broader range of free exercise than at Jerusalem. Reviewing the pleadings, before the Jews could even make a case, the judge threw it out of court. "If it were a matter of wrong or wicked lewdness, O ye Jews . . . I should bear with you. But if it be a question of . . . your [ecclesiastic] law, look ye to it, for I will be no judge of such matters." (Acts 18:15) "And he drave them from the judgment seat." (Acts 18:16) The Greek Christian Jews of the city are subsequently able to invoke the Jewish community's own law against blasphemous libel against its corrupt representatives in Achaia. (Exod 22:28) They scourge the ruler of the synagogue for filing false charges against Paul. (Acts 18:17) In Achaia it is not legal to smear another church with a kind of religious libel that one is actually guilty of oneself.[71]

Once Paul comes to Ephesus, he is falsely accused there as well. Here he is accused of defaming the goddess Diana. Here the town mayor judges sentiently as well. "For ye have brought hither these men, which are neither robbers of churches, nor yet blasphemers of your goddess." (Acts 19:37) He then advises them that should they have a serious rather than frivolous "matter against any man, the law is open, and there are deputies: let them implead one another." (38) He then

---

71. See Rowe, *World Upside Down*, 57–62 for a discussion of Roman-Jewish relations in Corinth and in this case.

Captivity in the New Testament

advises them that they are in danger of an offense against public order themselves if they do not disband. (40–41) It is in the interest of the town mayor to maintain order, lest Rome exact its famous vengeance against the city.[72]

Paul gives a spirited defense of the First Commandment in Rome at his trial there. He says, "There (is) no reason for the death penalty... I had done nothing against our people." (28:17–20)

In the Book of Revelation, written near the end of the reign of the Roman Emperor Domitian (96 CE), the theme of captivity is honed to a high science and applied to an alien ruler rather than a corrupt local one. It is virtually an underground handbook for active Christian resistance to political and religious tyranny. In this book, both the political and religious "powers that be" are obvious enemies of humanity.[73] The writer, John, is exiled on the island of Patmos. Roman historians are clear that the rule of Domitian was marked by his suspicion of disloyalty among his subjects, and his fear of retribution by those groups.[74]

In this book the Roman imperial state is described using the image of two beasts, who exemplify political and religious oppression of emperor worship (Rev 13, 17), and also a great whore, who seduces and defiles the people of the known world. (Rev 17) The text appeals to the people of the empire who believe in a more ethical way of living. As if in a new Exodus, they are "to come out of her," leaving behind the totalitarian state. (Rev 18:4) But Christians are not to use the methods of the commandment-less Roman state: "If any man has an ear, let him hear. He that leadeth into captivity shall go into captivity. He that killeth with the sword must be killed with the sword." (Rev 13:9–10) Roman methods include forced exile, which John himself apparently is familiar with.

PERSECUTION OF NEW LIGHT POLITICS AND RELIGION

In an earlier essay I argued that ancient society historically reacted with violent hostility to the advent of a new prophetic messenger, even in a nation like Israel, which had a tradition of tolerating them.[75] The

---

72. Rowe, *World Upside Down*, 45–49.
73. Pilgrim, *Uneasy Neighbors*, 145.
74. Ibid, 146.
75. Shinkoskey, *Do My Prophets No Harm*, 60–80.

mainstream churches in Jesus' day, as in the days of previous prophets, taught, and perhaps believed, that the heavens had been sealed up against any further incursions of God's voice into the world. One like Jesus, who disputes that notion, cannot have a legitimate calling from God: "Have any of the rulers or of the Pharisees believed on him?" (John 7:48) They say he works by the devil instead. (Matt 9:34, 12:24) He warns his apostles to "beware of men: for they will deliver you up to the councils, and they will scourge you in their synagogues . . ." (Matt 10:17) He foretells his own death based on their inflamed disbelief in the notion of new revelation. (Matt 16:21, 17:22, 20:17) He ruefully remarks in prayer, "I have given them thy word, and the world hath hated them." (John 17:14)

Generations of Jews up until the present day generally, though begrudgingly, conceded authority to the literary prophets strung out over the nine centuries after Elijah. But things seemed to change palpably at the time of John the Baptist. "The prophets . . . prophesied until John came . . ." (Matt 11:13) Then the official stance turned more vicious than usual: "and from the days of John the Baptist until now the kingdom of heaven suffereth violence, and the violent take it by force." (Matt 11:12) Of John, who eats or drinks little, it is said, "He has a devil." (Matt 11:18) Of Jesus, who eats and drinks like most people, they say "he casteth out devils through the prince of the devils." (Matt 9:34) The prophets are damned if they do, and damned if they don't. There is no longer any way to reason with the authorities. The present conundrum is "like children . . . calling to one another, 'We played the flute for you and you did not dance.'" (Matt 11:16–17) This is as much to say, this generation has forgotten who they are . . . they are Jews in a millennium long tradition of recurring prophecy. But now when John and Jesus prophesy, the scribes, priests, and lawyers forget how to play the game.

In a sense it is easy to see why they no longer want to play. The Herodians have for decades served Rome as sycophants of Roman power. The Sadducees are tight with Rome as well. To an extent they have appropriated the imperial Roman civic religion for themselves. That religion increasingly is emperor worship as a replacement of God worship. Jesus does not worship the high priest, and the high priest is therefore incensed. The Pharisees themselves, though less cozy with Rome, have adopted an end-of-prophecy doctrine too. For generations they have been working on the assumption that there will be no new additions to scripture, and by a generation after Jesus will have solidified their closed canon, if they have not done so already. Therefore, it is in the interests of both the political and ecclesiastic powers to shun prophecy and jealously guard the authority the Romans have given each to govern in their separate spheres. They want to monopolize political and religious power, and to do so "by force," as Jesus says. (Matt 11:12) On the other hand, prophets announce that God wishes ethical leaders to govern instead.

Jesus' "kingdom" parables indicate what the world is like before, during, and after efforts to restore constitutional values. Jesus' Parable of the Sower is an extended metaphor on the difficulty of new oracular revelation taking root in society in view of aggressive, entrenched political and religious power. The seed/word that falls by the wayside is that which is diverted from good soil by an interpretation of the law that excludes ongoing revelation. The seed that falls into stony places represents revelation that first is received by the people, but then is recanted when persecution begins. Religious captivity prevails. (Matt 13:21) Seed that falls among thorns is new gospel that gets suffocated by riches, which prevent attachment to a lifestyle of moderation. (Matt 13:1–23)

The Parable of the Mustard Seed and the Parable of Leaven are messages about the difficulty of living in the midst of imperial captivity or orthodox oppression of pluralism. There is a maturation process that both the seed and the loaf must undergo, in order to once again apprehend constitutional values. Small concepts (seed), or small additions (leaven), can synergize a polity, which can then grow to great proportion. Indeed, the blessing of a great nation coming from Abraham's loins took quite a long time to be effectuated.

The Parable of the Wicked Husbandman, also known as the Parable of the Vineyard, is an allegory of a nation under secure the patronage of a "householder," clearly seen to be God. God gave it into the custody of husbandmen, politicians and priests, and went away. In due time he sends political reformers, the prophet constitutionalists, to harvest fruit. The placemen tending the property destroy the reformers, so that in the end the householder must "miserably destroy those wicked men." This parable recalls Nebuchadrezzar putting out the eyes of Zedekiah after killing the king's children before his face. It also recalls Shalmaneser's destruction of Samaria, and Pompey's obliteration

Biblical Captivity

of a recalcitrant faction of Hasmoneans, all of whom fail to act in the interests of God. These are days of comeuppance known as "days of the Lord," where captivity is earned and deserved. (Matt 21:33–41)

When Jesus asks his disciples to be baptized with water, he is asking them to immerse themselves in God's word for the present day. "He would have given thee living water . . ." (John 4:10) Revelation is that which flows down from high places like a river from a mountain: "Everyone that thirsteth, come ye to the water." (Isa 55:1) "Let judgment run down as waters, and righteousness as a mighty stream." (Amos 5:24) When Jesus asks them to remember his body and blood by means of bread and wine, he uses two of the most important Old Testament metaphors for continuing revelation. Bread and wine (both sweet and fermented) are the lifeblood of the Israelite economy. They are symbols of independence and prosperity. (Micah 4:4) Both are taken by the mouth. The bread of Ezekiel is the scroll of new revelation that God asks Ezekiel to eat, and which tastes like honey to him. (Ezek 2:8—3.3) This kind of "food" is like the words God puts in Jeremiah's mouth to deliver to the people. (Jer 1:9)

Yet in the day of Jesus, it is blasphemy against the ruling Sadducee faith—the official/public religion of the Jews—to claim a messianic connection with God. The Sadducees claim they have a "living God," but also that God speaks no longer. (Matt 26:63) The one variety of prophet the Sadducees accept is a shadowy Messiah who sets all things in order and establishes the high priesthood in an even more exalted place than it now occupies. This, Jesus does not do. He disparages that priesthood instead. Thus, the priests accuse him of blasphemy and condemn him to death. Then the priestly enclave belittle the version of prophesy Jesus claims to represent, prophesy linked to everyday events: "Prophesy unto us, thou Christ, who is he that smote thee?" (Matt 26:68) Jesus, on the other hand, elsewhere taught a different law of blasphemy. It is blasphemy to deny the power of God to speak anew: "Blasphemy against the Holy Ghost shall not be forgiven unto men." (Matt 12:31)

Jesus's second temptation in the wilderness is the same one he faces on the cross when he asks God if he might be spared the "bitter cup"—the temptation to abandon the prophetic duty and lifestyle. In the wilderness, Satan asks Jesus to cast himself down from the pinnacle of the temple. (Matt 4:5–7) This is tantamount to asking him to give up

Captivity in the New Testament

his work, to end his own life before he can share God's new word with others. This scene recalls a similar temptation experienced by Ezekiel, who is encouraged by God to understand that if a prophet declines a legitimate calling, he will face death as a consequence of that refusal, just as surely as he faces death by accepting it. (Ezek 33:6–7)

THE PROPHET'S CALLING: STAND UP AGAINST OPPRESSION

The purpose of a prophet's calling is to agitate like the drum of a washing machine, to try to get the dirt out of society. The way to a clean or make a society "holy," in Old Testament terms, is to enact constitutional government that has a full slate of human rights. The object of Jesus' calling is like that of Moses and the other prophets: to re-establish the original intent and meaning of the law, and to make reforms in favor of that law. Thus Jesus says, "Think not that I am come to destroy the law, or the prophets: I am not come to destroy, but to fulfil." (Matt 5:17) Here, there is a sense of filling up a jar to the top, when its oil has been depleted or emptied.

Jesus devotes himself to a critique of the existing powers in both the secular and religious sectors, which have combined in an unholy alliance with the illegitimate power of Rome. He contrasts the plain-clothed, yet highly ethical, John the Baptist with "those who live in royal palaces" and are clothed in "finery."[76] (Matt 11:7–8; REB) The royals "live in luxury." (Luke 7:25) These are the same who put good people to death (Matt 14:1–12), and deprive the poor or their rights. (Mark 12:40; Matt 17:24–27, 26:11)

Jesus' method to accomplish his judgmental instructional program is to use his right to observe, learn and speak. He uses conversations, sermons, responses to questions, disputations, and stories as a "sword" to cut away false knowledge and reveal deceit, treachery, pretention, and malevolent intention, and replace it with a positive vision of human capacity and existence. (Matt 10:34) The sword is thus the sword of controversy, not violence. Families often love tradition, pageant and culture more than freedom and revelation, and thus members of a household may become at variance politically with one another. A true seeker

---

76. Pilgrim, *Uneasy Neighbors*, 52–53.

must "take (up) . . . his cross" (Matt 10:38) and be prepared to suffer indignities meted out by those who are mere sheep in the ruler's pen.

Jesus judges the institutions of the day, and especially the leaders of those institutions. However, he is reluctant to judge or condemn individuals, primarily because "They know not what they do." (Luke 23:34) They have not been taught well. The judgment that Jesus is about elevates the lowly with both knowledge and political power, and abases the mighty, whose world is made of cloth that is corruptible: "For judgment I am come into this world, that they which see not might see; and that they which see might be made blind." (John 9:39) Those who were ignorant of their rights have their eyes opened and now assert their rightful powers, and those who deprived their neighbors of those rights are rendered immobile and inert so they cannot continue on such a course.

His parables speak carefully, though in somewhat veiled fashion, of the need to stand up for fundamental values. The Parable of the Pearl of Great Price encourages individuals to seek out a more sophisticated way of life than mere economic subsistence and political dependence. Once this life is discovered, one will happily abandon the goals of gaudy physical luxury in favor of that new life. (Matt 13:45–46) The Parable of the Ten Pounds stresses the importance of citizens actively seeking out this political, social and economic sophistication rather than standing pat with what they have. (Luke 19:11–27) His Lesson to Guests and a Host (Luke 14:7–11) and his Parable of the Great Supper (Luke 14:16–24) stress the inevitability of God's replacement of a once elect people, who now refuse to participate in their own salvation, with a new people who do actively wish to participate.

The kingdom of God are those people who accept and revere the legitimate messengers of God, and do not fear to enter with the prophet into criticism of the perquisites of the elite, especially when those privileges clash with the laws of the Decalogue. For example, John the Baptist criticized the adulterous kingship of Herod Antipas, and in the Sermon on the Mount Jesus affirmed the sacredness of the bonds of marriage as well. John lost his life for supporting age-old values, and Jesus did as well. The message of the story of the New Testament is that death should not be the price of truth-telling in a decent society.

The cleansing of the temple is a deeply personal act of protest, apparently devoid of collaboration with any of his disciples. It expresses Jesus' utter dismay and indignation about the situation of life in

Palestine. It is the out-breaking of anger, disappointment, revolt, revulsion, fear, courage, instruction, and obedience to God. It is a protest against the unholy alliance between church and state in the form of the Herodian/high priestly nexus that spreads its pall of orthodoxy across the land, forces new light religion to an immediate grave, and deprives the people of their First Commandment right to speech and religion. Here is the political passion of Jesus Christ. The crucifixion is the price he paid for exercising good citizenship. But Christ turned that punishment into an example of submission to a God of non-violence, and drew enough attention to the injustice of the event that it motivated his disciples to stand up against domineering political elites wherever they subsequently went.

The prophet Hosea elaborated a political theory of oppression and release which can be taken as an analysis of ancient history in his own day. That Hosea knew the political lore of Mesopotamia and of Egypt is evidenced by his mention of Israel's earlier encounters with those two great traditions. (Hos 9:1–6, 11:5, 12:12) Hosea posits that there is a cyclical and general chronology in the affairs of men, to which he attaches the name of Israel's God, who, after all, takes credit, whether it tarnishes his name or not, for all that happens in the world that he has created. There are three days, or periods of time, in this grand cycle. The people of a nation are established in righteousness, or at least good intentions, in the beginning for a day. But they then fall into unrighteousness and/or oppression for two days, after which, with the help of a prophet, they stand a chance to return again to their ethical senses for a day of peace, local government, and toleration.

Such a pattern might roughly be held to have occurred before Hosea in the hundred years "day" of Moses' and Joshua's lifetimes. After the deaths of those two great foundational leaders, there was a 200 year decline during the time of Judges. A day of renewal was observed during the 100 year time span of the lives of Samuel and David. This day of political, economic, and social prosperity then gave way to a 200 year period of constitutional decline associated with Solomon and his offspring. Despite a minor renewal in the time of Elijah, this grand cultural decline was not addressed broadly until the time of the preaching and civic activity of Amos, Hosea, Isaiah, and Micah in the mid-to-late eighth century.

Biblical Captivity

As to his own day, if the people listened to what he had to say, things would not be too bad. Hosea suggests "Let us return unto the Lord . . . he hath torn . . . he hath smitten . . . After two days will he revive us . . . in the third day he will raise us up, and we shall live in his sight." (Hos 6:1–3) On the other hand, if the people did not listen to reason, things would be much bleaker. Those citizens of the northern kingdom that he expected would soon be deported into captivity by Assyria would have to experience an aggravated and international version of the captivity the northern kingdom had imposed upon its own society. It was his hope that the children of the north would one day return, but he could not say when: "The children shall abide many days without a king [without political independence] . . . afterward shall the children of Israel return . . . in the latter days." (Hos 3:4–5) It was difficult for even a great prophet to trump the power of a huge imperial nation, as the experience of Moses had shown long before.

In Hosea's mind, the three-day cycle of decline and recovery in an elect nation can conceivably be a briefer period, but it can also be much longer, especially if no authentic prophet arises to assist God with his work of extricating the people. For example, in Egypt there was apparently a 400 year absence of prophetic intervention from the time of Joseph to Moses.

Because the southern kingdom was increasingly committed to the same ruinous policies that affected the north, the southern kingdom could not sustain the revival of freedom brought on by these literary prophets. Little more than a hundred years after the north lost its place in the world, the south succumbed to Babylon. The last Bible prophets, Joel and Malachi, spoke around 400 BCE, and once again there was a 400 year silence of prophetic activity in Judea until the time of John and Jesus—and all the while Israel was kept under the hand of a succession of great empires.[77]

There would be much less time of oppression and captivity if the people understood the need for new prophetic leadership, and if potential prophets properly prepare themselves for the calling. It is Hosea's view that Yahweh's faithfulness to the liberty lifestyle is effectively available not every 200 years, but as often as yearly, like "spring rain," and

---

77. The 200 year interval emerges again if we consider the works of Jesus ben Sira and the author of Wisdom of Solomon in the early second century BCE.

even daily, like "dawn."[78] (Hos 6:3) But communities of men cannot seem to muster the awareness of their own potential nearly so often as Yahweh stands ready to support it. Oppression must be onerous and very long standing before societies can figure out it is wrong. Nevertheless, Hosea is confident that eventually God "will place them in their houses" (Hos 11:10–11) and it will be said, "I returned the captivity of my people." (Hos 6:11)

The specific chronology of internal weakness and decline leading to international subjugation hinges on policy choices made with respect to the constitutional law, the Decalogue. When Moses gave his farewell address, he specified the consequences of neglect of the laws of right and responsibility—the cursings of social decline. Hosea enumerated these once again. (Hos 7:16, 9:13, 11:6, 10:9, 14, 8:14) In sum, if the people neglect to maintain the constitutional laws, it will be as if they returned to the oppression of Egypt. (Hos 8:13) The mentality of living as slaves in Egypt never has quite been purged from the culture. (Hos 11:5)

Jesus of Nazareth was impressed with Hosea's understanding of the cycle of captivity and liberty. He condensed it and used it to describe the period of consternation and concern that he believed would follow his own suffering and death (Matt 16:21, 17:23), and the resurrection of hope which would take place on the third day when his followers would comprehend the events of his ministry, find him in their sights once again, and undertake the great "day" of kingdom building to which he called them. But he also used Hosea's three days in its original sense, to apply to the long period of persecution and hostility that his followers now faced while nations about them seethed in violence against other nations—"until the times of the Gentiles be fulfilled." (Luke 21:24) About this coming stretch of violent history he warned them numerous times. (Luke 21:10–12; Mark 10:30; Matt 5:10, 10:16–23, 23:34) They must try to hold to personal and corporate peace, to be a remnant of righteousness, to live in the eye of the storm. (Luke 21:18) In this sense Jesus wished his followers to resist the trend of history, thriving by the wayside, or even underground, but still engaged in the polity, as Hosea wished his own followers to live. (Hos 2:14–15, 14)

In rough chronological terms, the day of Jesus' announcement of salvation and the kingdom-building resulting from it lasted from the time of John the Baptist through the life time of the apostles. After that there

---

78. Seow, "Book of Hosea," 296.

Biblical Captivity

was clearly enough a time of darkness and decline, wherein the people saw the destruction of the second temple and the end of Israel's frail existence as a nation under Greco-Roman hegemony. (Matt 24) Jesus suggests there is an unlikely possibility that the ensuing time of desolation would be abbreviated so as to save some people's lives, but, at least, for those who practice freedom, "those days shall be shortened." (Matt 24:22)

The son of man, a political liberator to come after the long "two days" of tribulation outlined above, will come in a time and in a place where the people least expect him. (Matt 24:26) Only then and there will the elect among the people, scattered much like in the prediction of Hosea, "gather together." (Matt 24:31) This time will be in a day of great wickedness, as in the day of Noah. (Matt 24:36–44)

Jesus made another variation on the captivity theme of Hosea. Salvation comes not merely every third day, but to every third man and woman. (Matt 24:40–41) Two of the three apparently care not for political and religious freedom, and are happy enough to live without it. The political cycles of Hosea and Jesus, then, together cover political/civic salvation in both time and space. The Sadducees and Pharisees of Jesus have already returned to Egypt, because they willingly accept life empowered by Roman imperial rule of Judea. The Zealots, on the other hand, are equally short-sighted in that they hope to pull off a physical revolt that cannot succeed. Only education and promotion of the Decalogue in Judea and throughout the nations can hope to bring about peace and self-government. (Matt 5:17–20, 19:17, 23:23; John 14:15) The worst condition of all is when the people replace the "worship" of the freedom commandments of God with worship of the person and perquisites of a despotic king, the "abomination of desolation" spoken of in the book of Daniel. (Matt 24:15; Dan 9:.27, 11:31, 12:11)

Jesus makes clear his concern about the inevitable spiritualization of the sacred story of good news he reports to the people—the removal of its interpretation from the civic and political realm. He says it is persecution of ethical political thought and practice that forms the content of the two days tribulation, and that it is perpetrated by two people out of three. In order to fix in the minds of his hearers that political captivity is the focus of his doctrine and message, he indicates that whoever his followers "shalt loose on earth shall be loosed in heaven." (Matt 16:19, 18:18) By this he suggests that loosing the bonds of captivity on earth is the kind of loosing that is promoted by and hoped for in heaven.

Bibliography

Albertz, Rainer. *A History of Israelite Religion in the Old Testament Period: From the Beginnings to the End of the Monarchy*. Translated by J. Bowden. Louisville: Westminster John Knox, 1994.
Albright, William F. *From the Stone Age to Christianity: Monotheism and the Historical Process*. Baltimore: The Johns Hopkins Press, 1946.
Anderson, Bernhard W. *Understanding the Old Testament*. 3d. ed. Englewood Cliffs, NJ: Prentice Hall, 1975.
——— "Covenant." In *OCB*, 139.
Avalos, Hector. *Fighting Words: The Origins of Religious Violence*. Amherst, New York: Prometheus, 2005.
Bailey, Kenneth E. "Trace and Transport." In *OCB*, 748.
Barr, James, "Politics and the Bible." In *OCB*, 599–600.
Bauer, Susan Wise. *The History of the Ancient World: From the Earliest Accounts to the Fall of Rome*. New York: W.W. Norton, 2007.
Bellah, Robert. "Civil Religion in America," Daedalus 96:1, 1–22.
Braund, David C. "Herodian Dynasty." In *ABD* 3:174.
Brichto, Herbert C. *The Problem of "Curse" in the Hebrew Bible*. Philadelphia: Society of Biblical Literature and Exegesis, 1963.
Brueggemann, Walter. *The Land: Place as Gift, Promise, and Challenge in Biblical Faith*. Minneapolis: Fortress, 2002.
———, *Genesis*. Atlanta: John Knox, 1982.
Cockerill, Gareth L. "Judges." In *ABD* 3:1090–91.
Cohen, Nick. "God Spare Us the Queen," Time, May 16, 2011, 56.
Collins, J.J. *Does the Bible Justify Violence?* Minneapolis: Fortress, 2004.
Conrad, Edgar W. "Curse." In *OCB*, 144–45.
Coogan, Michael D. *The Old Testament: A Historical and Literary Introduction to the Hebrew Scriptures*. New York: Oxford University Press, 2006.
Cowles, C.S. et al. *Show Them No Mercy: 4 Views on God and Canaanite Genocide*. Grand Rapids: Zondervan, 2003.
D'Emilio, Frances. "Pope calls Christians the most persecuted." *Yahoo! News*, December 16, 2010.
Dorsey, David A. *The Roads and Highways of Ancient Israel*. Baltimore: Johns Hopkins University Press, 1991.
Eichler, Barry L. "Nuzi Tablets." In *OCB*, 563.
Eidsmoe, John. *God and Caesar: Christian Faith and Political Action*. Westchester,

Bibliography

IL:Crossway, 1984.
Ehrlich, Carl S. "Law, Israelite." In *OCB*, 421.
Ehrman, Bart D. *The New Testament: A Historical Introduction to the Early Christian Writings*. 3d. ed. New York: Oxford University Press, 2004.
Ellis, Elisabeth G., and Esler, Anthony. *World History: Connections to Today*. Upper Saddle River, NJ: Prentice Hall, 2003.
Ellis, Robert R. *Learning to Read Biblical Hebrew: An Introductory Grammar*. Waco, TX: Baylor University Press, 2006.
Garnsey, P.D.A., and C.R. Whittaker, eds. *Imperialism in the Ancient World*. Cambridge: Cambridge University Press, 1978.
Goldenberg, Robert. *The Nations That Know Thee Not: Ancient Jewish Attitudes Toward Other Religions*. New York: New York University Press, 1998.
Gottwald, Norman K. *The Politics of Ancient Israel*. Louisville: Westminster John Knox, 2001.
——, *All the Kingdoms of the Earth: Israelite Prophecy and International Relations in the Ancient Near East*. New York: Harper & Row, 1964.
——, *The Tribes of Yahweh: A Sociology of the Religion of Liberated Israel, 1250–1050 BCE*. Sheffield: Sheffield Academic Press, 1999.
Habel, Norman C. *The Land Is Mine*. Minneapolis: Fortress, 1995.
Halpern, Baruch. *The First Historians: The Hebrew Bible and History*. San Francisco: Harper and Row, 1988.
——, "Kenites." In *ABD*, 4:17–22.
Healy, Gene. *The Cult of the Presidency: America's Dangerous Devotion to Executive Power*. Washington D.C.: Cato, 2008.
Hendawi, Hemza, "Christian-Muslim clashes in Egypt kill 13," *Yahoo! News*, March 9, 2011.
Herring, George C. *From Colony to Superpower: U.S. Foreign Relations since 1776*. New York: Oxford University Press, 2008.
Herzog, Chaim, and Mordechai Gichon. *Battles of the Bible: A Military History of Ancient Israel*. New York: Fall River, 2006.
Hiebert, Theodore. "Warrior, Divine." In *ABD*, 6:877.
Hoffmeier, James K. *Israel in Egypt: The Evidence for the Authenticity of the Exodus Tradition*. New York: Oxford University Press, 1996.
Horsley, Richard A. *Jesus and Empire: the Kingdom of God and the New World Disorder*. Minneapolis: Fortress, 2003.
——, *Bandits, Prophets, and Messiahs: Popular Movements at the Time of Jesus*. Harrisburg: Trinity, 1999.
Hutton, Rodney R. "Korah." In *ABD*, 4:101.
Isaac, Benjamin, and Aharon Oppenheimer, "Bar Kokhba." In *ABD*, 1:599.
Janzen, Waldemar. *Old Testament Ethics: A Paradigmatic Approach*. Louisville: Westminster John Knox, 1994.
Jenni, Ernst, and Claus Westermann. *Theological Lexicon of the Old Testament*. Translated by M. Biddle. Peabody, MA: Hendrickson, 1997, 2004.
Josephus, *Jewish Antiquities*.
Josephus, *Jewish War*.
Jurgensmeyer, Mark. *Terror in the Mind of God: the Global Rise of Religious Violence*. 3d. ed. Berkeley: University of California Press, 2003.
Kent, Charles Foster. *Israel's Laws and Legal Precedents; From the Days of Moses to*

the Closing of the Legal Canon. New York: Charles Scribner's Sons, 1925.
Kiernan, V.G. *America The New Imperialism; From White Settlement to World Hegemony.* New York: Verso, 1978, 2005.
Kitchen, K.A. "The Exodus." In *ABD*, 2:708.
Klassen, William. "War in the New Testament." In *ABD*, 6:868.
Knauf, Ernst A. "Manahath." In *ABD*, 4:493.
Knight, Douglas A. "Hebrews." In *OCB*, 273.
Kuhrt, Amelie E. *The Ancient Near East: c. 3000–330 BC.* London: Routledge, 1995.
Levine, L.I. "Herod the Great." In *ABD*, 3:168.
Lewis, Sian, ed. *Ancient Tyranny.* Edinburgh: Edinburgh University Press, 2006.
Mathews, Victor H., and Don C. Benjamin. *Old Testament Parallels: Laws and Stories from the Ancient Near East.* 3rd. ed. Mahwah, NJ: Paulist, 2006.
Meyers, Carol. *Exodus.* New York: Cambridge University Press, 2005.
Milgrom, Jacob. *Leviticus.* Minneapolis: Fortress, 2004.
Millard, A.R. "Abraham." In *ABD*, 1:37–40.
Miller, J. Maxwell. "Israel, History of." In *OCB*, 330.
Nielsen, Eduard. *The Ten Commandments in New Perspective: A Tradition-historical Approach.* Translated by David J. Bourke. Naperville, IL: Allenson, 1968.
Noss, John B. *Man's Religions.* 5th ed. New York: Macmillan, 1974.
Pilgrim, Walter E. *Uneasy Neighbors; Church and State in the New Testament.* Minneapolis: Fortress, 1999.
Plumley, J. Andrew. "Egypt." In *OCB*, 181.
Pritchard, James B., ed. *Ancient Near Eastern Texts Relating to the Old Testament.* 3d. ed. Princeton: Princeton University Press, 1969.
Propp, William H. "Wilderness." In *OCB*, 798–99.
Rajak, Tessa. "Hasmonean Dynasty." In *ABD*, 3:67–76.
Redford, Donald B. "Hyksos." In *ABD*, 3:341.
Riley, Patrick G.D. *Civilizing Sex: On Chastity and the Common Good.* Edinburgh: T&T Clark, 2000.
Rowe, C. Kavin. *World Upside Down: Reading Acts in the Graeco-Roman Age.* New York: Oxford University Press, 2009.
Schipper, Jeremy. *Parables and Conflict in the Hebrew Bible.* Cambridge: Cambridge University Press, 2009, reviewed in Review of Biblical Literature by the Society of Biblical Literature, April, 2011.
Schwartz, Regina M. *The Curse of Cain: The Violent Legacy of Monotheism.* Chicago: The University of Chicago Press, 1997.
Segal, Ben-Zion, and Gershon Levi, eds. *The Ten Commandments in History and Tradition.* Jerusalem: Magness, 1990.
Seow, C.L. "Hosea, Book of." In *ABD*, 3:296.
Shane, Scott. "Hearing Puts Muslims in Hot Seat." *New York Times News Service*, March 12, 2011.
Smith-Christopher, Daniel L. *A Biblical Theology of Exile.* Minneapolis: Fortress, 2002.
Smith, Morton. *Palestinian Parties and Politics That Shaped the Old Testament.* New York: Columbia University Press, 1971.
Speiser, E.A. *Genesis: A New Translation with Introduction and Commentary*, New York: Doubleday, 1964.
Spinoza, Baruch. *Theological-Political Treatise (Gebhardt Edition)*, 2nd ed. Translated by S. Shirley. Indianapolis: Hackett, 2001.

Bibliography

Strange, James F. "Magdala." In *ABD*, 4:463–64.
Strassler, Robert B. ed. *The Landmark Herodotus: The Histories*. Translated by A.L. Purvis. New York: Anchor, 2009.
Stuart, Douglas. "Curse." In *ABD*, 1:1218.
Terrien, Samuel. *The Elusive Presence: Toward a New Biblical Theology*. Eugene, OR: Wipf and Stock Publisher, 2000.
Trible, Phyllis. *Texts of Terror: Literary-Feminist Readings of Biblical Narratives*. Philadelphia: Fortress, 1984.
Vaux, Roland de. *Ancient Israel: Its Life and Institutions*. Translated by John McHugh. Livonia, MI: Dove, 1997.
Walzer, Michael. *Exodus and Revolution*. Basic, 1985.
Weinfeld, Moshe. *Social Justice in Ancient Israel and in the Ancient Near East*. Jerusalem; Magness, 1995.
———, "Deuteronomy." *In Anchor Bible Dictionary*, 1:292.
Wells, Bruce, and F. Rachel Magdalene, eds. *Laws from the Tigris to the Tiber: the Writings of Raymond Westbrook*, vol. 1, Winona Lake, IN: Eisenbrauns, 2009.
Wendorf, Fred, and Angela E. Close. "Egypt, History of." In *ABD*, 2:333.
Westbrook, Raymond, and Bruce Wells. E*veryday Law in Biblical Israel; An Introduction*, Louisville: Westminster John Knox, 2009.
Williams, James G. *The Bible, Violence, and the Sacred: Liberation from the Myth of Sanctioned Violence*. Eugene, OR: Wipf and Stock, 2007.
Witherington, Ben III. "Herodias." In *ABD*, 3:175.
Zevit, Ziony. *The Religions of Ancient Israel: A Synthesis of Parallactic Approaches*. London: Continuum, 2001.

Index

A

Aaron, 59–60, 76n49, 115–16, 118–23, 141
Abel, 8, 16–17, 53–55
Abiathar, 44
Abimelech, 4–7, 57, 80–81, 126, 143
Abiram, 115, 118–23
Abomination of Desolation, 139, 142, 187
abomination theory, 70–73
Abraham
    curses of, 114
    family quarrels of, 50
    intrigue against, 61–62
    Lot and, 56–57, 80, 84
    migration to Canaan, 1–3, 82, 99–100
    as patriarch, 49
    peaceful coexistence sought by, 16–17
    sister ruse used by, 62–65
    socio-political ethics of, 10–11, 56–57
Absalom, 94n17, 127–28, 143
Achaia, 188
Achaioi Phthiotai, 40
Achan, 126
Acts, book of
    bondage vocabulary in, 23
    captivity in, 186–89
    rebellions in, 161–62
    themes in, 18
Adad-nirari, 39, 132
Adam, 53–54
Adonijah, 128, 143

Adullamites, 126
Afghanistan, 84
aggression, in ancient Israel, xxiii
Agni, 34
Agrippa I and II, 153, 161
Ahab
    captivity narrative and, 8, 43–44
    civic government and, 143
    revolt against, x, xvi, 84, 130–31
    tyranny of, 145–46, 152
Ahaz, 43, 133, 146, 153
Ahijah, 95, 128–30
Akhtoy I, xvii, 45
Alexander Jannaeus, 150
Alexander of Pherae, 40, 142
Alexander the Great, 83, 134, 138–39
alliances, captivity and formation of, 16–18
Amalekites, 17, 123–24, 125, 127
Amaziah, 132–33
Amenhotep III, 31
Amenmhet, 61–62
Amish, 82
Ammi-Saduqa, 100
Ammonites, 123–24, 127, 132–33, 136
Amorites, 4–7, 123–24
Amos, 132–33, 195
ancient Near East
    early historical science in, 109–14
    fear of internal captivity in, 41–47
    molten idolatry in, 140–43
    religious and political violence in, 24–47, 52–61
    religious liberty in, 98–101
ancient world, dual menaces in, xvii–xviii

203

Index

Anthony, Marc, 155
Antiochus Epiphanes, 42, 43, 139, 142, 154
Antipater, 160
apiru/Hapiru, 71
apocalyptic curses, Biblical language of, 22–23
Apostles, captivity in work of, 186–89
Arabah rift valley, 122n15
Arabs, 132
Arad, King of, 123–24
Archelaus, 153
Ares (Greek god), 29
Aristotle, 28
Asa, King, 130, 132, 145
Ashurnasirpal, 39–40
Asoka, 40
Assyria
    captivity narratives and, 9–10, 70, 103
    expansion of, 84–85, 133–34
    human rights in, 99–100
    imperial violence of, 36–37
    Israeli alliance against, 25
Athaliah, 130, 132, 143, 146
Athronges, 158, 182
Augustus Caesar (Octavian), 151, 155–56
autocratic conditions, in ancient Israel, 25
Avalos, Hector, xiv–xv
Azariah (Uzziah), 133, 146

B

Baalism
    Biblical opposition to, xi–xii
    cruelty of, 34–35
    indigenous Canaanite culture of, 4–7
    in Israel, 32–33
    as Israeli state religion, 132
    in Judah, 130
    Moabite establishment of, 8
    Seth (Egyptian diety) and, 35, 50, 69, 73
    terminology of, xiin12
Baasha, 130–31
Babylon
    ancient Israel's conflict with, 9–10, 19, 25, 36
    Assyrian oppression of, 31
    expansion by, 134
    as firstborn culture, 30–31
    hegemony over Judah of, 136, 196
    internal captivity in, 43–44, 85
    Israeli assimilation in, 137–40
    Persian conquest of, 40
Balaam, 124
Balak of Moab, 123–24
baptism, 186, 192
Bar Kokhba revolt, 158, 159, 163
Barr, James, xxiii
Bashaan, 123–24
battles, Biblical vocabulary concerning, 21
Bel and the Dragon, 58
Benedict XVI (Pope), xix
Benhadad, 130–31
Benjamin, 44
Benjaminites, 44, 83, 126
Bernice, 153
Bible. See also New Testament, Old Testament, and specific books
    captivity as focus of, 15–18
    compilations of, 76–77
    curses in, 109–14
    fear of internal captivity in, 41–47
    imperial captivity in Second temple period and, 135–40
    political lessons for modern nations in, xviii–xxiii
    violence in, ix–xi
    vocabulary of fear in, 19–23
Biblical religion and politics, xi–xiii
Bill of Rights, 97
"bitter water" test, 112–13
body counts, in Bible, 10
bondage, Biblical vocabulary of, 22–23
Book of the Covenant, 92–93
boundary formation, monotheism and, xiii–xiv
Bourne, Randolph, 26

Index

bread and wine, Jesus' use of, 192
Buddha, xvn20
burning bush, narrative of, 67–69
Bush, G. W., 32

C

Cain, 8, 16–17, 53–55, 60, 119–21
Caligula, 142–43, 156, 161
Cambyses, 40, 137
Canaan
    dissidents and indigenous populations in, 77–86
    geography of, 78–79
    Hebrew history in, 70–73
    internal captivity in, 42
    Israeli community in, 24, 53
    Joshua's expansion into, 124–25
    migrations to, 1–7, 13–14
    religious rivalries in, 57–61
    tribal settlements in, 14–15
    violence in, x–xi, xin5
    war and oppression in, 1–7
captivity
    Apostles' view of, 186–89
    Biblical focus on, 15–18
    constitutional law curbs on, 106–9
    cruelty in, 34–41
    curses and, 109–14
    fear of, 19–23, 37–38
    foundational stories, 48–86
    imperial captivity in Second Temple period, 135–40
    Jesus' concern over, 169–77
    in King James Bible, 6–7, 6n10
    in New Testament, 8–18, 148–98
    in Old Testament era, 115–47
    permanence of, 102–3
    prevention in Israel of, xxii, 8–15
    tyranny in Mediterranean and, 146–47
Cassius, 142–43
central government structure
    Biblical references to, 11
    internal captivity and, 16
    Jesus' criticism of, 177–82

Chaldea, 31
Cheops (Kahfre), 45
China
    political dissoluteness in, 45–47
    religion and politics in, 34
    slavery in, 39
Christian apocrypha, 158
Christian persecution
    apostles' account of, 186–89
    in modern Muslim countries, xix–xx
    new light politics and, 189–93
    in Roman empire, 155–56
Chronicles, book of, 17
    genealogies in, 70–71
    socio-political ethics in, 24–25
    vocabulary of fear in, 19
Cicero, 28
circumcision, 39, 76–77, 163
citizenship
    in Decalogue, 96–98, 108–9, 177–78
    Jesus' view of, 175–77
    Jesus' vision of, 178–82
    resistance to oppression and, 194–98
    salvation through, 182–85
civic government and society
    Biblical sources for, 7
    Israeli descriptions of, 10–15
    Jesus' concern over, 164–77
    Jesus' political method and, 177–82
    religion and, 141–43
    Ten Commandments and, 5–7
class politics, Biblical political lessons concerning, xxi–xxiii
Claudius, 156
cleansing of the temple, Jesus' act of, 194–95
client-friendships
    Jesus' criticism of, 177–82
    Roman empire and, 147–54
Clinton, Hillary, xix
Code of Hammurabi, xvn20
coins
    king's images on, 142, 151
    minting of, 150

205

Index

colonialism, migration patterns and, 82
Common Era, 84
Confucius, xvn20
Constantine, 156
constitutional kingship, freedom, and corruption, xviii
constitutional law
    Canaan settlements and, 3–7
    Exodus and Sinai experiences and, xxii–xxiii
    hospitality principles in, 83–84
    Israeli disregard of, 24–25
    Jesus' view of, 163–77
    neglect of, 197–98
    prevention or restriction of captivity and, 106–9
    Sinai and establishment of, 89–98
    Ten Commandments as, 5–7
    threats to, 124–35
"corvee" (conscripted) labor, xvii, 43–47, 89–99
Covenant Code, 91–93, 177
Covenant Code curses, 101–5
Crassus, 160
creation narrative, 53, 60–61
cross-religion political aggression and intolerance, in ancient Israel, 9–10
crucifixion, 157–61
cruelty of imperial gods, 34–41
curses and cursing
    in Decalogue, 101–5
    political and corporate cursing, 109–14
Cyrus, 31, 43, 134, 136–37

D

Dagon, 35
Damascus, 127–28, 131
Daniel, 58, 114, 137, 139, 198
Darius, 40
Dathan, 115, 118–23
David (Biblical king)
    Absalom and, 94n17, 127–28
    decline of, 143
    expansion of monarchy by, 30n18
    forced labor under, 44
    government of, 94–95
    life of, 50
    national draft registration of, xvii
    religious rivalry and, 60
    Saul and, 60, 82, 127
    Sinhue compared with, 62
    tyrannical practices of, 145–47, 153
day of renewal, 195–98
Dead Sea Scrolls, 173
death, Biblical promise of, x–xi
Deborah, 42, 84, 125, 159
Decalogue. *See* Ten Commandments
Demetrius II, 149
democratic society
    ancient Israel as, 25, 28–29
    constitutional law and, 89, 106–9
    Decalogue provisions for, 91
    Moses' vision of, 75–77, 115–17
    in Rome, 154–56
    Shasu people, 71
    Yahweh's identification with, 69
Demosthenenes, 28
Deuteronomy, book of, 17
    curses in, 110
    Decalogue in, 90, 92–93
    history in, 96–97
    Kadesh narrative and, 117–18
    monotheism in, 27–29
    Moses' discussion of, 102
    oppression discussed in, 56
    political theory in, 29
    Sermon on the Mount influenced by, 168–71
    on slavery and servitude, 107–9
    vocabulary of fear in, 19
Diaspora uprisings, 159
Dinah, 59, 62, 81
Diocletian, 156
disabled, in Biblical narratives, 51–52
Do My Prophets No Harm: Revelation and Religious Liberty in the Bible (Shinkoskey), xvii–xviii, xxi
Domitian, 156, 188
droit de seigneur (right of the Lord), 63

Index

Ducetius, 146

E

Eannatum, 38
Eber, 70–71
Ecclesiastes, Book of, 18, 139
ecclesiastic diversity, Biblical focus on, 14–15
economic conditions
    in Decalogue, 106–9
    fear of decline in, 20–23
    imperialism and, 33–34
Edom, 93, 123–25, 127–28, 132–33
education
    for citizenship, 182–85
    in Decalogue, 177–78
    Jesus' use of, 178–82
Egypt
    Amarna age in, 32
    circumcision practices in, 76
    cruelty of leaders in, 39
    First Dynasty of, 35, 44
    as firstborn nation, 31–32
    gods of, 33–34, 50
    internal captivity in, 44–45
    internecine violence in, 26
    Israeli alliance with, 24–25
    legal code of, 90
    Middle Kingdom of, 45
    minorities in, 70–73
    Moses in, 66–69
    New Kingdom of, 32
    Old Kingdom of, 45
    oppression of Israelites in, xvii–xviii, 36–41
    Persian conquest of, 40
    political marriages in, 145
    religious liberty in, 98
    Second Dynasty in, 44
    Sinuhe story in, 61–62
    war and religion in, 27–28
Egyptian (Jewish) prophet, 158
Ehud, 125
Elah, 131
Elam (Aratta), 35, 38, 70

Eleazar, 159–60
Eli, 44
Elijah, x, 84, 130, 131, 159, 195
end-of-prophecy doctrine, 190–93
Enlil (god), 35, 44
Enmerker, 33
Enmetena of Lagash, 99
Ephraim, 78, 83–84, 133
Ephraimites, 126
Epiphanes, 176
Esarhaddon, 41, 100
Esau, 49, 58–59, 80
Eshnunna, 99
Essene community, 82, 138, 150–51, 158, 162–63, 171, 173
Esther, story of, xin6, 18, 63, 137
ethnicity and religious affiliation, 76–77. See also minority groups
Euphron, 146
Eve, 53
exile
    Biblical vocabulary concerning, 22–23
    captivity vs., 6–7
Exodus, book of
    bondage vocabulary in, 22–23
    captivity narrative in, x, 9, 17
    Decalogue in, 89–90, 92–93
    internal captivity in, 43
    Kadesh narrative in, 117
    political ethics in, 65–69, 74–77
    secession narrative in, 60–61
external captivity
    Biblical focus on, 15–18
    in New Testament, 172–77
    permanence of, 103
Ezekiel, book of, 41, 43, 104–5, 110, 136, 192–93
Ezra, 14, 18, 92n15, 137–38

F

Fadus, 161
faith, Jesus on, 171
family quarrels
    Biblical depictions of, 47–52, 57–61

207

Index

family quarrels (*continued*)
    in Kadesh, 117–23
    sibling rivalries, in Bible, xiii–xiv, 48–54
fear
    ancient court of, 61–62
    of internal captivity, 41–47
    vocabulary of, 19–23
Felix, 161
Festival of Booths, 19
Fifth Commandment, religious freedom and local government in, 13–15, 179–80
First Commandment
    apostles' invocation of, 186–89
    blasphemy in, 89–90
    civil rights protected by, xviii
    freedom politics in, 12–13
    government guidelines in, 93–94
    humane law in context of, xxii
    interpretations of, 76–77, 96–97
    Jesus' teaching and, 167, 172, 175, 195
    monotheism in, 27–28
    political ethics in, 96
    religious liberty in, 76n49, 106n44, 107–9
    separation of church and state in, 92
First Dynasty of Kish, 45
First Jewish War, 158–59, 162–63
firstborn nation, political concept of, 30–34
Flaminus, 31
flight, Biblical vocabulary concerning, 21–22
flood narrative, 55–56, 88–89
foreign policy, 93
foundational stories
    captivity in, 48–86
    day of renewal in, 195
    Jesus' interest in, 166–77
    politics and violence in, xxii–xxiii
    religious rivalry in, 52–61
Fourth Commandment, 106n44, 107–9
freedom
    fear over loss of, 20–23
    internal captivity and deprivation of, 43–47
    Jesus' proclamation of, 171–77
    prophets' advocacy of, xviii, 12–15
    of religion, 7–15, 92–101
    Ten Commandments emphasis on, 91–98
friendship treaties, fear of, 41

G

Galilee, 157, 159–60
Gamaliel, 187
Garden of Eden, 53, 110
Gedaliah, 136
genealogies, in Bible, 70–73
genealogies in Genesis, 70–71
Genesis, book of, 16–17, 60–61, 70–71
Gerar of Canaan, 61–62
Gesius Florus, 162
Ghandi, Mahatma, 51–52
Gibeon, 43, 126
Gideon, 12, 84, 125–26, 159
Gilead, 126, 131
Gilgamesh, xvii, 33, 63
God. *See also* Yahweh
    consequences of disobedience to, 110–14
    Jesus' vision of, 170–71
    secular rights guaranteed by, 94n16
gods. *See also specific gods and cults*
    bickering of, 50
    captivity of, 107–9
    cruelty of, 34–41
    imperialism of, 32–34
    war among, 26–29
Golden Calf, 59–60, 115–16
Goshen, Moses in, 74–77
Gospels
    Jesus ministry in, 165–77
    political ethics in, 18
Gottwald, Norman K., 135–36
government. *See also* central government structure; civic government and society; local

government; Mosaic covenant
of government; self-government
Decalogue guidelines for, 91–98
Jesus' concern over, 164–77
limited government, Biblical ideal
of, 11
Gracchus brothers, 155
Greece
internal captivity under, 42, 46
Israel under, 9–10, 97–98, 138
judges in, 144
molten idolatry in, 141–43
Persian conflicts with, 38
political theory in, 28–29
Roman oppression of, 31
tyranny in, 143–47
war epics in, 27

H

Habakkuk, 173
Hadad, 34, 128
Hadrian, 156, 163
Hagar, 49, 57–58
Haggai, 137
Ham, 70
Hamath, 127
Hammurabi, 30–31, 91, 100
Hasidim, 172–73
Hasmonean dynasty, 44, 134, 140, 143, 149–51, 192
Hebrews
curses of, 112
history of, 70–73
Hellenism, pagan, 151
Heraclitus, 25–26
Herod, 42, 44, 151–56, 160, 190
Herod Antipas, 153
Herod Phillip, 153
Herodias, 153
Herodotus, 44–45, 63
Hesiod, 28, 29, 46
Hezekiah, 24, 133–34, 146, 159
Hieron, 142
Hiram of Tyre, 145
Hittites, 71–72, 98, 100

Holiness Code, 93
holocaust, memory of, 19
Homeric epics, 27
homicide, in Biblical foundation
narratives, 52–61
Horus, 26, 35
Hosea, 22, 82, 133, 195–98
Hoshea, 133, 181
hospitality, in Biblical narratives, 82–86
human rights
in ancient Near East, 98–101
culture in ancient Israel of, xvi
internal captivity and deprivation
of, 43–47
Jesus' concern over, 164–77
in Ten Commandments, 96–97
tyranny and, 146
Hurrians, 72
Hyksos, 35, 71–72
Hyrcanus II, 150
Hyrcanus, John, 150

I

idolatry
laws against, 89, 95n19, 137
molten idolatry, 140–43
imperialism
of ancient deities, 34–41
justification for, in ancient Near
East, 30–34
Inanna, 34–35
independence, Biblical references to, 11
India
kings in, 40
village politics in, 28–29
internal captivity
Biblical focus on, 15–18
Biblical vocabulary concerning, 20–23
fear of, 41–47
in New Testament, 172–77
permance of, 103
political secession and, 60–61
international marriages, xiii–xvi, 145–47

Index

international trade
   in Biblical era, 78–79
   between Greece and Israel, 143–44
Ireland, religious violence in, xx
Isaac
   Ishmael and, 57–58, 80
   migrations of, 82
   as patriarch, 49
   peaceful coexistence sought by, 16–17
   sacrifice of, 52
   sister ruse used by, 62–65
Isaiah (prophet), 166–67, 173, 195
Isaiah I, 104, 133
Isaiah II, 43, 60, 136, 137, 141, 167
Ishmael, 49, 57–58, 60, 80
Ishme-Dagan, 38, 44, 99
Israel
   Baalism in, 32–33
   Canaan settlements of, 77–86
   internal captivity in, 43–47
   intolerance and aggression in, 9
   prevention of captivity in, 8–15
   religious violence in modern state of, xx
"ius primae noctis" (law/right of the first night), 63

J

Jacob
   in Canaan, 81–82
   Hebrew genealogy and, 71
   as patriarch, 49
   rivalry with Esau, 58–59, 61–62, 65
Janus, 35
Jefferson, Thomas, 28
Jehoahaz, 132
Jehoash, 132
Jehoiakim, King, 108, 136, 181
Jehoshaphat, 130–32
Jehu, x, 81, 84, 114, 130–32, 159
Jephthah, 125–26
Jeremiah, 82, 86, 105, 108–11, 134, 136, 168–69
Jeroboam, 81, 94n17, 95, 128–31, 141

Jeroboam II, 132–33
Jerubbabel, 134
Jerusalem
   Assyrian siege of, 8–9
   Jesus in, 165–77
Jesus ben Hananiah, 158
Jesus Ben Sira, 140, 196n77
Jesus of Nazareth
   avoidance of violence by, 114
   captivity narratives and, 9, 18, 42
   on citizenship as salvation, 182–85
   cleansing of the temple by, 194–95
   on curses, 111–12
   on Hosea's prophecies, 197–98
   hospitality of, 83
   on human rights, 92n15
   Judaic constitutional culture and, 153–54
   on laws, 102
   new light politics and, 189–93
   persecution of, 186–89
   political method of, 177–82
   religious rivalries and, 52
   resistance to oppression and, 193–98
   Roman rule and story of, 154–63
   socio-political protests of, 60
   temptations and Sermon of, 163–77, 192–93
   Ten Commandments and, 148–54
Jethro, 119
Jezebel, xvi, 8
Joash, 132
Job, book of, 18, 60
Joel, 79, 196
John (apostle), 186–87
John the Baptist
   captivity narrative and, 9, 18, 42
   constitutional law and, 153
   end-of-prophecy doctrine and, 190, 193
   on freedom, 171–73
   political ethic of, 82, 158–63
   Ten Commandments and, 148
Jonah, 22
Jonathan, 149–50
Joram, King, 130, 132

Index

Joseph, 8, 49, 59–60, 103
Josephus, 153, 159, 162
Joshua
    blessings and curses described by, 101
    heroism of, 137
    internal captivity and, 43
    occupation of Canaan planned by, 124–25
    political resistance of, x–xi, 84
    religious rivalry and, 17, 59–60
Josiah, 24, 81, 92n15, 95, 118n11, 134, 159
Jotham, 110n5, 133
Jubilee law, 95
Judah, 128–35, 137–40
Judas Maccabee, 81, 149, 157–59, 182
Jude, book of, 119
Judea
    conquests of, 9, 78, 134–35, 149–54
    Rome and, 155–63, 178
Judges, book of, 84
    constitutional government in, 124–35
    decline of Israel in, 195
    politico-religious jealousy in, 17
    socio-political ethics in, 24–25, 81–83
judgment
    Biblical days of, 95–96
    governance as, 28–29
    of Jesus, 194–98
Jesus on, 171
Judith, story of, xin6
Julius Caesar, 25, 155
justice, political theory concerning, 25–26

K

Kadesh, sojourn in, 89, 93, 117–24
Kahfre (Cheops), 45
Kenites, 71, 101, 119
Kennedy, John F., 31
Khufu, 45

King James Bible, captivity vocabulary in, 6–7, 6n10, 23
kings and kingship
    Canaanite migration and, 3–7
    captivity of, xxii
    democratic antipathy to, 125–35
    gods' behavior resembling, 27
    human rights policies and, 99–101
    internal captivity under, 41–47
    Jesus' prophesies concerning, 173–77
    molten idolatry and, 141–43
    political theory and, 28–29
    sister ruse against violence by, 63–65
    state religion and, 12
    terror and capricious justice in, 61–62
    tyranny in Mediterranean world and, 143–47
    violence and cruelty of, 35–41
Kings, book of
    constitutional government in, 124–35
    covenant laws in, 17
    political power in, xv
    socio-political ethics in, 24–25
Korah, 61, 82, 118–23
Kurdish culture, 63, 84

L

labor
    "corvee" (conscripted), xvii, 43–47, 89–99
    in Ten Commandments, 106–9
Lamech, 54–55
Lamentations, book of, 41, 136
land allocation
    in Decalogue, 108–9
    political power and, 3–7, 11
latifundia, 155
laughter, in Bible, 57–58
Laws of Deuteronomy, 92–93
Laws of Manu, xvn20
Lenin, V. I., 25

Index

Lesson to Guests (Jesus), 194
Levi, 59, 121
Levites, 14, 67, 83, 117, 126
Leviticus, book of, 17, 95, 108
Libnah, 132
limited government, Biblical ideal of, 11
Lipit-Ishtar, 99
literary prophets, xvi
Livy, 28
local government
  Israeli political ethic of, 9–15
  Jesus' promotion of, 179–82
  Moses' vision of democracy and, 117–23
  tribal commitment to, 121n14
Locke, John, 28
Lot
  Abraham and, 56–57, 80, 84
  capture of, xin5, 9, 49
  political preferences of, 11
Lugulannemundu, 38
Luke, gospel of, 168, 174–76, 186

M

Maccabees, book of, 95, 134–35
Maccabees, revolt of, 9, 42, 84, 138, 140, 149, 159–60, 176
Macedonia, 31, 139
Machiavelli, 25
Magdala (Migdal), 160
Magi, visit of, 153–54
Malachi, 196
Manasseh, xvi, xvii, 44, 100, 133, 143, 153
Manetho, 45
manufacturing, in Biblical era, 79
manumission
  in constitutional law, 106–9
  language in Decalogue of, 93, 95
Marcus Aurelius, 156
Marduk, 34, 69
Mari, 95
martyrdom, Jesus' discussion of, 183–85

Mary Magdalene, 160
Masada, 160
Mattathias, 84, 149
Matthew, gospel of, 22–23, 153–54, 168, 174–75
Medes, 40
Melchizedek, 80
Menahem, 133, 146
Mennonites, 82
Mephibosheth, 51–52, 60
mercenaries, in tyrannical regimes, 143–47
mercy, Jesus on, 171
Merneptah, 83, 117, 125
Merodach-baladan, 31
Mesha, King, xvi
Mesopotamia
  creation theory in, 106–7
  Hebrews in, 70–73
  history of gods in, 32
  human rights in, xvii, 99–100
  imperial ideology in, 25
  Israel threatened by, 9, 125–26
  kings and kingship in, 28–29
  legal code in, 90–91
  violence in, 39
messianic kingship, Israelite dream of, 158
Micah (householder), 141
Micah, book of, 46, 131, 133, 195
Midian and Midianites
  Moses and, 61–62, 66, 88, 90, 119
  threat to Israel from, 125
Migdal (Magdala), 160
migration
  Biblical images of, 82–86
  as socio-political-economic event, 88
Min (god), 98
minority groups
  in Biblical narratives, 55–56
  Hebrews as, 71–73
  inter-political relations and, 32
  Jesus concern over, 164–77
  oppression of, 150
Minos, King of Crete, 38
Miriam, 82, 115, 118

Index

Moab and Moabites, 4, 8–9, 93, 123–25, 127, 131–32
modern nations
    Biblical political lessons for, xviii–xxiii
    minority groups in, 32
    power theories in, 25
monetization, in ancient Israel, 33–34
monotheism
    ancient embrace of, 69
    Israel theology of, 27–29
    Mosaic monotheism, 1n1
    political ethics and, xii–xvi
Mosaic covenant of government
    Canaan migration and, 4–7
    Jesus' view of, 185
Mosaic monotheism, 1n1
Moses
    Aaron and, 59–60
    blessings and curses described by, 101
    on captivity, 103–5
    Exodus narrative and, 74–77
    Golden Calf and, 115–16
    Jesus' teachings influenced by, 174–77
    life of, 50–52
    Midian and, 61–62, 66, 88
    migration of, 3–7, 63–64
    oppression of, xvii–xviii, 10
    political ancestors of, 71–73
    political ethics of, 88–98, 159
    secular mission of, 65–69
Mu (king), 34
Muslims, and violence in modern era, xix–xxiii

N

Nabonidus, 31
Naboth narrative, 131, 146
Narmer, 39
Nathan, 145
nature worship, 73n41
Nebuchadnezzar, 9, 37, 40–41, 43, 83, 136, 146–47, 191–92
Neco (pharaoh), 134
Nehemiah, 42, 134, 137–38
Nero, 156, 162
new light politics, 189–93
The New Republic, 26
New Testament
    captivity as focus of, 148–98
    captivity narratives in, 8–18
    Christian view of, 163–77
    civic mission in, 18
    curses in, 111
Nicean Creed, 156
"Nine Bows" of Egypt, 32
Ninlil, 44
Ninurta, 44
Nippur, 33
Nisroch, 8
Noah, 88
Numbers, book of, 17, 112–13, 117
Nuzi tablets, 71

O

Obadiah, 85
Obama, Barack, 32
Octavian (Augustus Caesar), 151, 155–56
Old Testament
    captivity as focus of, 15–18, 115–47
    captivity narratives in, 8–15
    curses in, 112–14
    Sermon on the Mount influenced by, 168–69
    violence in, xi–xii
    vocabulary of fear in, 20–23
Omri, 114, 131–32
oppression
    of ancient Israelites, xxiii, 1–7, 24–25
    in ancient Near East, 148
    apostles' account of, 186–89
    Jesus concern over, 163–77
    justification for, in ancient Near East, 30–34
    prophet's calling concerning, 193–98

Index

oppression (*continued*)
    Ten Commandments and prevention of, xvii–xviii
Osiris (Egyptian god), 50, 98
Othniel, 125

P

pagan Hellenism, 151
Pakistan, 84
Palestine
    annexation to Syria, 151
    as bridge to Canaan, 78–79, 85–86
    captivity in Second Temple period of, 135–40
    Greek occupation of, 42, 169
    Hebrews in, 70–73
    political division and disunity in, 79–80
    Roman occupation of, 42, 156–63, 169
Parable of the Great Supper, 194
Parable of Leaven, 191–93
Parable of the Mustard Seed, 191–93
Parable of the Pearl of Great Price, 194
Parable of the Prodigal Son, 60
Parable of the Sower, 191–93
Parable of the Ten Pounds, 194
Parable of the Wicked Husbandman, 191–93
parent *vs.* child nation theory, 32–34
Passover, ritual of, 27, 76–77
patriarchal stories
    religious rivalry in, 49, 52–61
    religious tolerance in, 69
    sister ruse in, 62–65
Paul, 23, 148, 158, 161–62, 169–70, 172, 187–89
peace
    Biblical concepts of, 16–17, 49
    ethical law and, 29
    in foundational and patriarchal narratives, 52–61
    Jesus' vision of, 170–77, 177–82
Pekah, 133
Peloponnesian Wars, 38

penalty, curses as stipulations of, 111
Pentateuch
    captivity as focus of, 16–18
    secession narrative in, 60–61
Pentecost, 186
Peor people, 81
Pepi II, 28, 98
Pericles, 144
Persia
    conquest of Babylon, 40, 136–37
    expansion by, 134
    Greek conflict with, 38
    internal captivity under, 41–42
personal property, fear of assault on, 20–23
Peter, 172, 180–82, 186–87
Phalaris of Acragas, 141
Pharaoh. *See* specific Pharaohs, e.g. Ramses II
Pharisees, 138, 150, 173, 181–82, 187, 190, 198
Philistines/Philistia
    campaigns against, 127, 132–33
    Israel threatened by, 9, 125–26
    Samuel and, 97–98
Phillip the Tetrarch, 153
physical ordeal, practice of, 113–14
Pilate, Pontius, 27, 160–61, 182
Pisistratus, 144
pluralism
    Biblical support for, xiv–xvi
    first commandment promotion of, 13n17
    parables of Jesus and, 191–93
    in Ten Commandments, 93–98
Plutarch, 40
political ethics
    of Abraham, 10–11, 56–57
    in Bible, 24–25
    Biblical religion and, xi–xvi
    in Canaan, 77–86
    in Decalogue, 87–98, 91–98
    in Exodus, 65–69, 74–77
    Exodus and Sinai experiences and, xxii–xxiii
    in Gospels, 18
    of Jesus, 177–82

monotheism and, xii–xvi
in Second temple period, 135–40
violence in ancient Near East and, 24–47
political idolatry, and Canaanite migration, 4–7
Polybius, 25, 44
polytheistic imperialism, theory of, 26
Pompey, 25, 134–35, 150, 155, 191–92
power
    dispersion in Israel of, 125–35
    imperial examples of, 34–41
    Jesus' discussion of, 177–82
    political theory concerning, 25
    Roman concepts of, 155–63
    tyranny of kingship and, 143–47
presidential politics, and war, 26
Price, Richard, xv*n*21
prophets and prophecy
    curses outlined by, 105, 110–14
    freedom and corruption and described by, xviii
    on internal captivity, 41
    in Jesus' teachings, 175–77
    political ethics of, 10, 14–15, 158–63
    on prevention of captivity, 18
    religious rivalry and, 60
    resistance to oppression and, 193–98
Protestant Bible, 58
Proverbs, 18
Psalms, book of, 17, 105, 169
    bondage vocabulary in, 22–23
    lamentations of loss in, 10
    religious rivalry in, 59–60
Ptolemaic Greece, 9, 138–40
Ptolemy IV Philopator, 95
Ptolemy V, 95
Ptolemy VIII, 95
Punic Wars, 38
Purim, festival of, 19

Q

Quirinius, 159

R

Rabshakeh, 5, 8
Rahab, 126
Ramah, 130
Ramses II, 32, 43, 65, 69, 71, 73–77
Rechabites, 82
Rehoboam, xvi, 44, 64, 94n17, 95, 129, 143, 152
religion
    ancient Near East violence over, 24–47
    conflict and oppression and, xix–xxiii
    establishment by kings, 131
    freedom of, 7–15, 92–101
    internal captivity and denominational competition, 16
    Jesus marginal interest in, 165–77
    political conflicts and, 27–29
    rivalry within, in foundation/patriarchal narratives, 52–61
    sacrificial practices and, 8
    war and, 26–27, 34–41
Reuben, 120–21
Revelation, Book of
    captivity in, 188–89
    cruelty of Rome described in, 37
    political ethics in, 18
    resistance to Rome in, 139, 188–89
    war described in, 169
Rezon, 128
Rome
    alliances with, 147–54, 190
    cruelty of, 37, 40–41
    defeat and sacking of, 156
    founding of, 50
    Greece invaded by, 31
    Hasmonean alliance with, 150
    imperial expansion of, 38, 139–40
    internal captivity under, 42, 46–47
    Jesus story in context of, 154–63, 183–85
    molten idolatry in, 142–43
    oppression of Israel by, 9, 27
    political theory in, 28

215

Index

Rome (*continued*)
  resistance to, 18
  Revelation image of, 188–89
  tyranny in, 144–47
Romulus and Remus, 50
Roosevelt, Theodore, 26
rule of ethical law, Jesus' teaching of, 170
Ruth, book of, 17–18, 83

S

sacralization of Bible
  Decalogue analysis based on, 11–12
  political lessons and, xxi–xxiii
sacrificial practices
  abomination theory and, 70–73
  Biblical descriptions of, 8, 52–53
Sadducees, 44, 138, 150–51, 170, 182, 187, 190, 192–93, 198
Salem, Massachusetts, testing for witches in, 113–14
salvation through citizenship, 182–85
Samaria, 133, 160–61, 191–92
Samson, 84, 125
Samsuiluna, 100
Samuel (prophet), 97–98, 126–29, 142, 159
Samuel, books I and II
  internal captivity as focus of, 17
  socio-political ethics in, 24–25
Sarah, 49, 56–58, 63–65
Sargon I, 37–38, 41, 113–14
Sargon II, 46
Saul, xvii, 60, 82, 97, 127, 129, 143, 145–46
Saul of Tarsus, 187–88
scapegoating, 50–51
Schwartz, Regina, xiii–xiv
scribal movements, 158
Sea People, 38
secession narrative, 60–61, 89–98
Second Commandment
  interpretations of, 96–97
  law contained in, 89–90

prevention of violence and oppression and, xvii–xviii
  separation of church and state in, 92
Second Jewish War, 157–58, 163
Second temple period, imperial captivity in, 135–40
sectarianism, accommodation of, 53–61
secular ideology
  civic salvation and, 13–15
  in Decalogue, 11–12, 91–98
  law and, 87–98
  of Moses, 65–69
  religious violence and, xx–xxiii
  self-government evolution and, 118–23
secular powers
  Biblical religion and politics and, xii
  violence and, xiii*n*13
Seleucid Greece, 9, 134–35, 138–40, 149–50
self-government
  Essenes' belief in, 173
  evolution of, 117–23
  Jesus' concern over, 164–77
  Jesus' teaching of, 179–82
Semerkhet, 44
Semites, 72–73, 76, 110–11
Sennacherib, 40, 133
separation of church and state
  Jesus' view of, 194–95
  in Ten Commandments, 92
Septuagint scripture, 58
Sermon on the Mount, 168–77
Servius Tullius, 46
Seshbazzar, 137
Seth (Egyptian diety), 35, 50, 69, 73
Seth (son of Adam), 54
Seti I, xii, 9, 74, 98, 103
Seventh Commandment, 90
sexual predation and violence
  Decalogue boundaries concerning, 90
  religious rivalries and, 59
  sister ruse against, 62–65
Shalmaneser I, 39

216

Index

Shalmaneser IV, 39–40, 46
Shalmaneser V, 43, 133
Shamgar, 125
Shang dynasty, 46
Shasu people, 71
Sheba, 127–28
Shechem, 58–59, 62, 81, 110n53
Shem, 70
Shi Huang-ti, 46–47
Shishak, 10, 64
"Shoah," memory of, 19
sibling rivalries, Biblical depiction of, xiii–xiv, 48–54
Sicily, tyrannical regimes in, 144–45
Sihon, King, 4–7, 123–24
Sima Qian, 45–46
Simeon, 59
Simon, 149–50
Simon bar Giora, 162
Simon bar Kokhba, 163
Sin (god), 35, 80
Sinai
    constitutional law formed at, xvii, 3, 60–61, 87–98
    dream culture of, 24
    Egyptian mining in, 33
    First Commandment at, 73–74
    national government formed at, 76
    religious and political freedom and, 77n50, 86
    Shasu in, 71
    threats against Israeli encampment in, 123–24
Sinuhe, 50, 61–62
sister ruse, in patriarchal narratives, 62–65
Sixth Commandment
    captivity in, 108–9
    prevention of violence and oppression and, xvii–xviii
    prohibition of killing in, 11
slavery
    constitutional law restrictions on, 106–9
    Covenant Code and manumission from, 93
    fear of, 19, 37–38
    freedom from, 98–99
    intermarriage with Jews of, 85
    records about, 39
socio-political norms
    captivity as pressure on, 16–18
    ethics, 24–25
    hospitality and, 82–86
    of Jesus, 163–77
    migration and, 88–98
    tribal threats to democratic governance and, 126–35
Solomon
    David and, 128–29
    forced labor under, 44
    marriage of, 64–65, 145
    political ethic of, 10, 86, 152, 195
Solomon, Song of, 18
Song of Lamech, 1–2, 55
state-mandated oppression, Biblical political lessons concerning, xix–xxiii
state religion, Biblical references to, 12–15
Stephen, 172, 187–88
suffering servant narratives, 51–52
Sumer, 28–29, 33
    curses in, 113–14
    First Dynasty of Kish, 45
    imperial gods in, 35
    violence in, 38–39
Sycthians, 40
Syria, 90
    Israel threatened by, 9, 133
    threats to Israel from, 132

T

Tacitus, 28, 162
Taliban, 84
talion, law of, 28–29
Tarquin, xvii, 46, 144
taxation
    government systems of, 95
    Jesus' teachings and, 175–76
    by kings, 133

Index

teachers and teaching, Jesus' vision of, 178–82
temple treasure, seizure of, 146–47
Ten Commandments
    ancient constitutional law and politics and, xvii–xviii
    anti-violence principles in, 11
    civic and prophetic activity in, 177–78
    curses and, 101–5
    government system of, xv
    humane law in context of, xxii
    idolatry admonitions in, 137
    internal captivity and, 44
    Jesus' teachings and, 167–77
    Kadesh sojourn as testing of, 117–23
    Moses mission concerning, 65–69
    New Testament neglect of, 148–54
    political nature of, xiv–xvi
    promise of death in, x–xi
    Protestant numbering of, 89n5
    resistance to, 61
    restrictions on captivity and, 106–9
    sacred and secular in, 11–15
    as secular constitutional law, 5–7
    secular interpretation of, 87–98
    transgressions against, 4–7
Tenth Commandment
    captivity in, 108–9
    prevention of violence and oppression and, xvii–xviii
    separation of church and state in, 92
Terah, 80
testimonial, law as, 97
Theudas the Prophet, 158
Tholomaus, 161
Thucydides, 25
Thut-mose III, 36
Tiberius, 156
Tibni, 131
Tiglath-Pileser, 34, 83, 133
Timni, 131
Titus, 162
Torah, 101–2
Trajan, 156
treaty instruments, Biblical depiction of, xiii–xvi
tribal structure, Israeli government and, 125–35
Tukulti-Ninurta, 39
Twelve Tablets of Rome, xvn20
two-kingdom theory, xii
tyranny
    Jesus' teachings concerning, 181–82
    kings and kingship and, 143–47

U

Ugarit, 100
United States, imperialism in, 31–33
Urgarit, 27
Urnammu, 99
Uruk (god), 35, 38
Urukagina, 28, 99–101
Utnapishtim, 88
Uzziah (Azariah), 133, 146

V

Varus (Roman general), 160
vengeance, of God, 21
village communities, political ethic in, 28–29
violence
    in ancient Near East, 24–47
    in Bible, misunderstandings concerning, ix–xvi
    captivity narrative in Bible and, 8–15
    causal factors in, 48–49
    historical incidents of, xx–xxiii
    modern religious and political violence, xix–xxiii
    Ten Commandments and prevention of, xvii–xviii
    war and oppression and, 1–7
Virgil, 25

W

war
　　between imperial gods, 34–51
　　Jesus' concern over, 169
　　political theory and, 26–27
War Scroll, 163
wilderness
　　in Biblical narrative, 82–86
　　self-government in, 117–23
Williams, Roger, 3n7

X

Xenophon, 95
Xia Dynasty, 46

Y

Yahweh
　　conflict with Baal, 35
　　cult of, in Israeli history, 12
　　indictment of slavery by, 106
　　Jesus' view of, 172–73
　　Moses' conversation with, 67–69, 75, 89
　　names for, 69
　　as warrior, 26

Z

Zealots, 84, 162, 198
Zechariah, 132, 137
Zedekiah, 37, 95, 109, 134, 146, 181, 191–92
Zerah, 130
Zerubbabel, 137–38
Zhou dynasty, 46
Zimri, 131
Zobah, 127

www.ingramcontent.com/pod-product-compliance
Lightning Source LLC
Chambersburg PA
CBHW070248230426
43664CB00014B/2446